TEMPLAR, ARIZONA.
3 – And a Stick to Beat the Devil With.

By Spike.

www.TemplarAZ.com

WWW.IRONCIRCUS.COM

This volume collects the third chapter of Templar, Arizona. More of the story is available at http://www.templaraz.com.

Write Spike: ironcircus@gmail.com

First Edition: April 2009

ISBN: 978-0-9794080-2-1

Printed in Canada

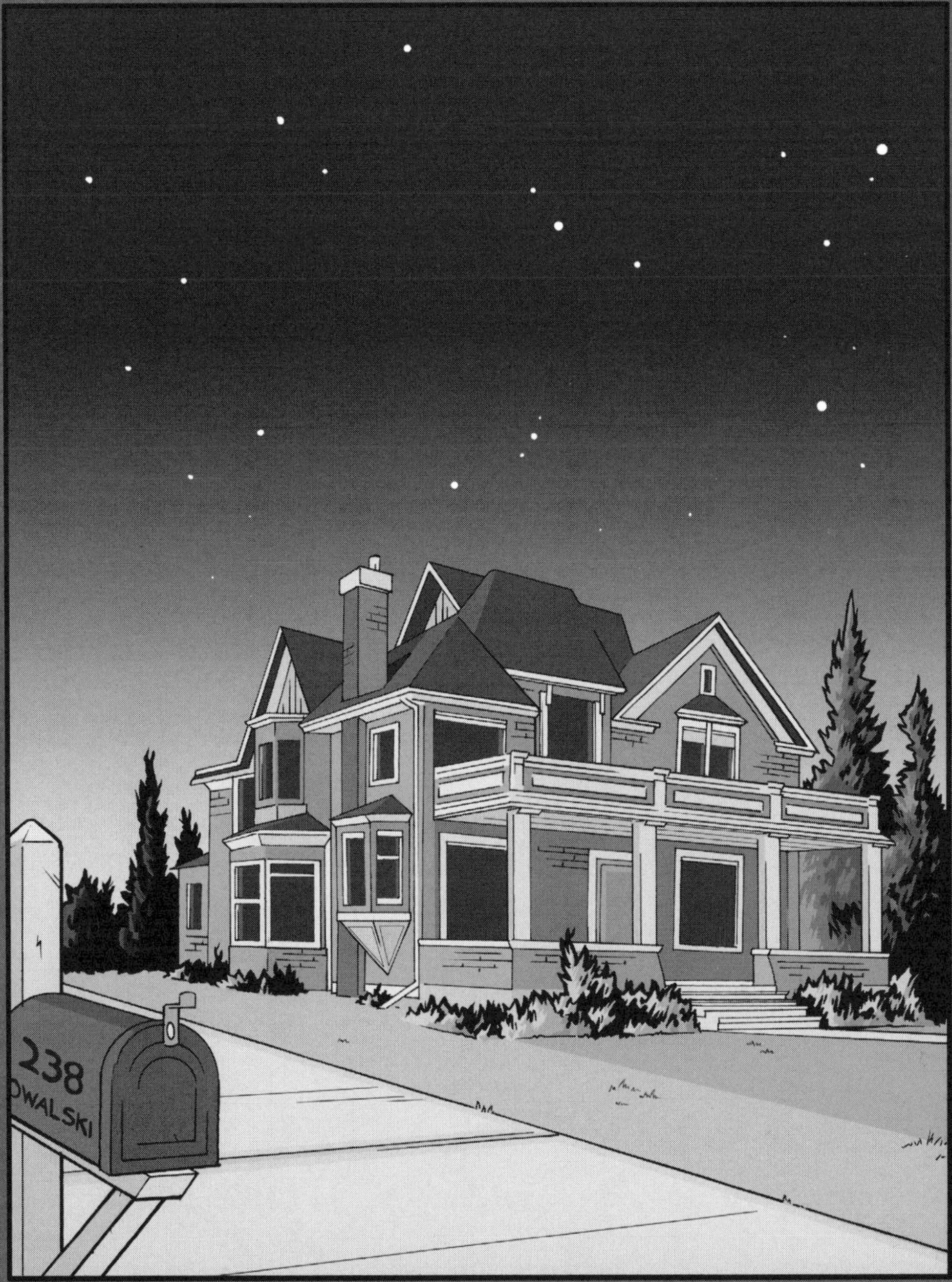
238
OWALSKI

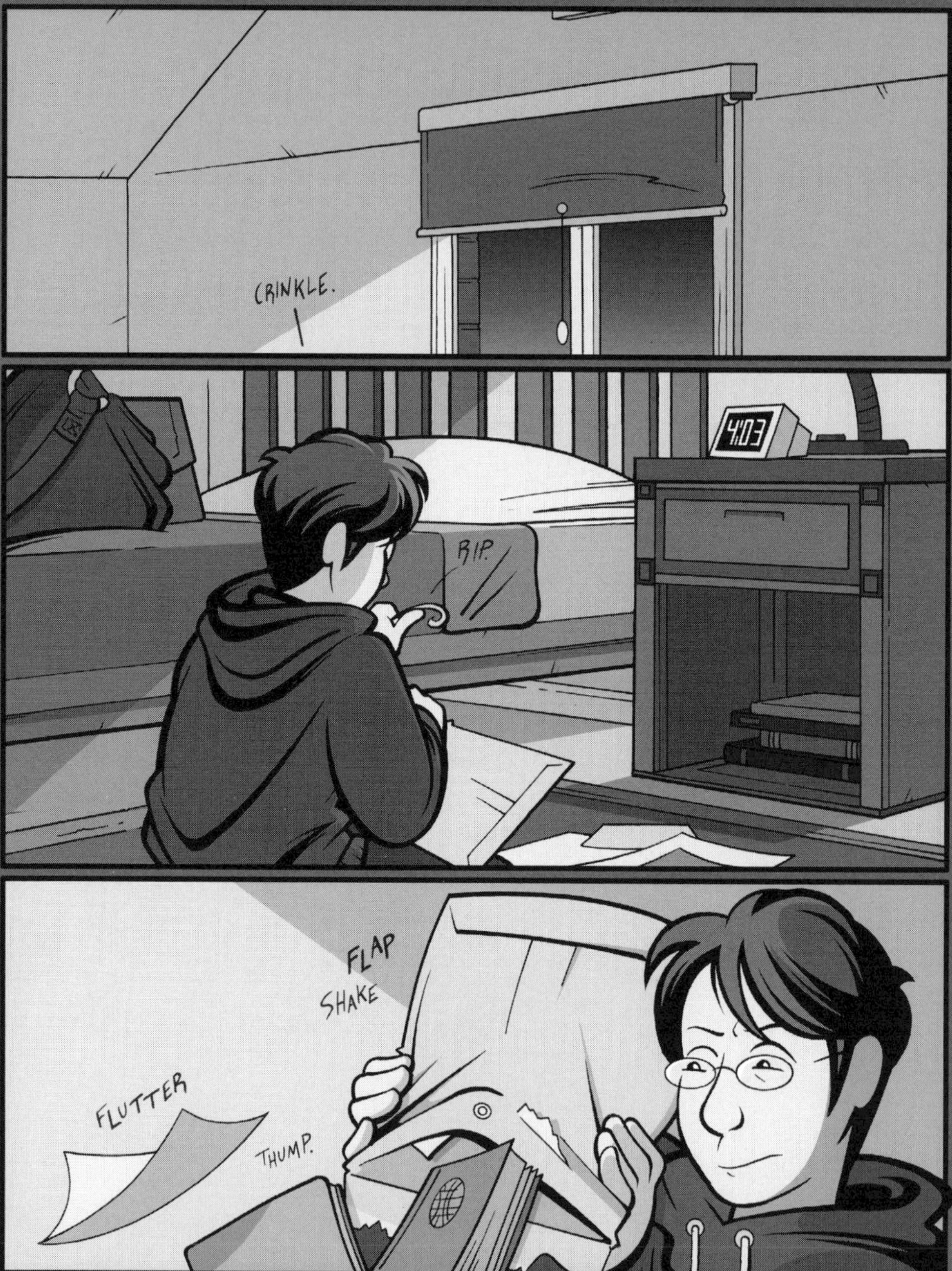
CRINKLE.
4:03
RIP.
FLAP
SHAKE
FLUTTER
THUMP.

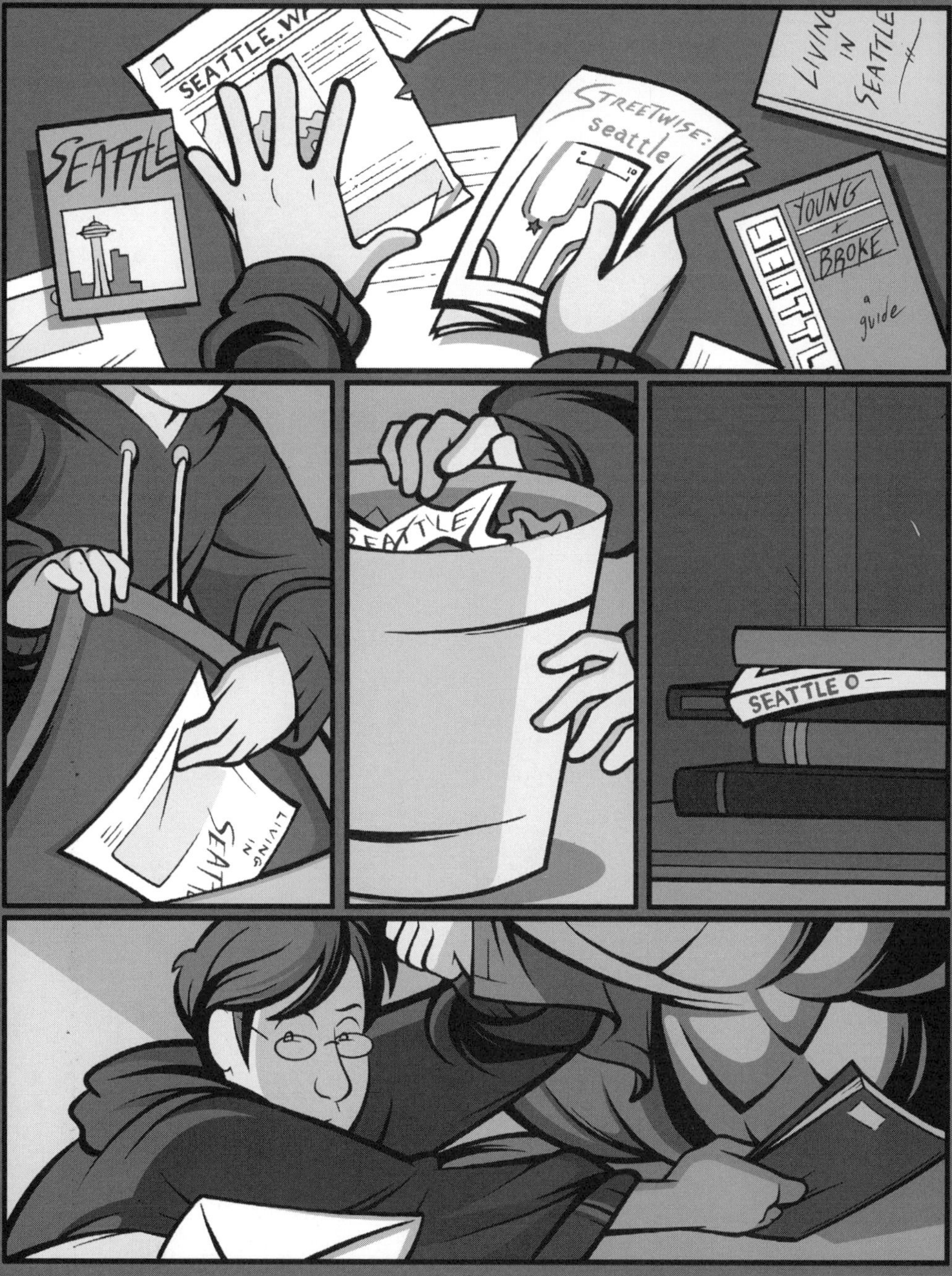
SEATTLE
SEATTLE.W
STREETWISE: seattle
LIVING IN SEATTLE
YOUNG + BROKE
SEATTLE
a guide
SEATTLE
LIVING IN SEATTLE
SEATTLE O

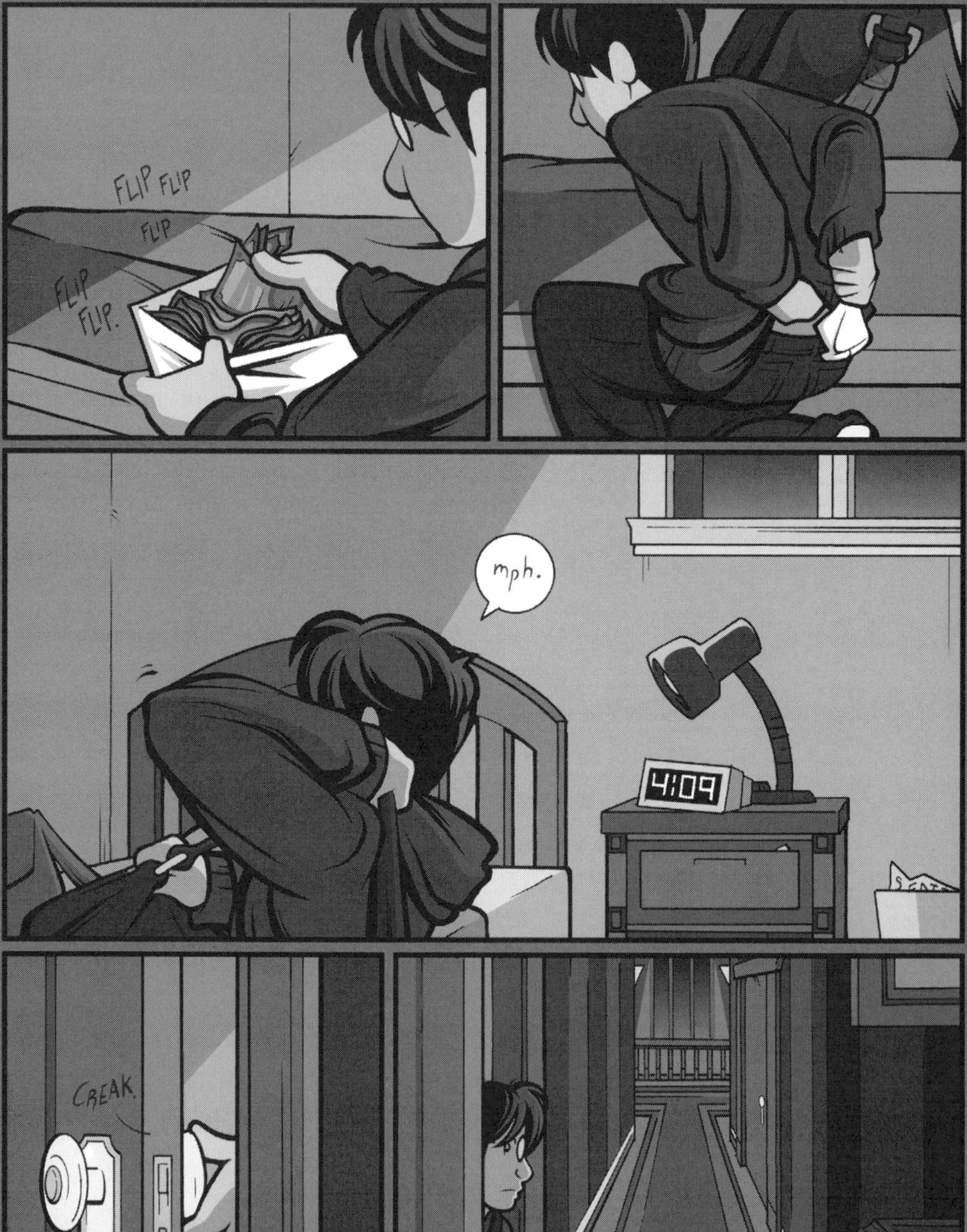
FLIP FLIP
FLIP
FLIP
FLIP.
mph.
4:09
CREAK.

ZIP.
SCRATCH SQUEAK.
MO
SCRATCH.
MOM + DAD

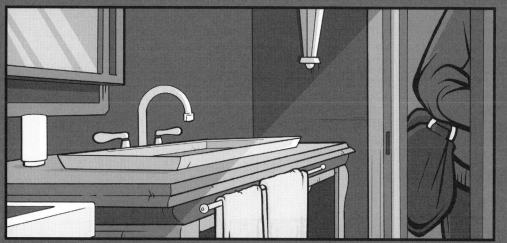

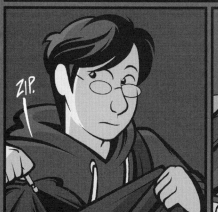

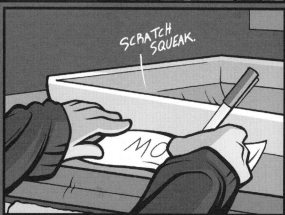

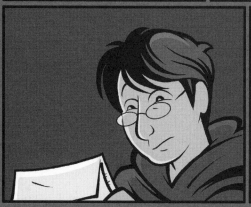

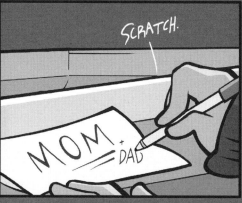

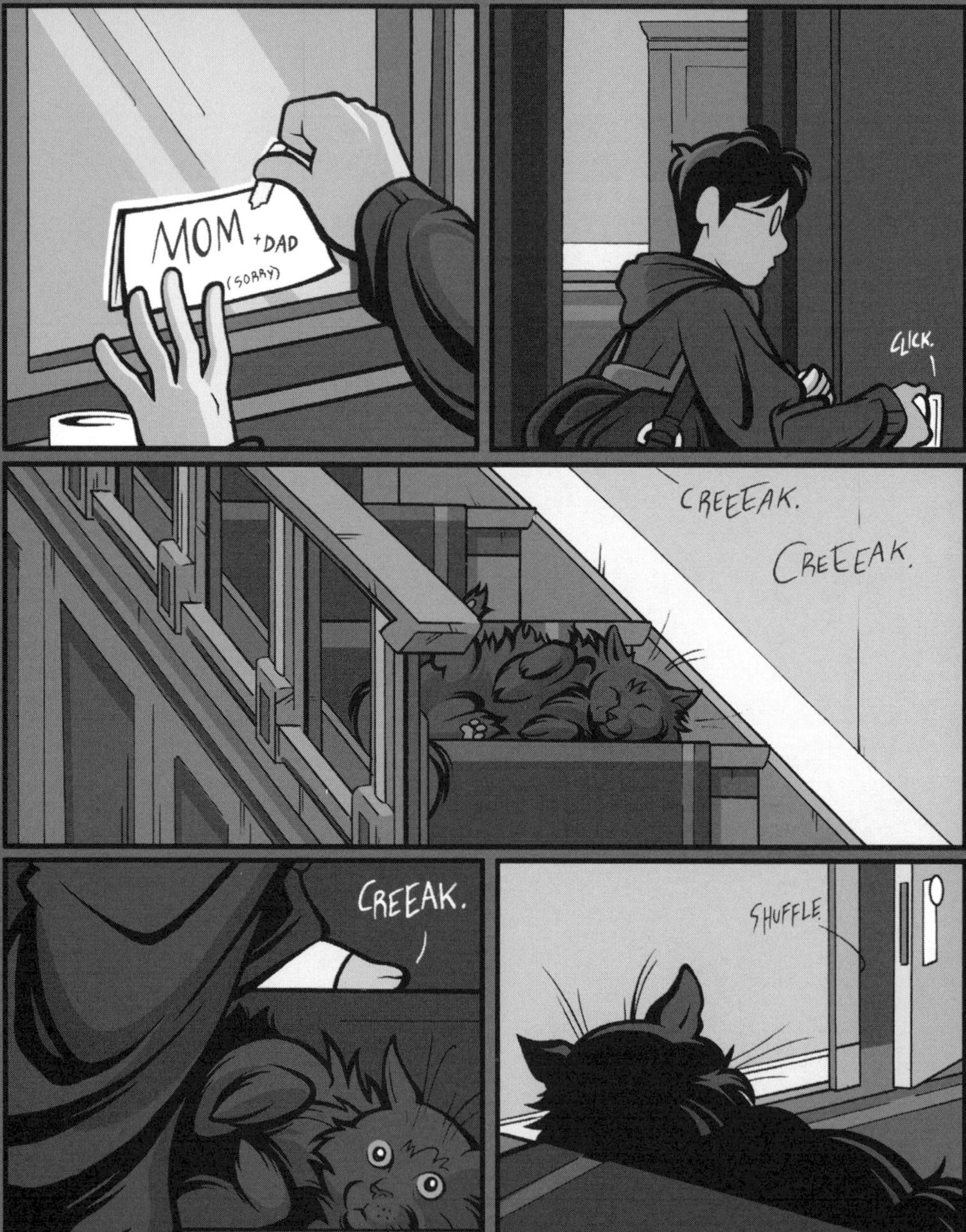
MOM +DAD
(SORRY)
CLICK.
CREEEAK.
CREEEAK.
CREEAK.
SHUFFLE

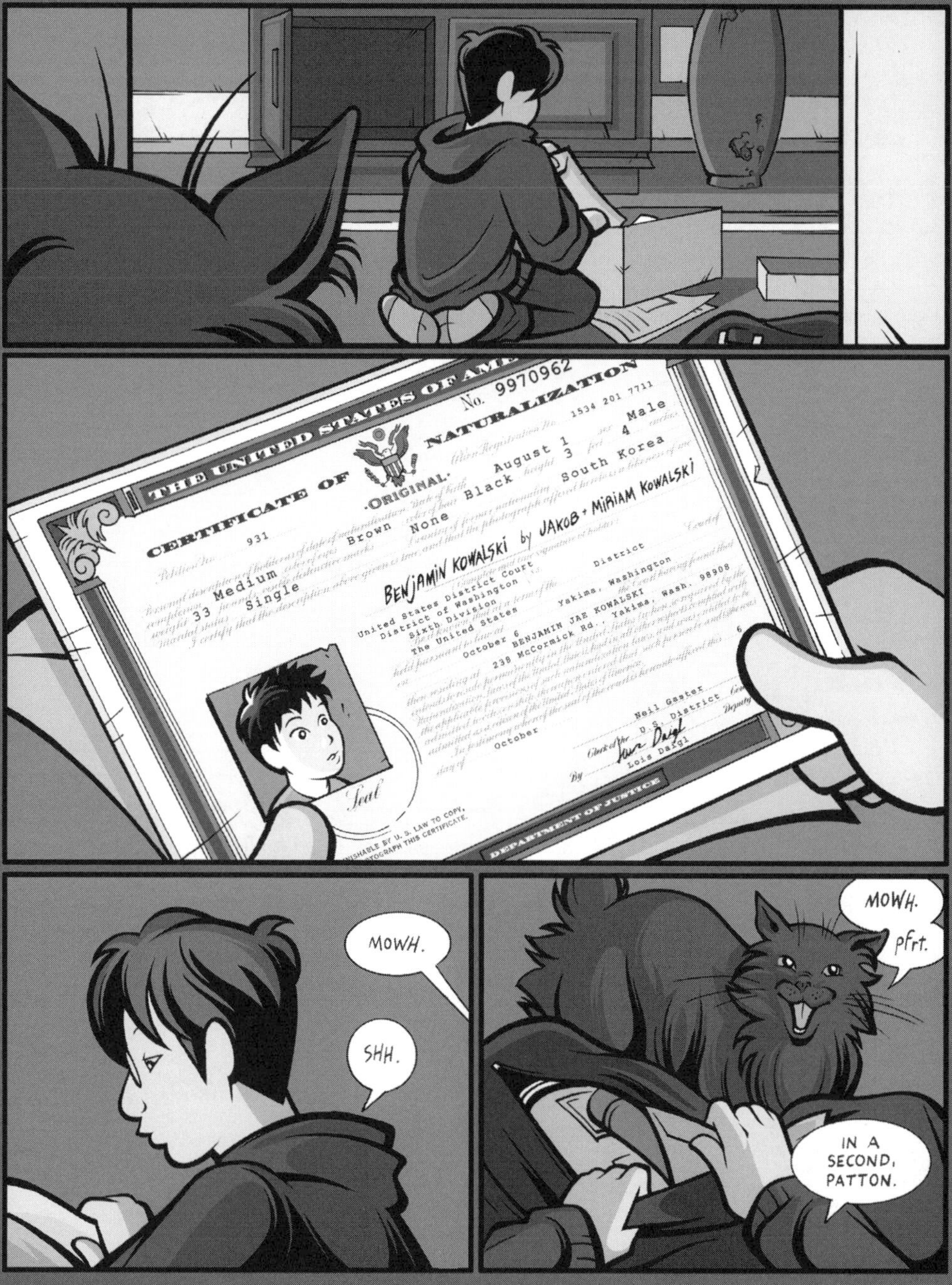
THE UNITED STATES OF AME
CERTIFICATE OF NATURALIZATION
No. 9970962
1534 201 7711
ORIGINAL
931
Male
August 1
4
3
Black
Brown
None
South Korea
33 Medium
Single
BENJAMIN KOWALSKI by JAKOB + MIRIAM KOWALSKI
District
United States District Court
District of Washington
Sixth Division
Yakima, Washington
The United States
October 6
BENJAMIN JAE KOWALSKI
238 McCormick Rd., Yakima, Wash. 98908
6
Neil Gaster
U.S. District
October
Lois Daigl
Seal
DEPARTMENT OF JUSTICE
MOWH.
SHH.
MOWH.
pFrt.
IN A SECOND, PATTON.

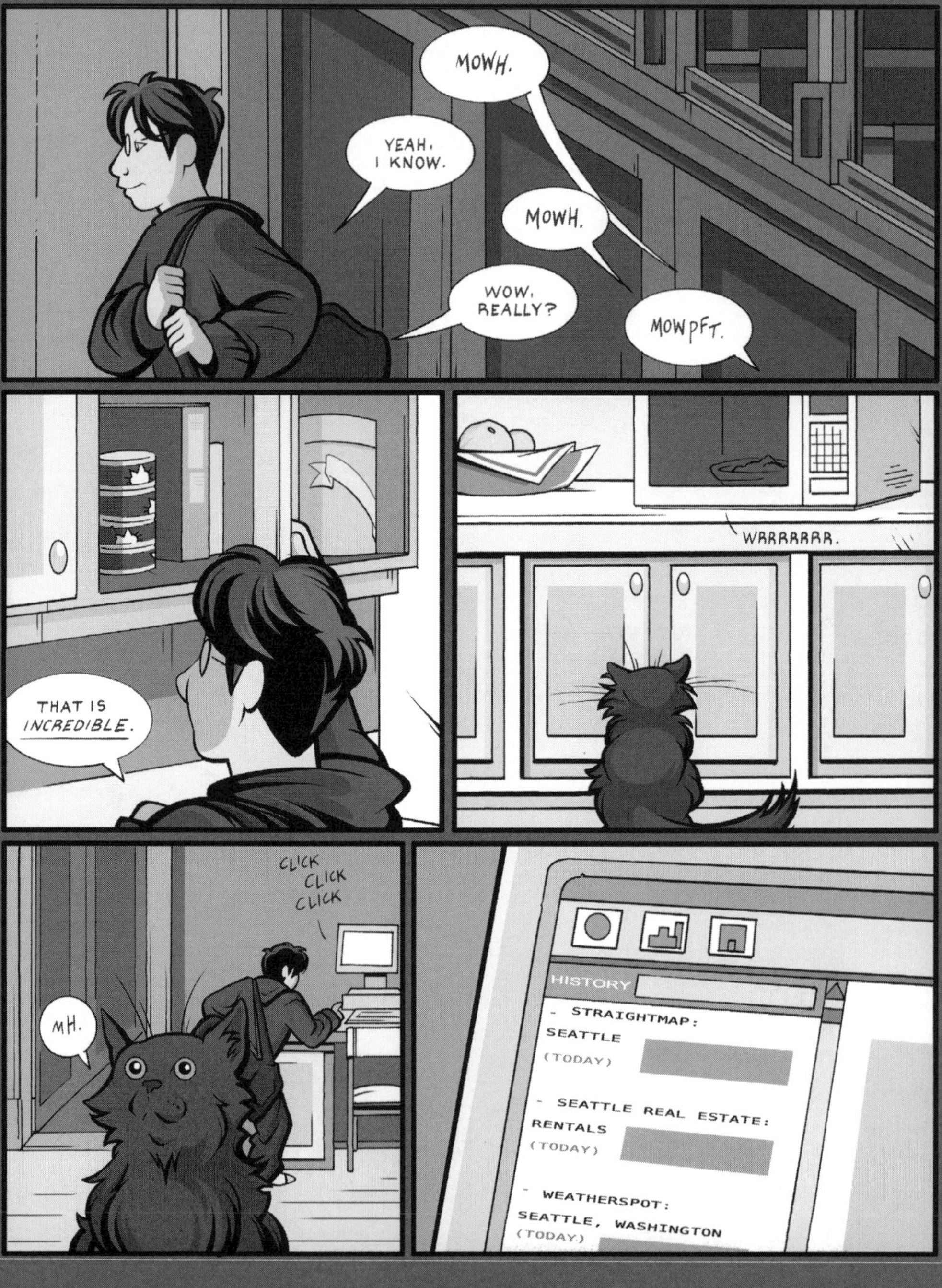
MOWH.
YEAH, I KNOW.
MOWH.
WOW, REALLY?
MOWPFT.
THAT IS *INCREDIBLE*.
WRRRRRRR.
CLICK CLICK CLICK
MH.
HISTORY
- STRAIGHTMAP:
SEATTLE
(TODAY)
- SEATTLE REAL ESTATE:
RENTALS
(TODAY)
- WEATHERSPOT:
SEATTLE, WASHINGTON
(TODAY)

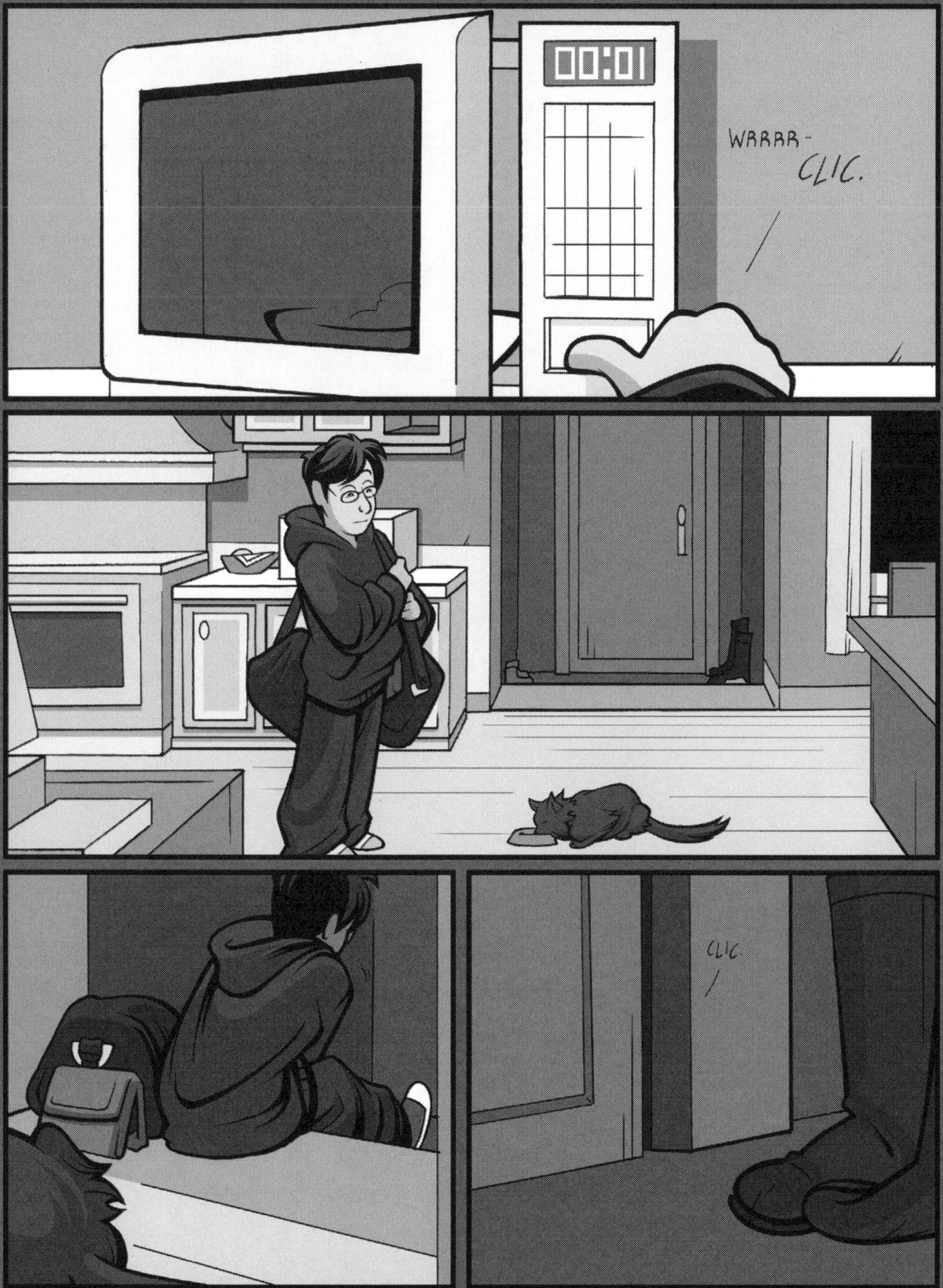
00:01
WRRRR-
CLIC.
CLIC.

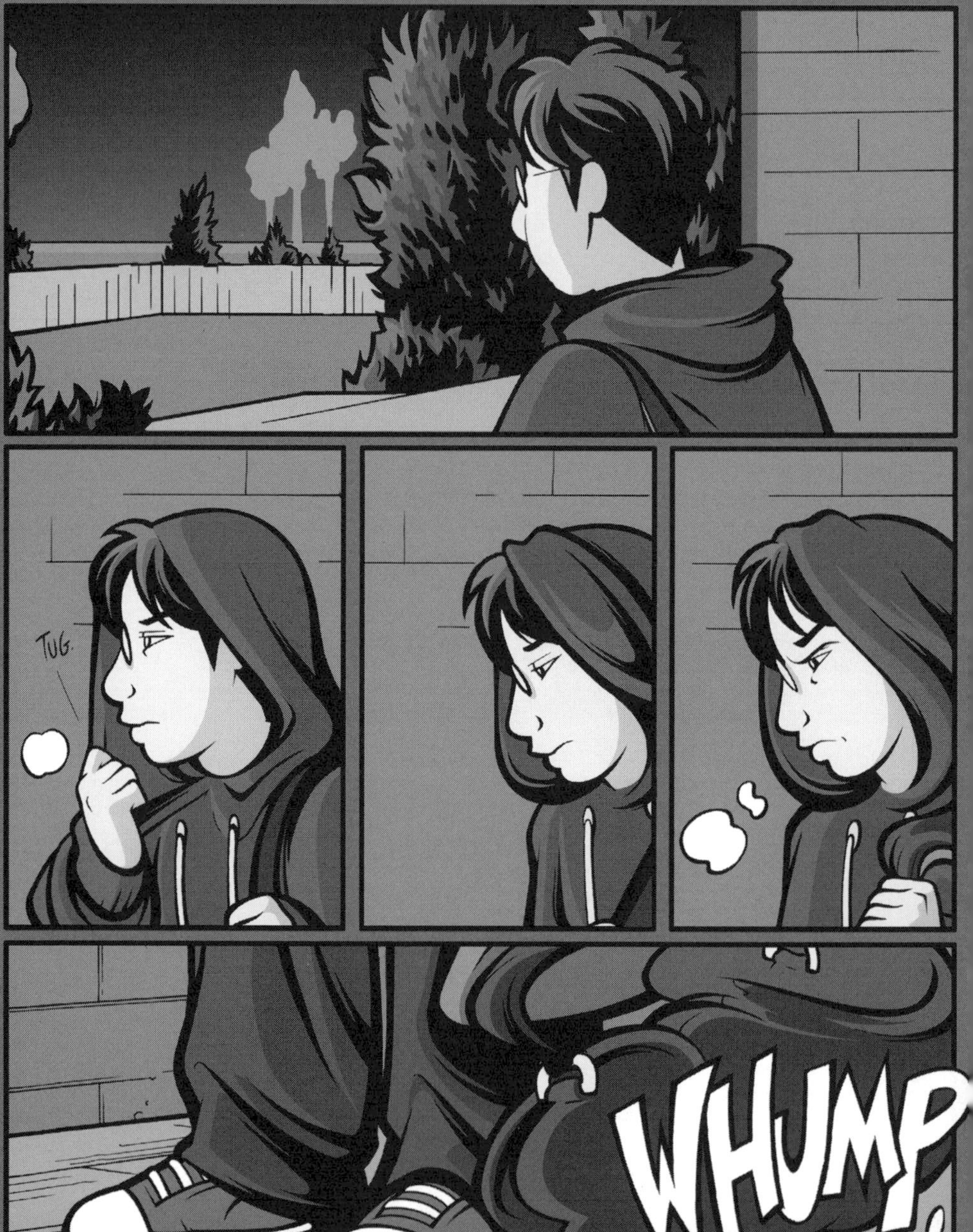
TUG.
WHUMP.

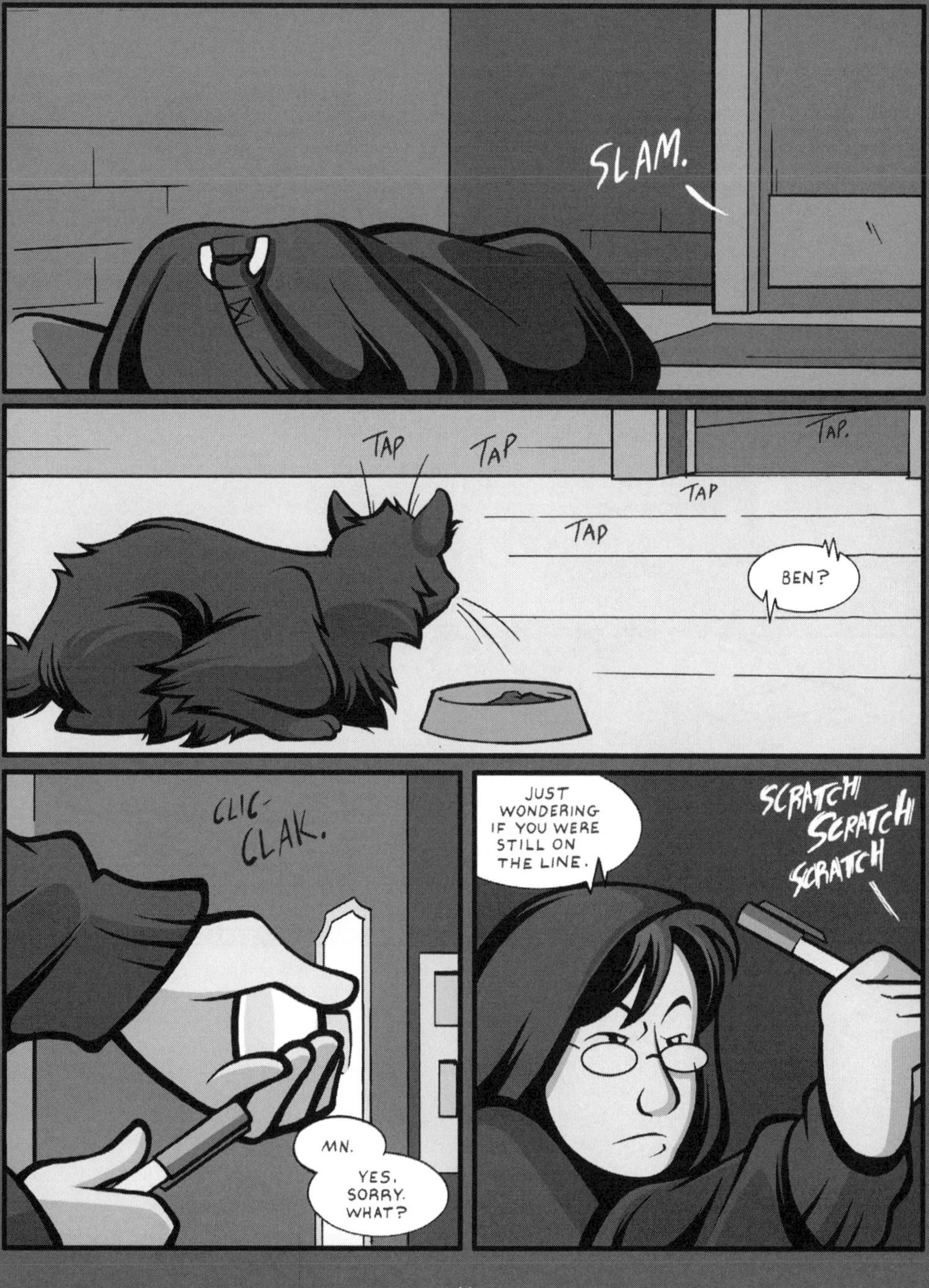
SLAM.
TAP
TAP
TAP.
TAP
TAP
BEN?
CLIC-CLAK.
MN.
YES. SORRY. WHAT?
JUST WONDERING IF YOU WERE STILL ON THE LINE.
SCRATCH SCRATCH SCRATCH

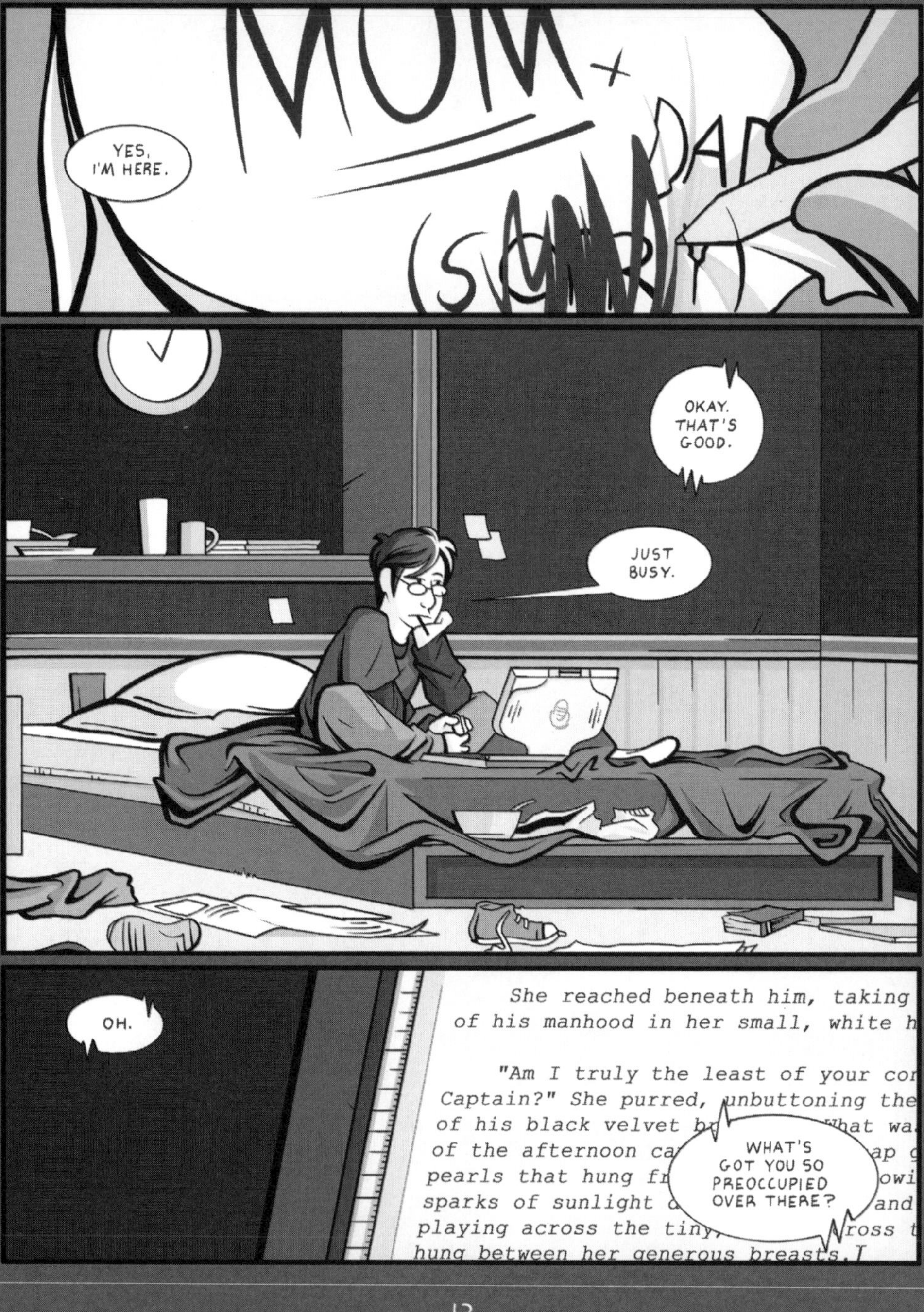
YES, I'M HERE.
OKAY. THAT'S GOOD.
JUST BUSY.
OH.
She reached beneath him, taking
of his manhood in her small, white
"Am I truly the least of your
Captain?" She purred, unbuttoning the
of his black velvet
of the afternoon
pearls that hung
sparks of sunlight
playing across the tiny
hung between her generous breasts.
WHAT'S GOT YOU SO PREOCCUPIED OVER THERE?

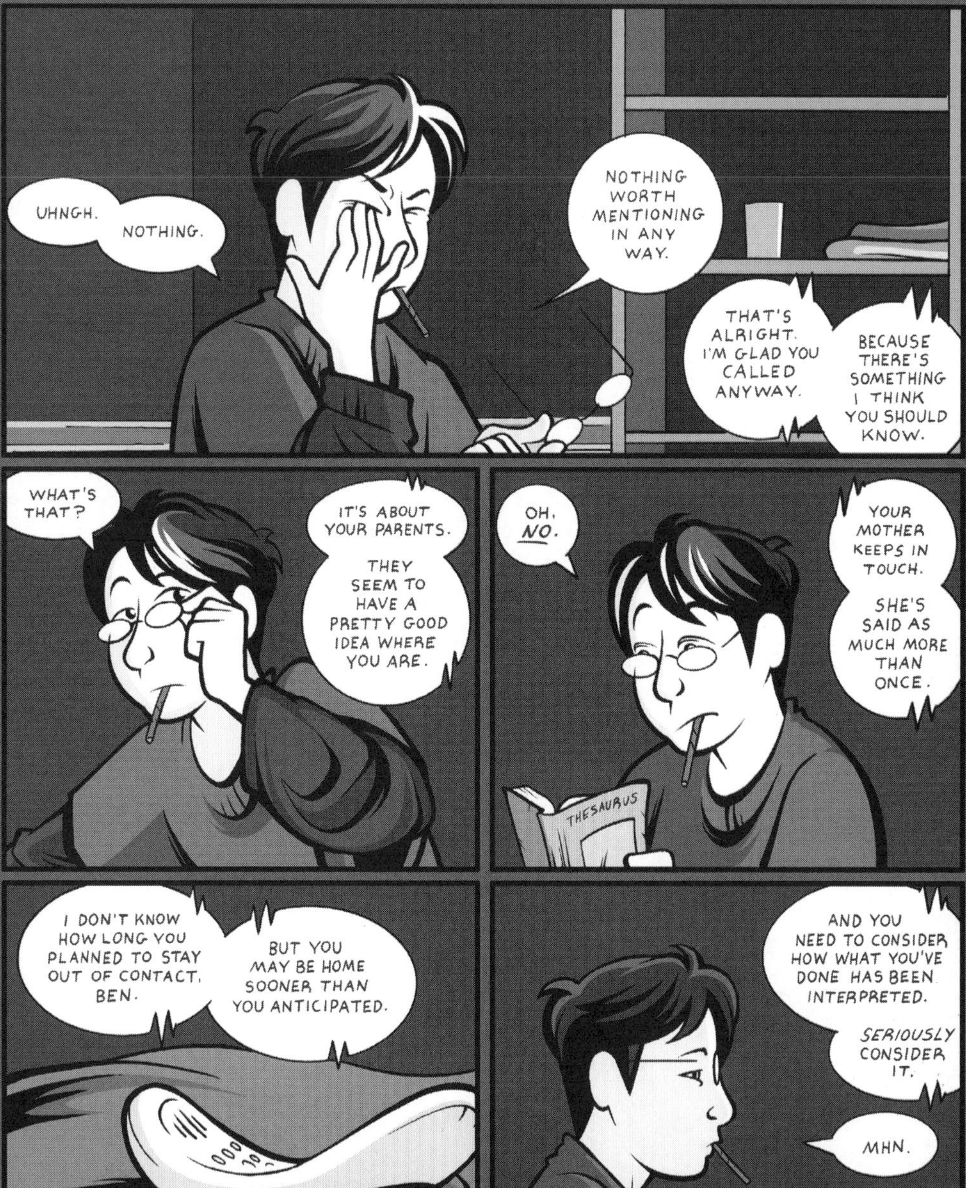
UHNGH.
NOTHING.
NOTHING WORTH MENTIONING IN ANY WAY.
THAT'S ALRIGHT. I'M GLAD YOU CALLED ANYWAY.
BECAUSE THERE'S SOMETHING I THINK YOU SHOULD KNOW.
WHAT'S THAT?
IT'S ABOUT YOUR PARENTS.
THEY SEEM TO HAVE A PRETTY GOOD IDEA WHERE YOU ARE.
OH. NO.
YOUR MOTHER KEEPS IN TOUCH.
SHE'S SAID AS MUCH MORE THAN ONCE.
THESAURUS
I DON'T KNOW HOW LONG YOU PLANNED TO STAY OUT OF CONTACT, BEN.
BUT YOU MAY BE HOME SOONER THAN YOU ANTICIPATED.
AND YOU NEED TO CONSIDER HOW WHAT YOU'VE DONE HAS BEEN INTERPRETED.
SERIOUSLY CONSIDER IT.
MHN.
TAP. TAP. TAP.

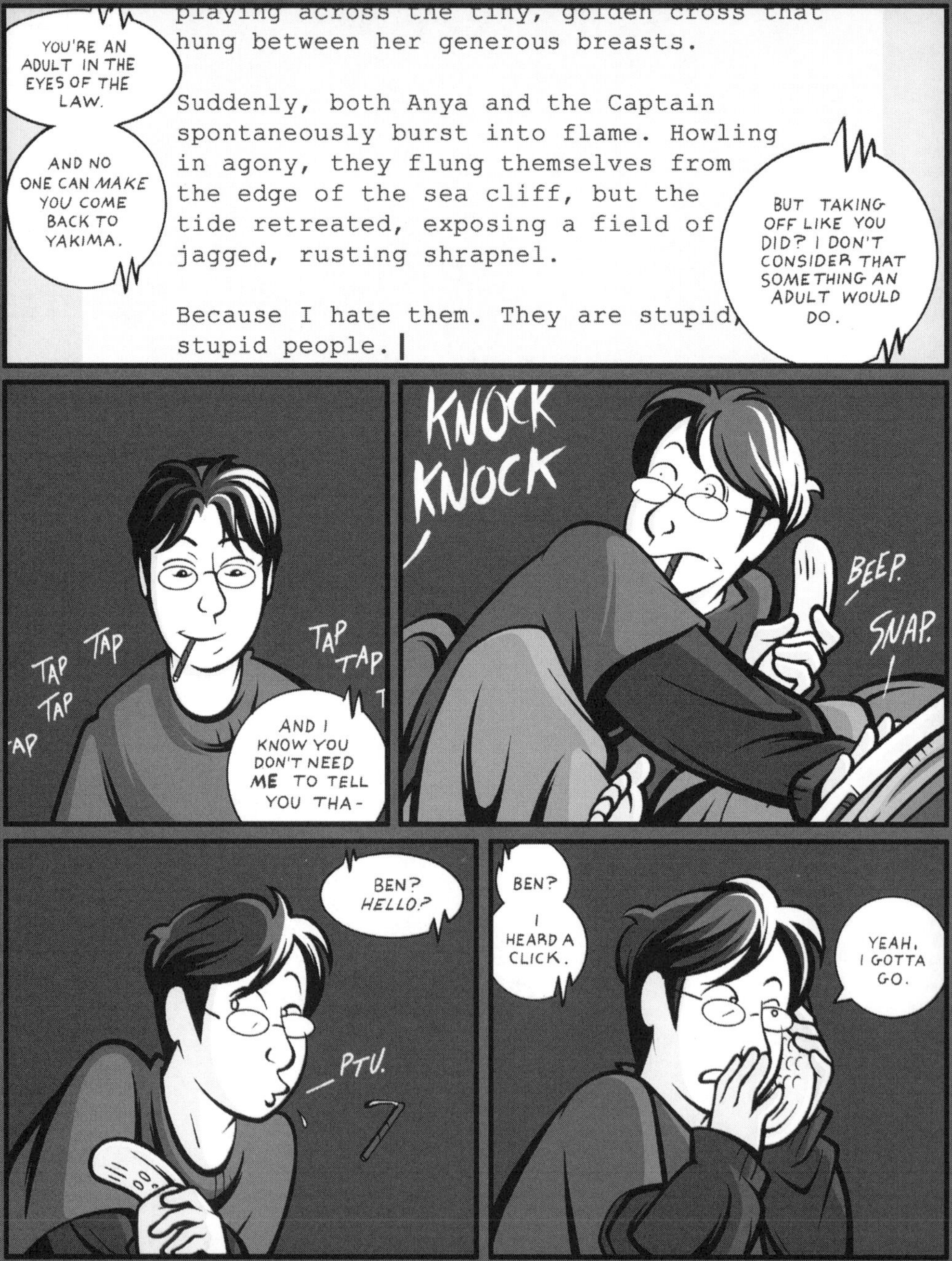
playing across the tiny, golden cross that hung between her generous breasts.
YOU'RE AN ADULT IN THE EYES OF THE LAW.
Suddenly, both Anya and the Captain spontaneously burst into flame. Howling in agony, they flung themselves from the edge of the sea cliff, but the tide retreated, exposing a field of jagged, rusting shrapnel.
AND NO ONE CAN MAKE YOU COME BACK TO YAKIMA.
Because I hate them. They are stupid, stupid people.
BUT TAKING OFF LIKE YOU DID? I DON'T CONSIDER THAT SOMETHING AN ADULT WOULD DO.
TAP TAP TAP TAP
TAP TAP
AND I KNOW YOU DON'T NEED ME TO TELL YOU THA-
KNOCK KNOCK
BEEP.
SNAP.
BEN? HELLO?
PTU.
BEN?
I HEARD A CLICK.
YEAH, I GOTTA GO.

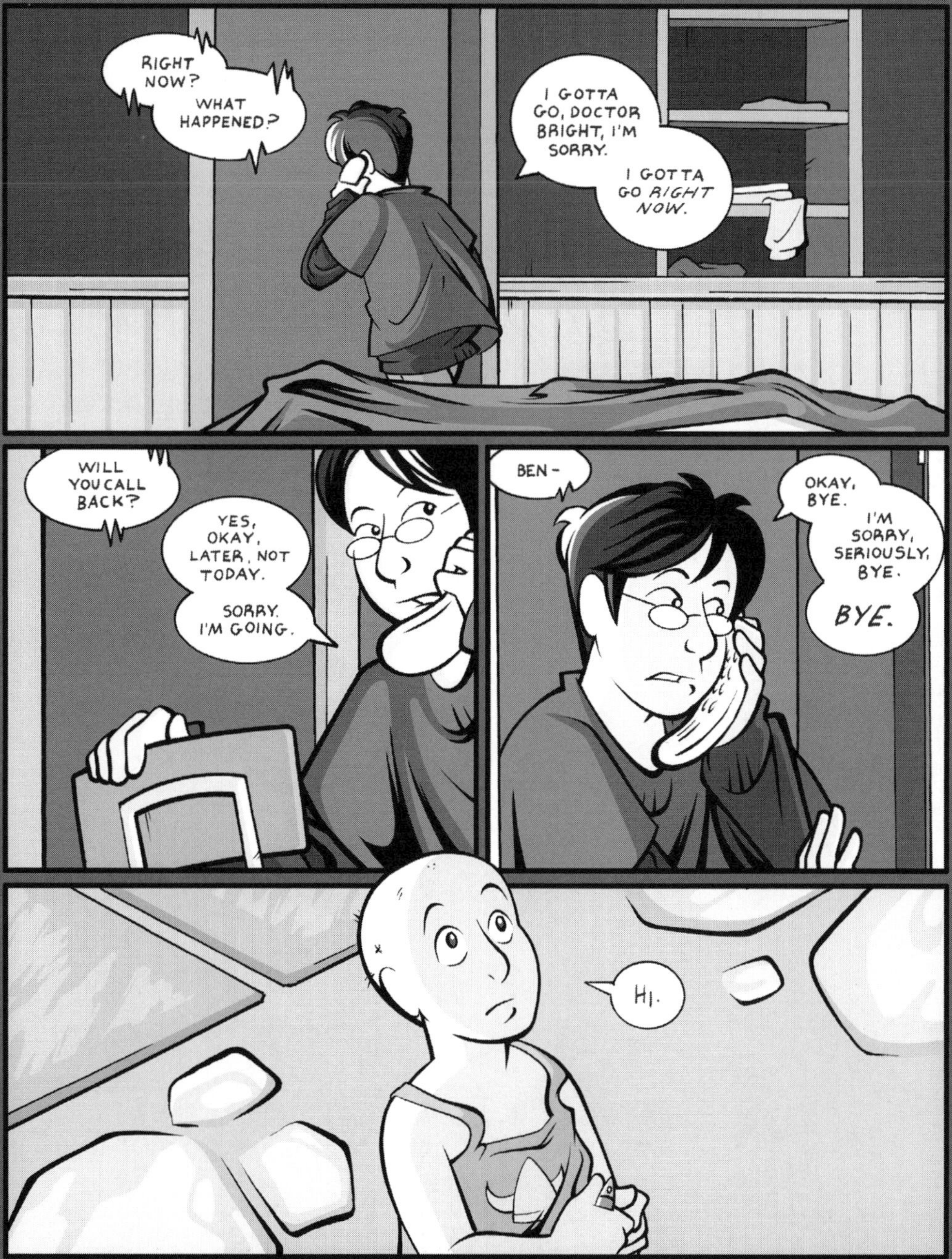
RIGHT NOW?
WHAT HAPPENED?
I GOTTA GO, DOCTOR BRIGHT, I'M SORRY.
I GOTTA GO RIGHT NOW.
WILL YOU CALL BACK?
YES, OKAY, LATER, NOT TODAY.
SORRY. I'M GOING.
BEN-
OKAY, BYE.
I'M SORRY, SERIOUSLY, BYE.
BYE.
HI.

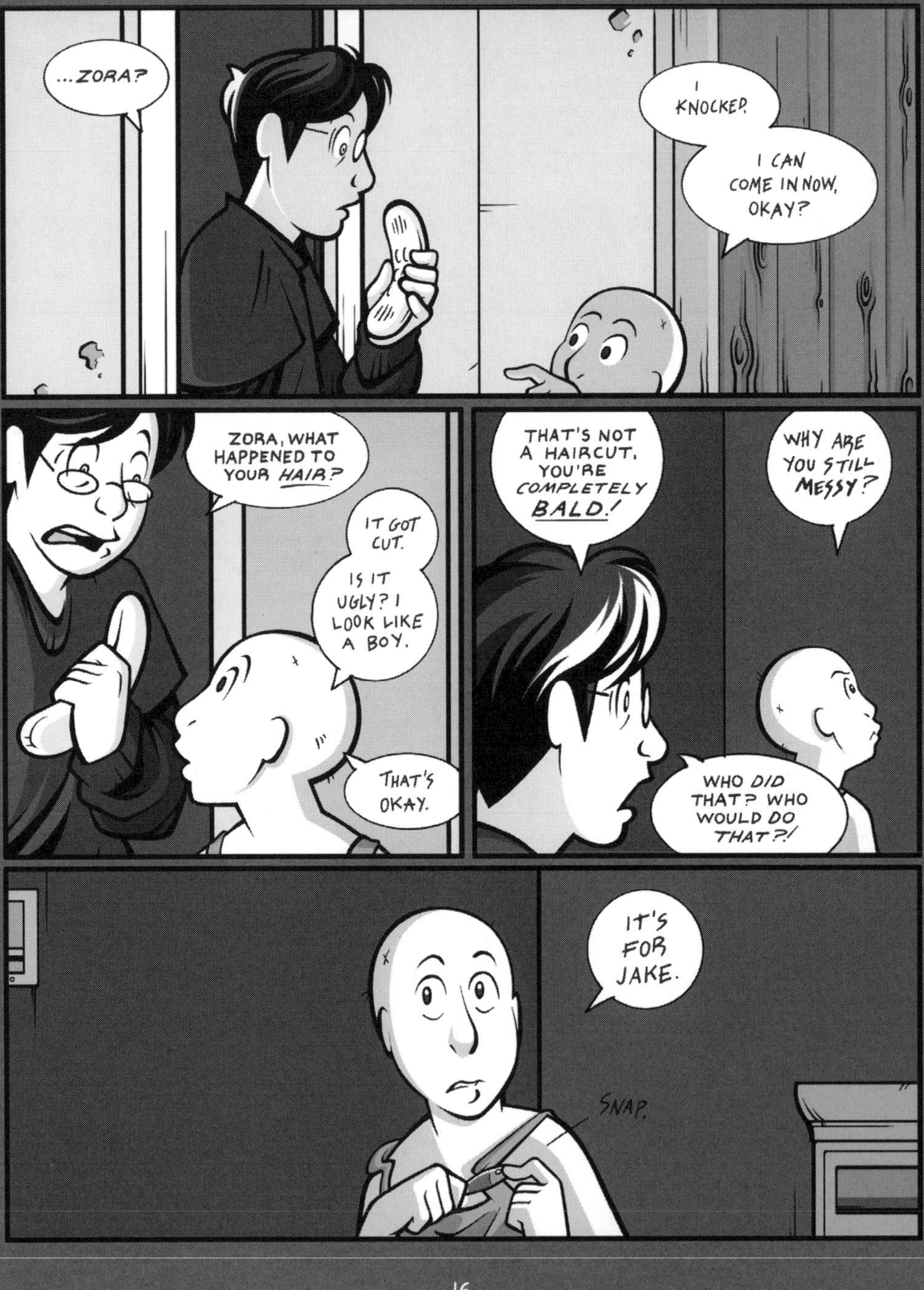
...ZORA?
I KNOCKED.
I CAN COME IN NOW, OKAY?
ZORA, WHAT HAPPENED TO YOUR HAIR?
IT GOT CUT.
IS IT UGLY? I LOOK LIKE A BOY.
THAT'S OKAY.
THAT'S NOT A HAIRCUT, YOU'RE COMPLETELY BALD!
WHY ARE YOU STILL MESSY?
WHO DID THAT? WHO WOULD DO THAT?!
IT'S FOR JAKE.
SNAP.

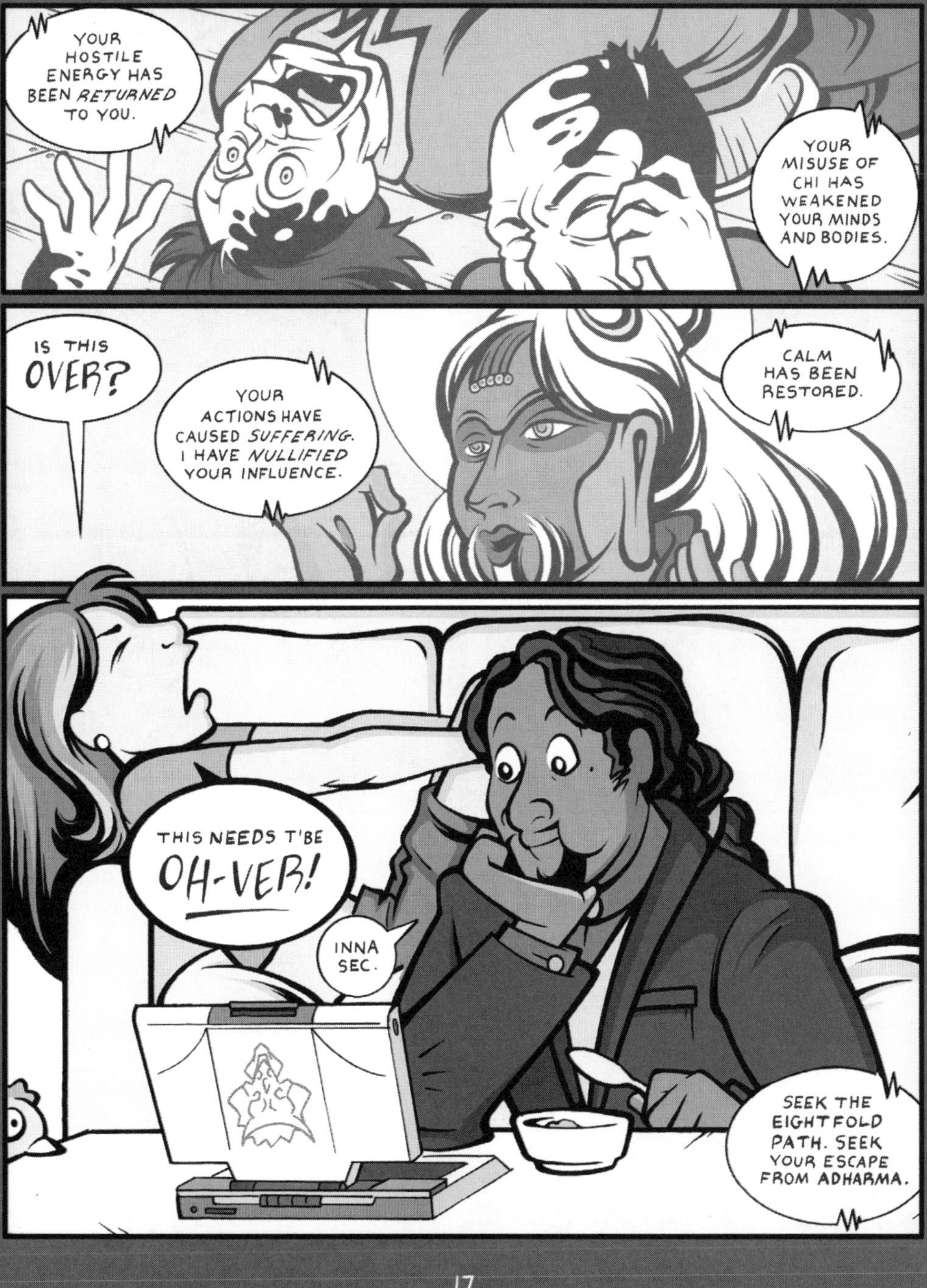
YOUR HOSTILE ENERGY HAS BEEN RETURNED TO YOU.
YOUR MISUSE OF CHI HAS WEAKENED YOUR MINDS AND BODIES.
IS THIS OVER?
YOUR ACTIONS HAVE CAUSED SUFFERING. I HAVE NULLIFIED YOUR INFLUENCE.
CALM HAS BEEN RESTORED.
THIS NEEDS T'BE OH-VER!
INNA SEC.
SEEK THE EIGHTFOLD PATH. SEEK YOUR ESCAPE FROM ADHARMA.

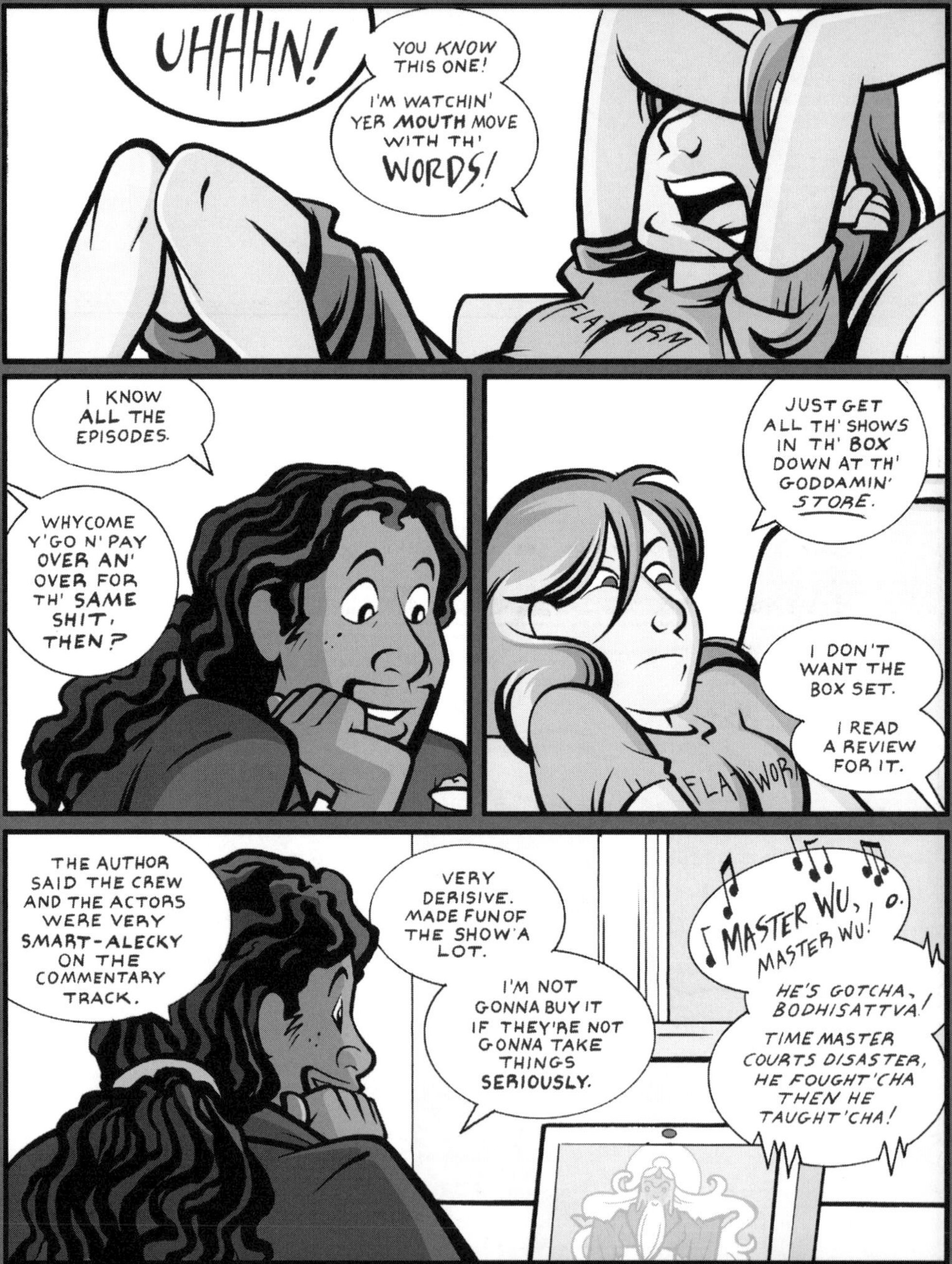
UHHHN!
YOU KNOW THIS ONE!
I'M WATCHIN' YER MOUTH MOVE WITH TH' WORDS!
FLATWORM
I KNOW ALL THE EPISODES.
WHYCOME Y'GO N' PAY OVER AN' OVER FOR TH' SAME SHIT, THEN?
JUST GET ALL TH' SHOWS IN TH' BOX DOWN AT TH' GODDAMIN' STORE.
I DON'T WANT THE BOX SET.
I READ A REVIEW FOR IT.
FLATWORM
THE AUTHOR SAID THE CREW AND THE ACTORS WERE VERY SMART-ALECKY ON THE COMMENTARY TRACK.
VERY DERISIVE. MADE FUN OF THE SHOW'A LOT.
I'M NOT GONNA BUY IT IF THEY'RE NOT GONNA TAKE THINGS SERIOUSLY.
MASTER WU, O. MASTER WU!
HE'S GOTCHA, BODHISATTVA!
TIME MASTER COURTS DISASTER, HE FOUGHT'CHA THEN HE TAUGHT'CHA!

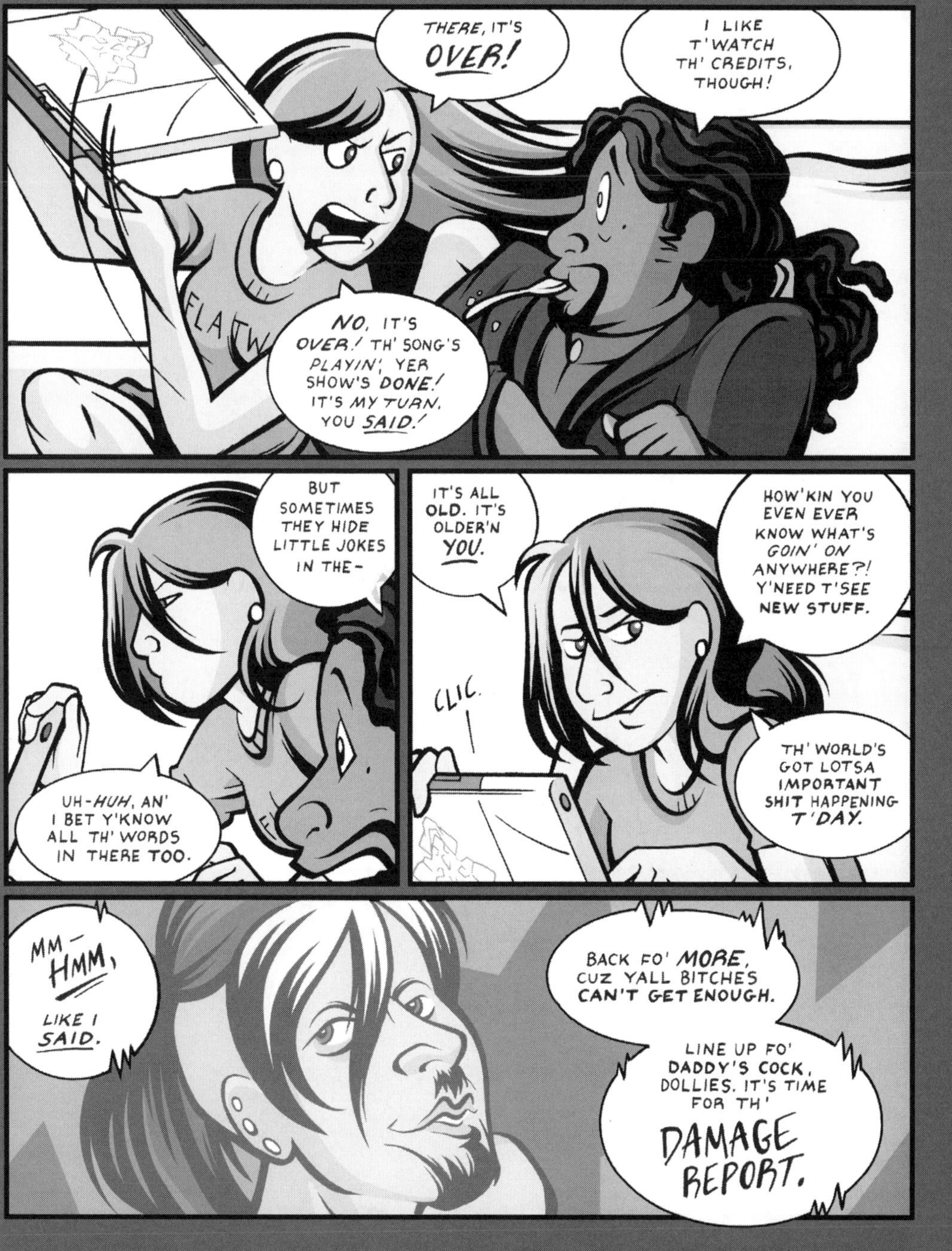
THERE, IT'S OVER!
I LIKE T'WATCH TH' CREDITS, THOUGH!
FLATW
NO, IT'S OVER! TH' SONG'S PLAYIN', YER SHOW'S DONE! IT'S MY TURN. YOU SAID!
BUT SOMETIMES THEY HIDE LITTLE JOKES IN THE-
UH-HUH, AN' I BET Y'KNOW ALL TH' WORDS IN THERE TOO.
IT'S ALL OLD. IT'S OLDER'N YOU.
HOW'KIN YOU EVEN EVER KNOW WHAT'S GOIN' ON ANYWHERE?! Y'NEED T'SEE NEW STUFF.
CLIC
TH' WORLD'S GOT LOTSA IMPORTANT SHIT HAPPENING T'DAY.
MM-HMM, LIKE I SAID.
BACK FO' MORE, CUZ YALL BITCHES CAN'T GET ENOUGH.
LINE UP FO' DADDY'S COCK, DOLLIES. IT'S TIME FOR TH' DAMAGE REPORT.

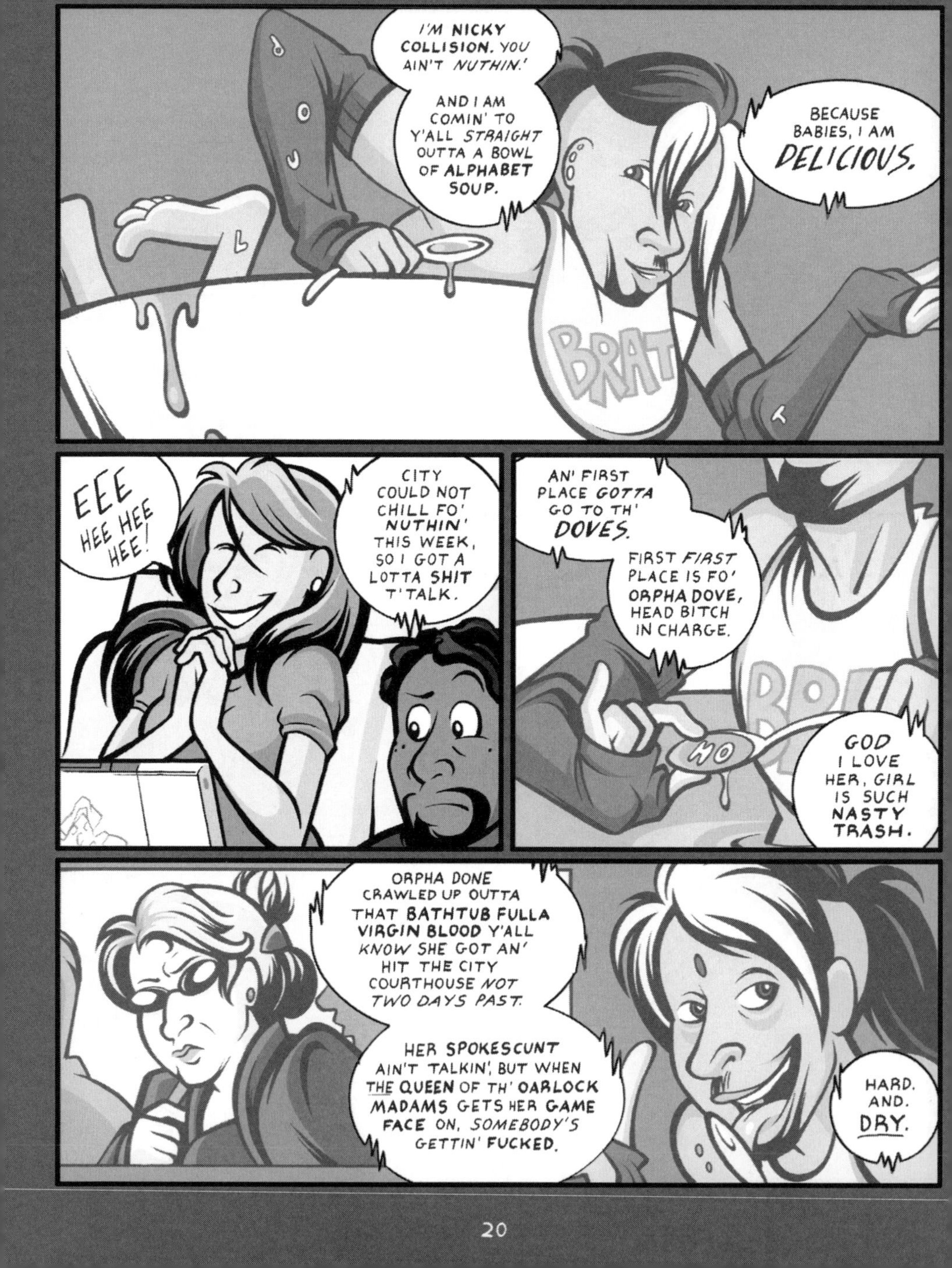
I'M NICKY COLLISION. YOU AIN'T NUTHIN.'
AND I AM COMIN' TO Y'ALL STRAIGHT OUTTA A BOWL OF ALPHABET SOUP.
BECAUSE BABIES, I AM DELICIOUS.
EEE HEE HEE HEE!
CITY COULD NOT CHILL FO' NUTHIN' THIS WEEK, SO I GOT A LOTTA SHIT T'TALK.
AN' FIRST PLACE GOTTA GO TO TH' DOVES.
FIRST FIRST PLACE IS FO' ORPHA DOVE, HEAD BITCH IN CHARGE.
GOD I LOVE HER, GIRL IS SUCH NASTY TRASH.
ORPHA DONE CRAWLED UP OUTTA THAT BATHTUB FULLA VIRGIN BLOOD Y'ALL KNOW SHE GOT AN' HIT THE CITY COURTHOUSE NOT TWO DAYS PAST.
HER SPOKESCUNT AIN'T TALKIN', BUT WHEN THE QUEEN OF TH' OARLOCK MADAMS GETS HER GAME FACE ON, SOMEBODY'S GETTIN' FUCKED.
HARD. AND. DRY.

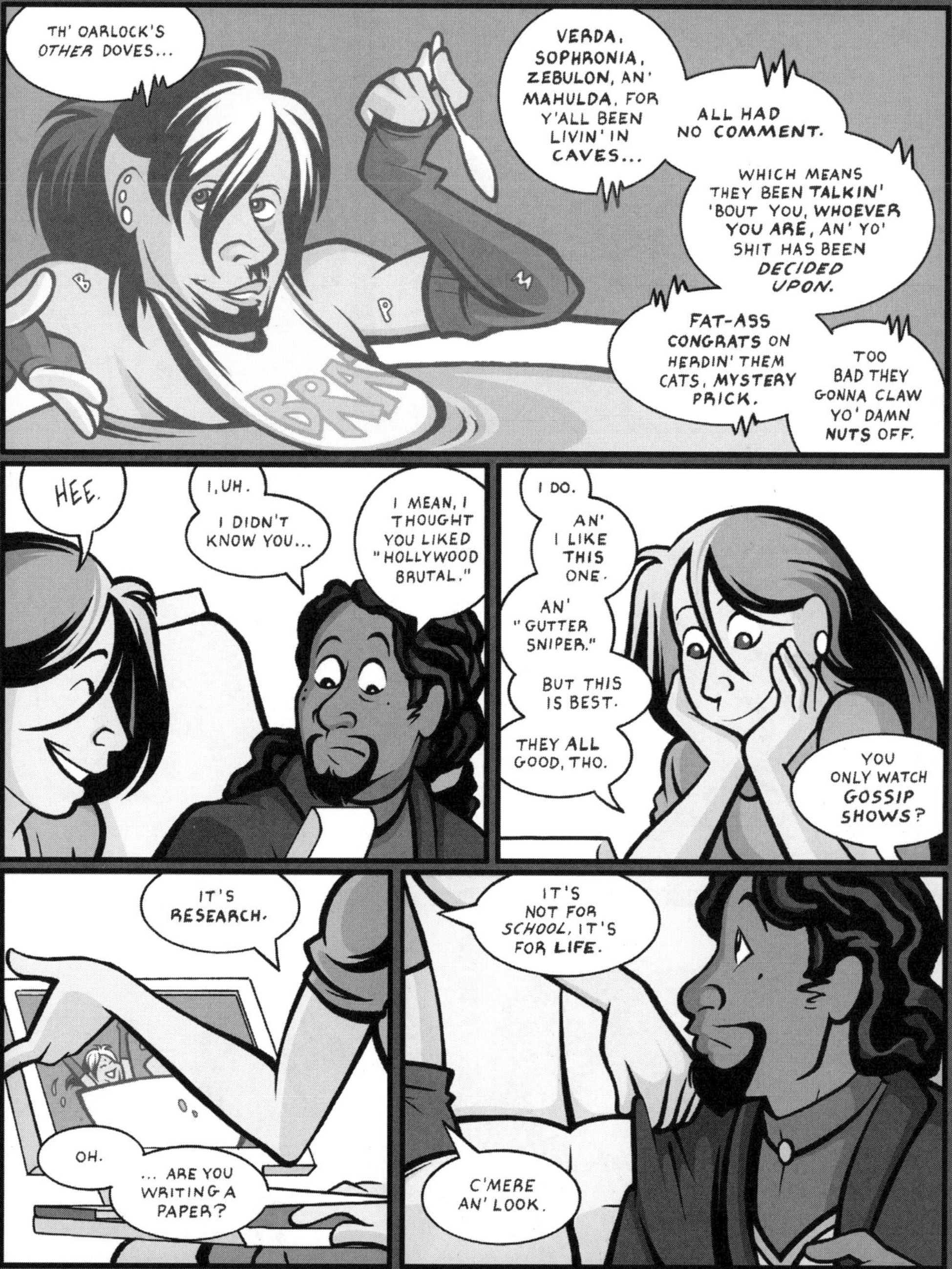
TH' OARLOCK'S *OTHER* DOVES...
VERDA, SOPHRONIA, ZEBULON, AN' MAHULDA, FOR Y'ALL BEEN LIVIN' IN CAVES...
ALL HAD NO **COMMENT**.
WHICH MEANS THEY BEEN **TALKIN'** 'BOUT YOU, **WHOEVER YOU ARE**, AN' YO' SHIT HAS BEEN *DECIDED UPON*.
FAT-ASS CONGRATS ON HERDIN' THEM CATS, **MYSTERY PRICK**.
TOO BAD THEY GONNA CLAW YO' DAMN **NUTS** OFF.
HEE.
I, UH.
I DIDN'T KNOW YOU...
I MEAN, I THOUGHT YOU LIKED "HOLLYWOOD BRUTAL."
I DO.
AN' I LIKE **THIS** ONE.
AN' "GUTTER SNIPER."
BUT THIS IS BEST.
THEY **ALL** GOOD, THO.
YOU ONLY WATCH **GOSSIP SHOWS**?
IT'S **RESEARCH**.
OH.
... ARE YOU WRITING A PAPER?
IT'S NOT FOR *SCHOOL*, IT'S FOR **LIFE**.
C'MERE AN' LOOK.

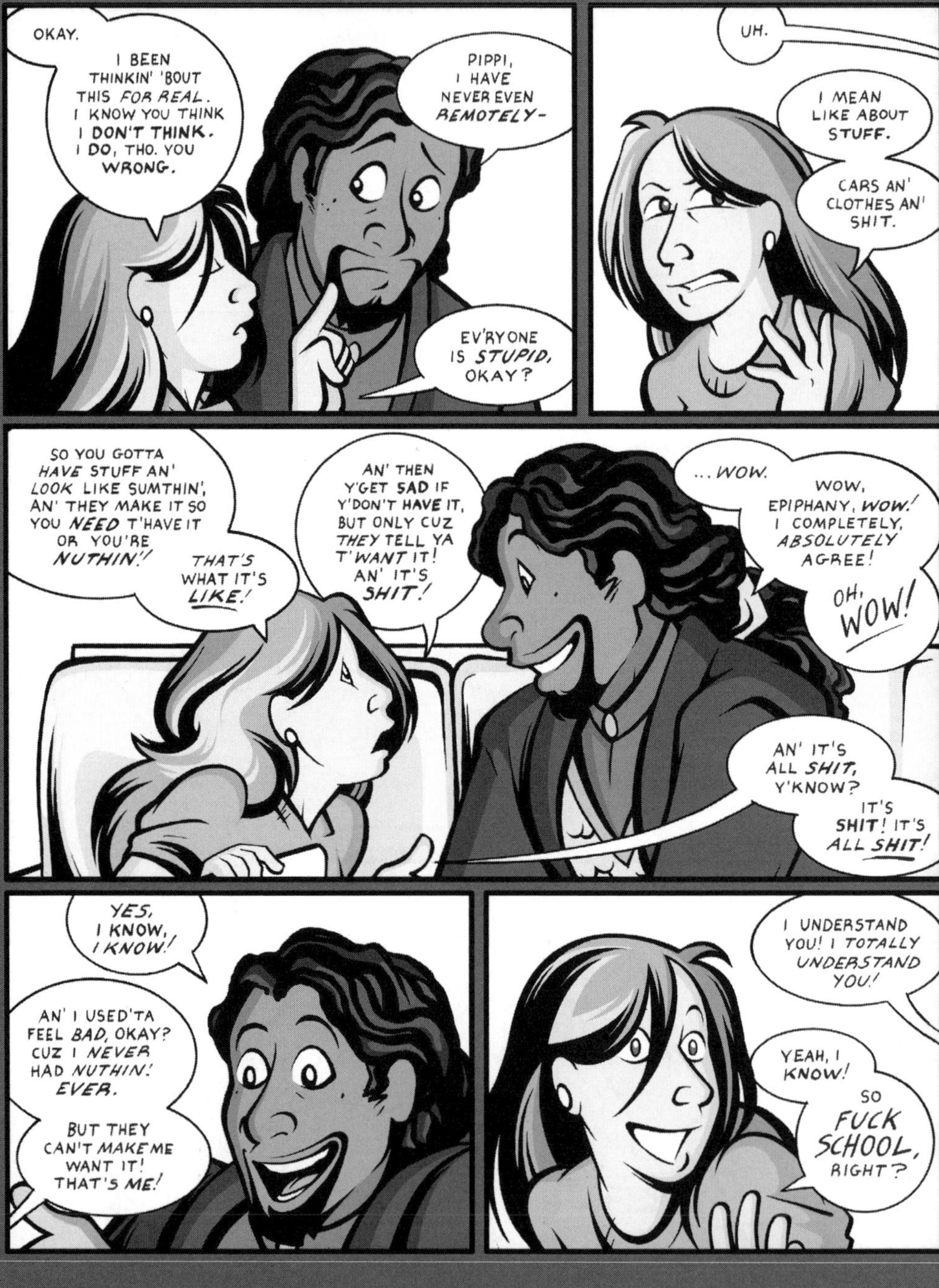
OKAY.
I BEEN THINKIN' 'BOUT THIS FOR REAL. I KNOW YOU THINK I DON'T THINK. I DO, THO. YOU WRONG.
PIPPI, I HAVE NEVER EVEN REMOTELY-
EV'RYONE IS STUPID, OKAY?
UH.
I MEAN LIKE ABOUT STUFF.
CARS AN' CLOTHES AN' SHIT.
SO YOU GOTTA HAVE STUFF AN' LOOK LIKE SUMTHIN', AN' THEY MAKE IT SO YOU NEED T'HAVE IT OR YOU'RE NUTHIN'!
THAT'S WHAT IT'S LIKE!
AN' THEN Y'GET SAD IF Y'DON'T HAVE IT, BUT ONLY CUZ THEY TELL YA T'WANT IT! AN' IT'S SHIT!
...WOW.
WOW, EPIPHANY, WOW! I COMPLETELY, ABSOLUTELY AGREE!
OH, WOW!
AN' IT'S ALL SHIT, Y'KNOW?
IT'S SHIT! IT'S ALL SHIT!
YES, I KNOW, I KNOW!
AN' I USED'TA FEEL BAD, OKAY? CUZ I NEVER HAD NUTHIN'! EVER.
BUT THEY CAN'T MAKE ME WANT IT! THAT'S ME!
I UNDERSTAND YOU! I TOTALLY UNDERSTAND YOU!
YEAH, I KNOW!
SO FUCK SCHOOL, RIGHT?

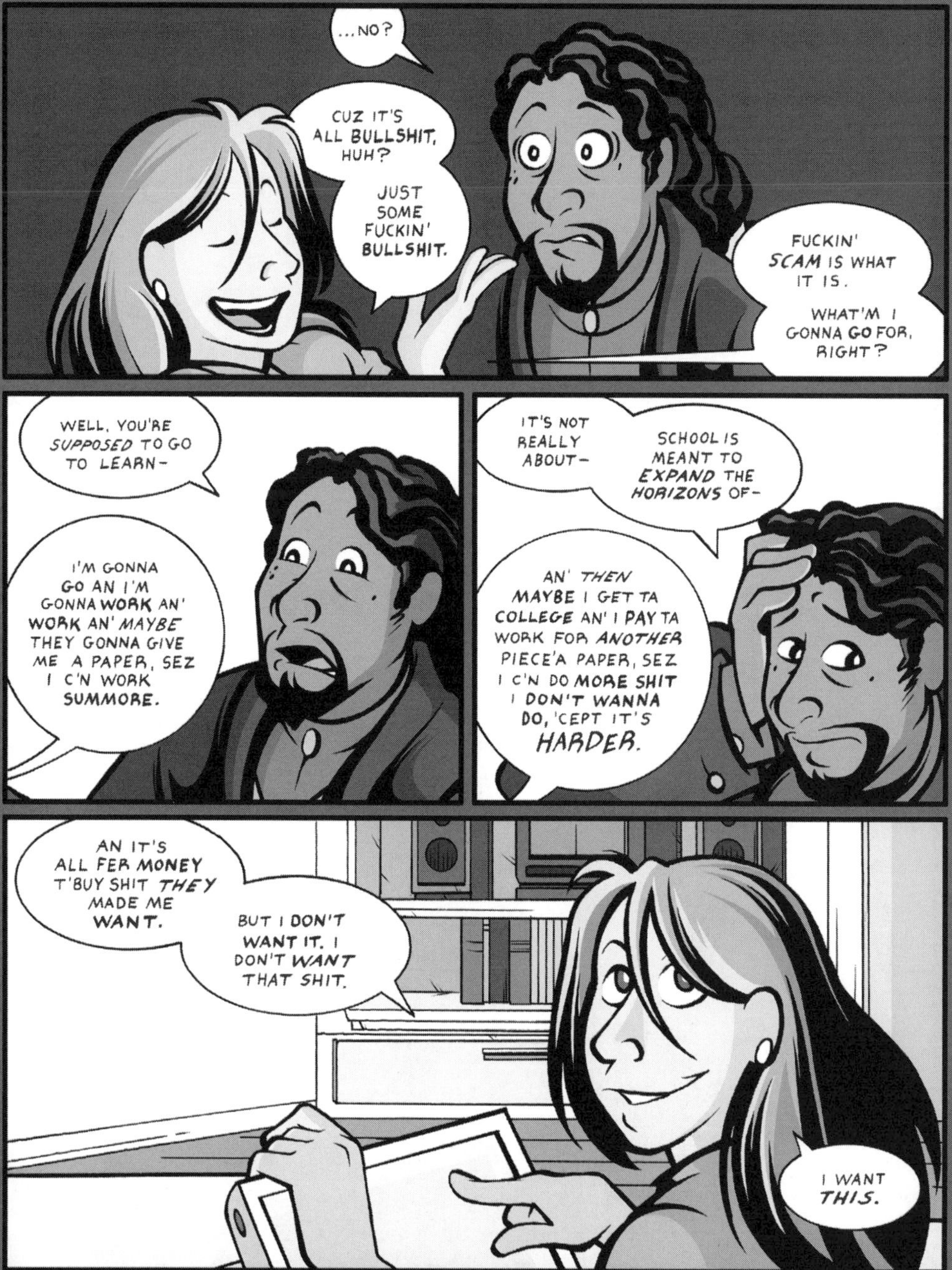
...NO?
CUZ IT'S ALL BULLSHIT, HUH?
JUST SOME FUCKIN' BULLSHIT.
FUCKIN' SCAM IS WHAT IT IS.
WHAT'M I GONNA GO FOR, RIGHT?
WELL, YOU'RE SUPPOSED TO GO TO LEARN-
I'M GONNA GO AN I'M GONNA WORK AN' WORK AN' MAYBE THEY GONNA GIVE ME A PAPER, SEZ I C'N WORK SUMMORE.
IT'S NOT REALLY ABOUT-
SCHOOL IS MEANT TO EXPAND THE HORIZONS OF-
AN' THEN MAYBE I GET TA COLLEGE AN' I PAY TA WORK FOR ANOTHER PIECE'A PAPER, SEZ I C'N DO MORE SHIT I DON'T WANNA DO, 'CEPT IT'S HARDER.
AN IT'S ALL FER MONEY T'BUY SHIT THEY MADE ME WANT.
BUT I DON'T WANT IT. I DON'T WANT THAT SHIT.
I WANT THIS.

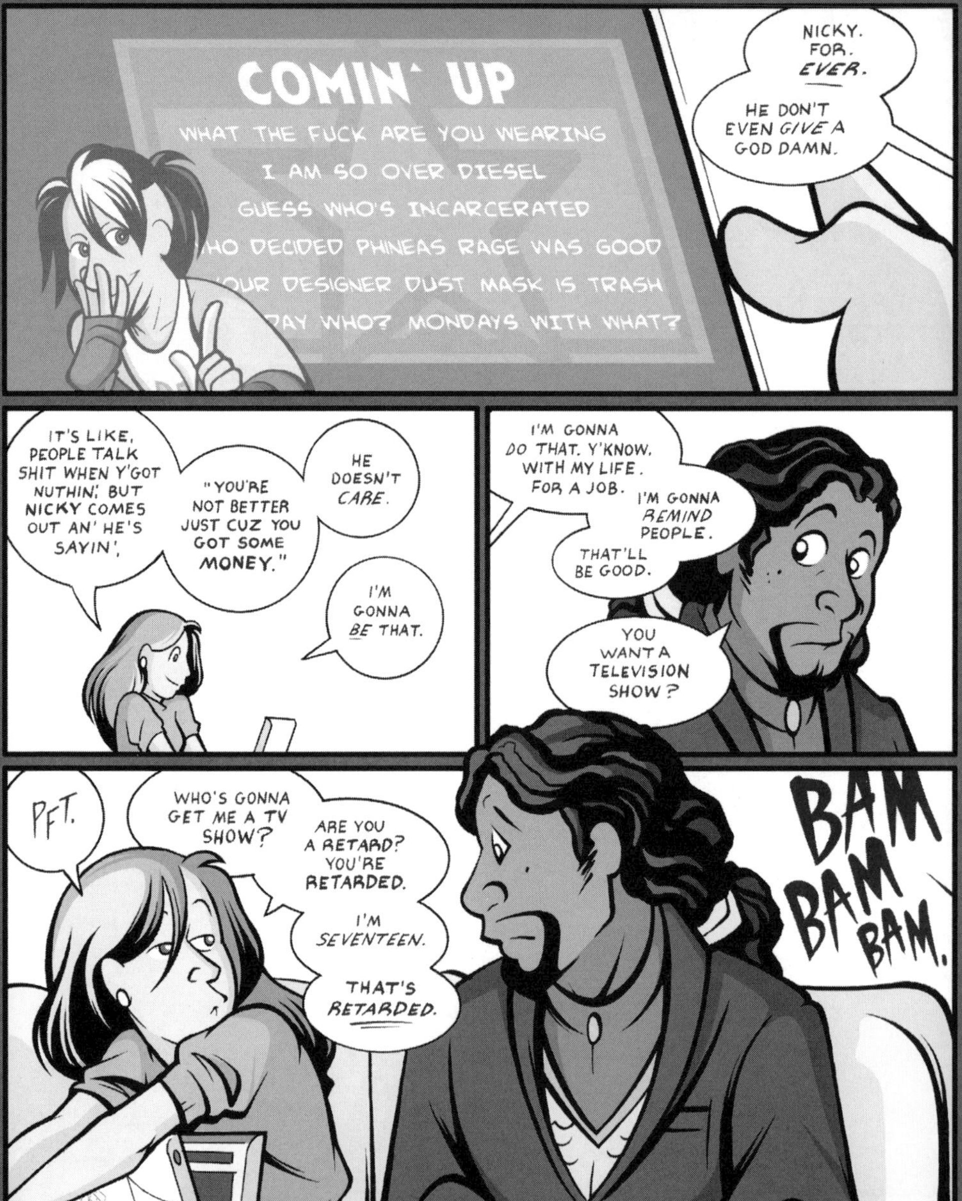
COMIN' UP
WHAT THE FUCK ARE YOU WEARING
I AM SO OVER DIESEL
GUESS WHO'S INCARCERATED
WHO DECIDED PHINEAS RAGE WAS GOOD
YOUR DESIGNER DUST MASK IS TRASH
DAY WHO? MONDAYS WITH WHAT?
NICKY. FOR. EVER.
HE DON'T EVEN GIVE A GOD DAMN.
IT'S LIKE, PEOPLE TALK SHIT WHEN Y'GOT NUTHIN', BUT NICKY COMES OUT AN' HE'S SAYIN',
"YOU'RE NOT BETTER JUST CUZ YOU GOT SOME MONEY."
HE DOESN'T CARE.
I'M GONNA BE THAT.
I'M GONNA DO THAT. Y'KNOW. WITH MY LIFE. FOR A JOB.
I'M GONNA REMIND PEOPLE.
THAT'LL BE GOOD.
YOU WANT A TELEVISION SHOW?
PFT.
WHO'S GONNA GET ME A TV SHOW?
ARE YOU A RETARD? YOU'RE RETARDED.
I'M SEVENTEEN.
THAT'S RETARDED.
BAM BAM BAM BAM.

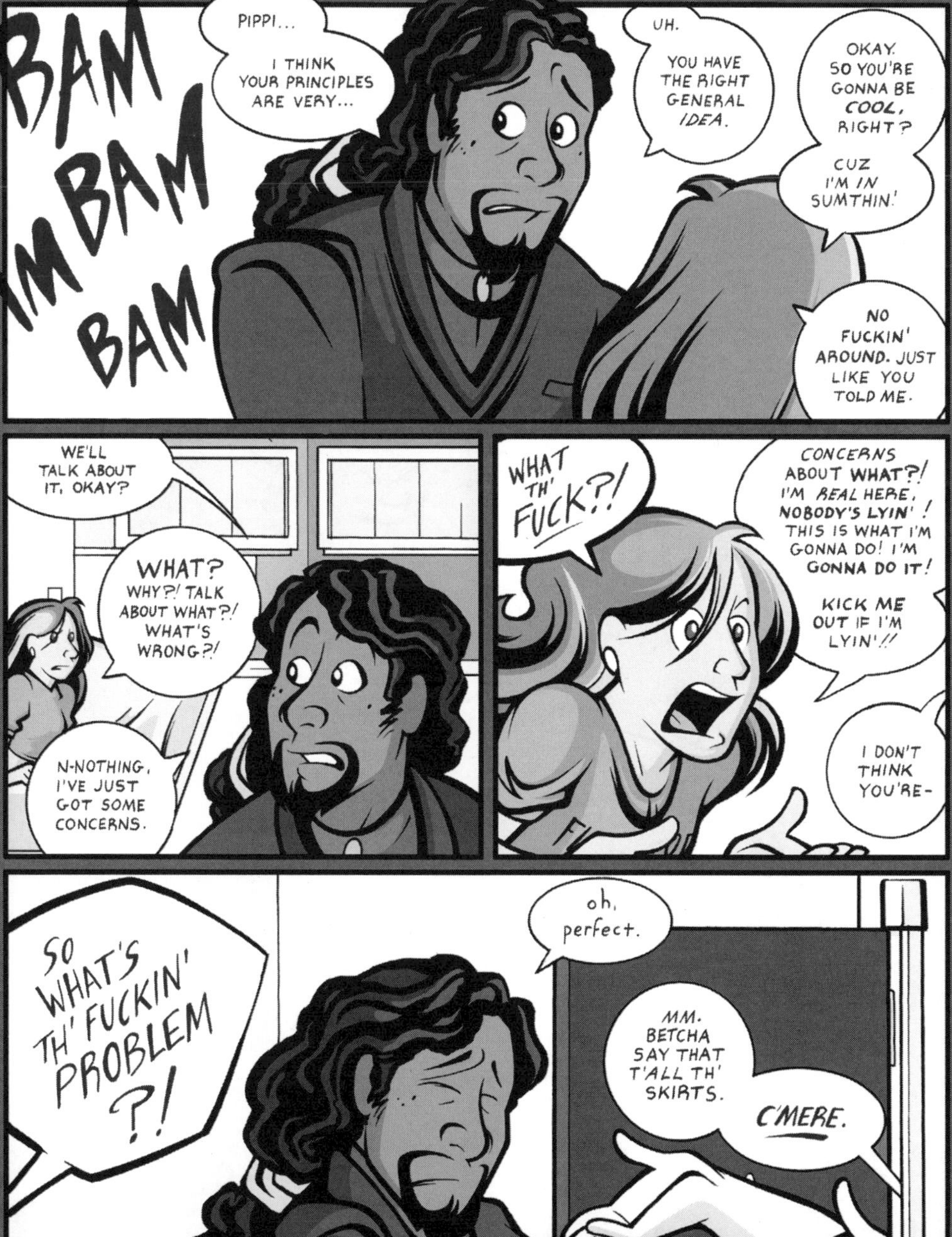
BAM BAM BAM BAM
PIPPI... I THINK YOUR PRINCIPLES ARE VERY...
UH. YOU HAVE THE RIGHT GENERAL IDEA.
OKAY. SO YOU'RE GONNA BE COOL, RIGHT?
CUZ I'M IN SUMTHIN'.
NO FUCKIN' AROUND. JUST LIKE YOU TOLD ME.
WE'LL TALK ABOUT IT, OKAY?
WHAT? WHY?! TALK ABOUT WHAT?! WHAT'S WRONG?!
N-NOTHING. I'VE JUST GOT SOME CONCERNS.
WHAT TH' FUCK?!
CONCERNS ABOUT WHAT?! I'M REAL HERE. NOBODY'S LYIN'! THIS IS WHAT I'M GONNA DO! I'M GONNA DO IT!
KICK ME OUT IF I'M LYIN'!!
I DON'T THINK YOU'RE-
SO WHAT'S TH' FUCKIN' PROBLEM?!
oh, perfect.
MM. BETCHA SAY THAT T'ALL TH' SKIRTS.
C'MERE.

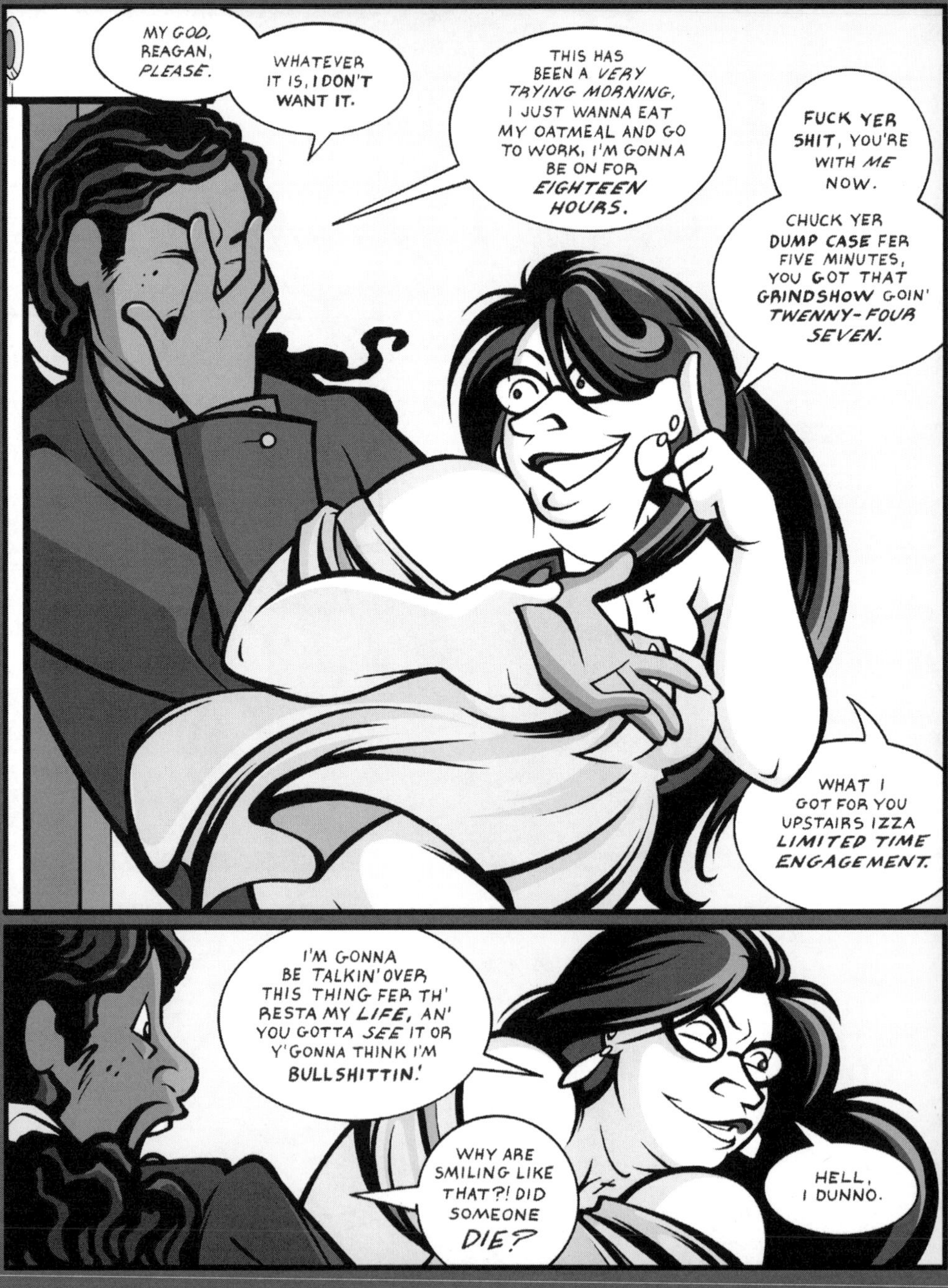

MY GOD, REAGAN, PLEASE.
WHATEVER IT IS, I DON'T WANT IT.
THIS HAS BEEN A VERY TRYING MORNING, I JUST WANNA EAT MY OATMEAL AND GO TO WORK, I'M GONNA BE ON FOR EIGHTEEN HOURS.
FUCK YER SHIT, YOU'RE WITH ME NOW.
CHUCK YER DUMP CASE FER FIVE MINUTES, YOU GOT THAT GRINDSHOW GOIN' TWENNY-FOUR SEVEN.
WHAT I GOT FOR YOU UPSTAIRS IZZA LIMITED TIME ENGAGEMENT.
I'M GONNA BE TALKIN' OVER THIS THING FER TH' RESTA MY LIFE, AN' YOU GOTTA SEE IT OR Y'GONNA THINK I'M BULLSHITTIN.'
WHY ARE SMILING LIKE THAT?! DID SOMEONE DIE?
HELL, I DUNNO.

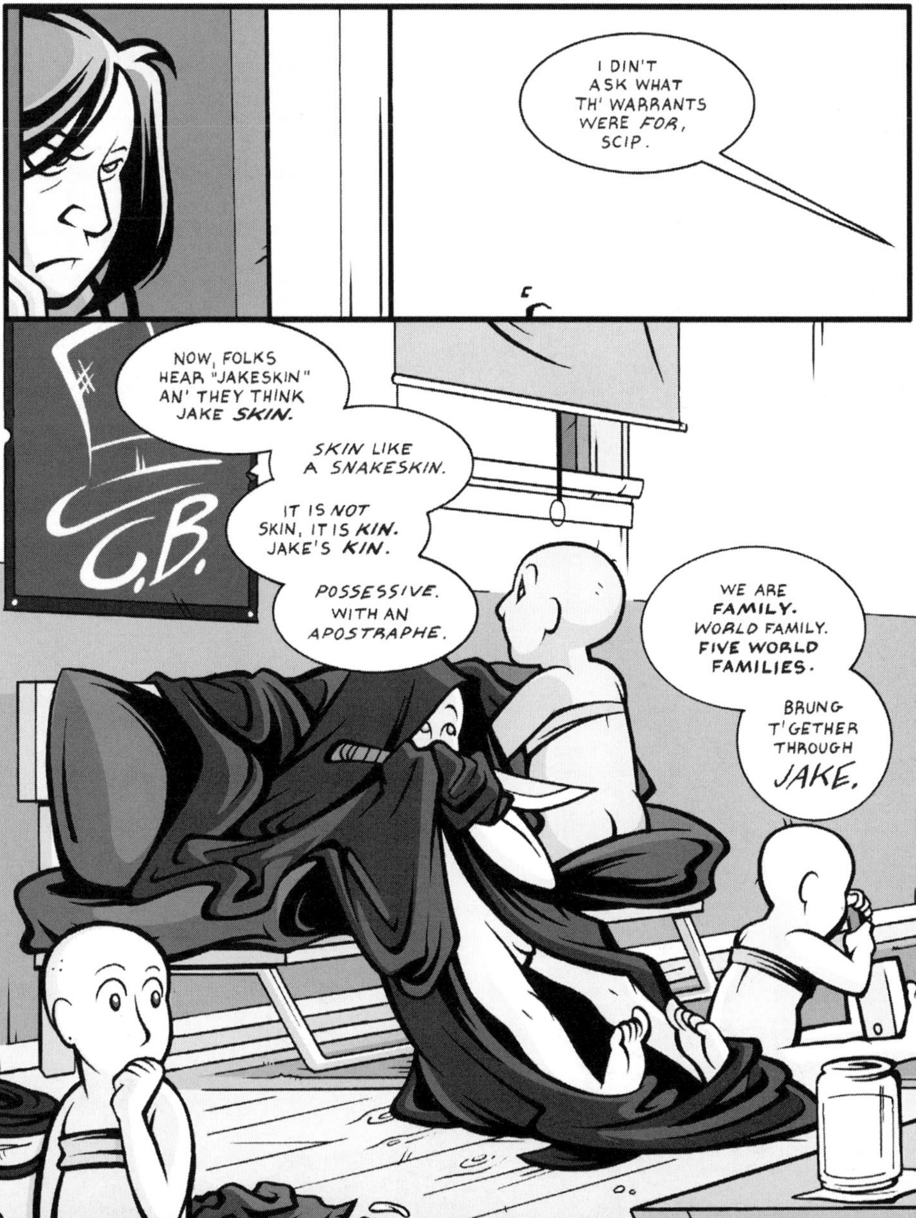
I DIN'T ASK WHAT TH' WARRANTS WERE *FOR*, SCIP.
NOW, FOLKS HEAR "JAKESKIN" AN' THEY THINK JAKE **SKIN**.
SKIN LIKE A *SNAKESKIN.*
IT IS *NOT* SKIN, IT IS **KIN**. JAKE'S **KIN**.
POSSESSIVE. WITH AN *APOSTRAPHE.*
WE ARE **FAMILY.** *WORLD* FAMILY. **FIVE WORLD FAMILIES.**
BRUNG T'GETHER THROUGH *JAKE.*
C.B.

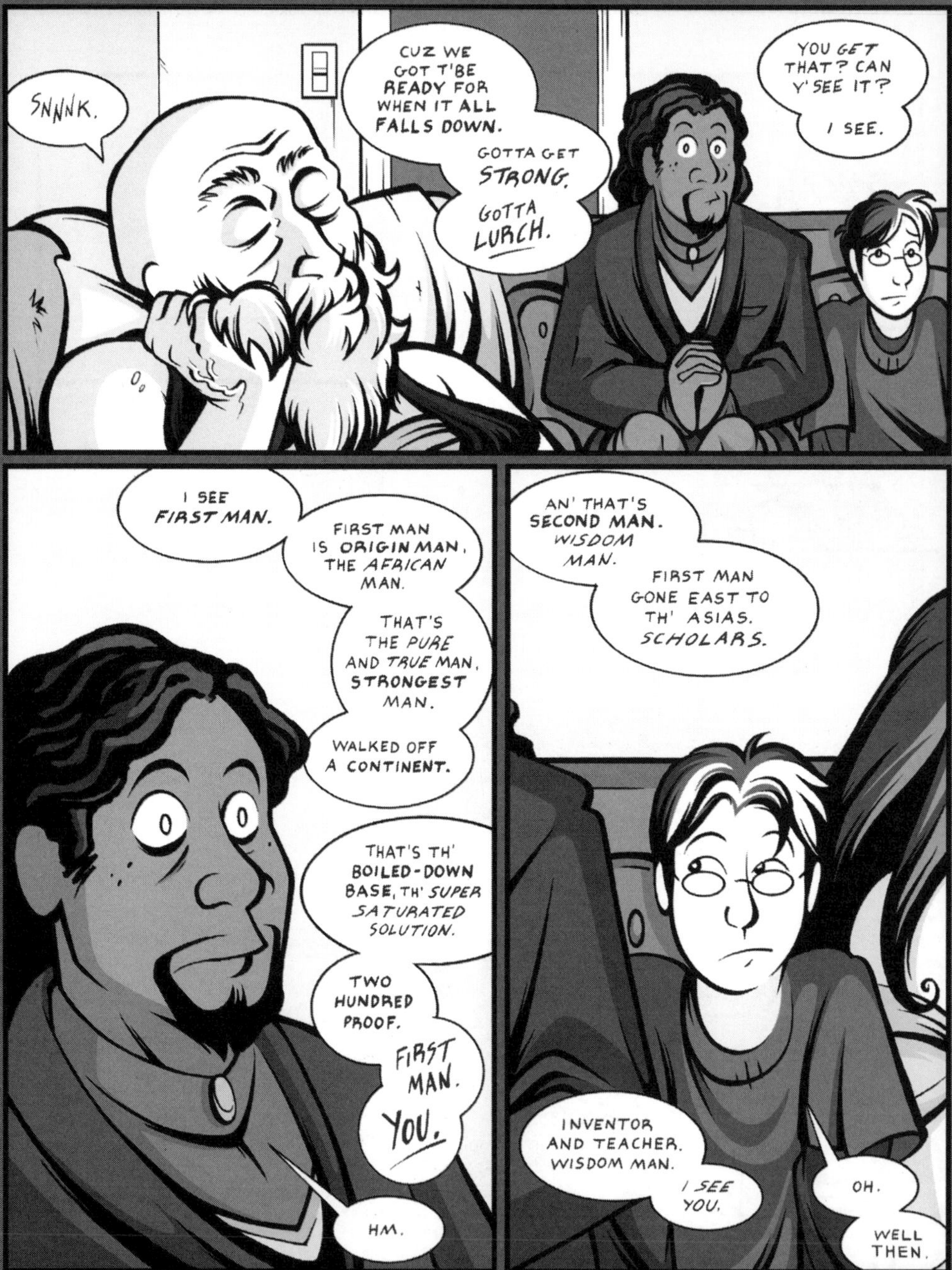
SNNNK.
CUZ WE GOT T'BE READY FOR WHEN IT ALL FALLS DOWN.
GOTTA GET STRONG.
GOTTA LURCH.
YOU GET THAT? CAN Y'SEE IT?
I SEE.
I SEE FIRST MAN.
FIRST MAN IS ORIGIN MAN, THE AFRICAN MAN.
THAT'S THE PURE AND TRUE MAN, STRONGEST MAN.
WALKED OFF A CONTINENT.
THAT'S TH' BOILED-DOWN BASE, TH' SUPER SATURATED SOLUTION.
TWO HUNDRED PROOF.
FIRST MAN.
YOU.
HM.
AN' THAT'S SECOND MAN. WISDOM MAN.
FIRST MAN GONE EAST TO TH' ASIAS. SCHOLARS.
INVENTOR AND TEACHER. WISDOM MAN.
I SEE YOU.
OH.
WELL THEN.

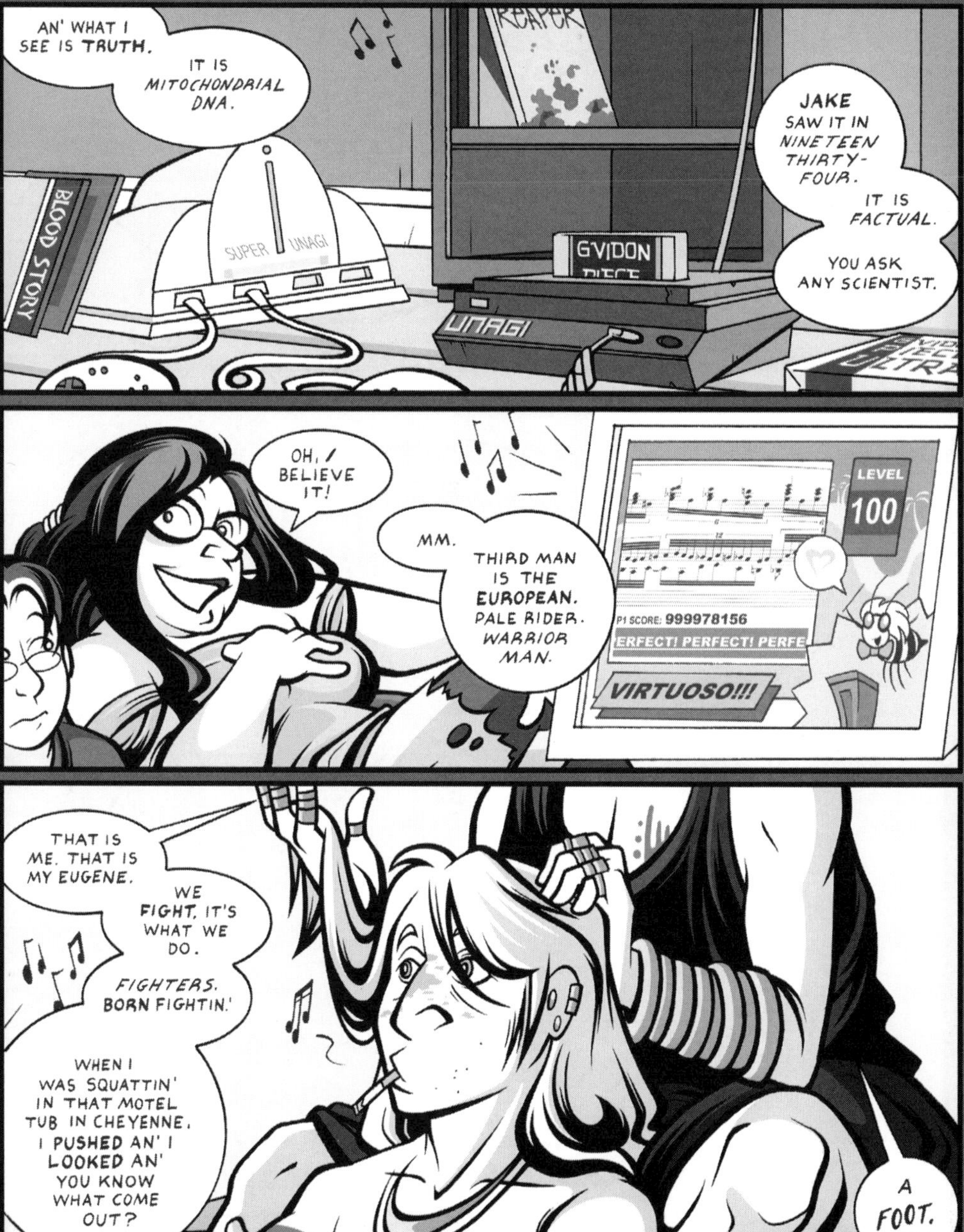
AN' WHAT I SEE IS TRUTH.
IT IS MITOCHONDRIAL DNA.
REAPER
BLOOD STORY
SUPER UNAGI
G'VIDON
UNAGI
JAKE SAW IT IN NINETEEN THIRTY-FOUR.
IT IS FACTUAL.
YOU ASK ANY SCIENTIST.
OH, I BELIEVE IT!
LEVEL
100
P1 SCORE: 999978156
ERFECT! PERFECT! PERFE
VIRTUOSO!!!
MM.
THIRD MAN IS THE EUROPEAN. PALE RIDER. WARRIOR MAN.
THAT IS ME. THAT IS MY EUGENE.
WE FIGHT. IT'S WHAT WE DO.
FIGHTERS. BORN FIGHTIN.'
WHEN I WAS SQUATTIN' IN THAT MOTEL TUB IN CHEYENNE, I PUSHED AN' I LOOKED AN' YOU KNOW WHAT COME OUT?
A FOOT.

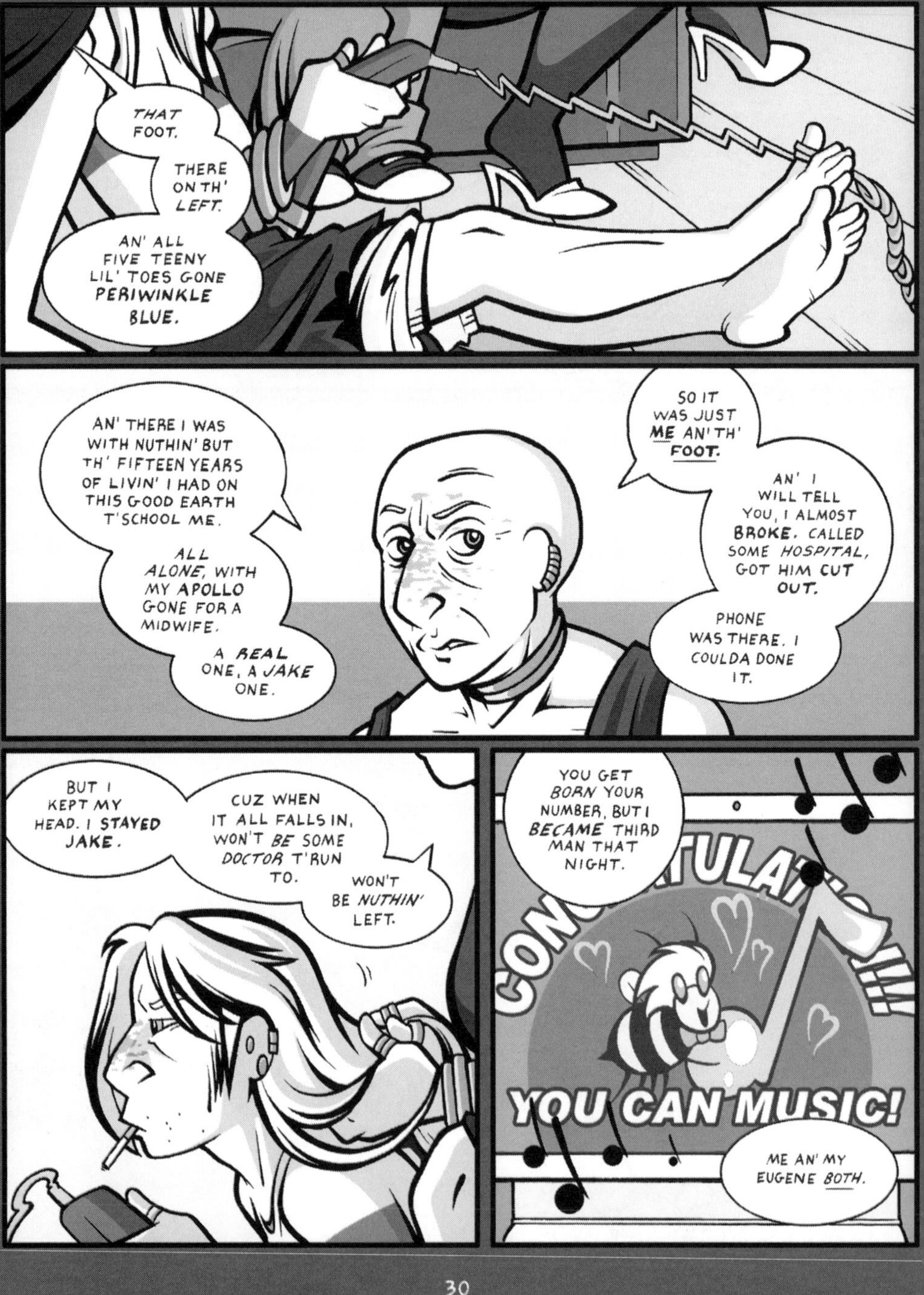
THAT FOOT.
THERE ON TH' LEFT.
AN' ALL FIVE TEENY LIL' TOES GONE PERIWINKLE BLUE.
AN' THERE I WAS WITH NUTHIN' BUT TH' FIFTEEN YEARS OF LIVIN' I HAD ON THIS GOOD EARTH T'SCHOOL ME.
ALL ALONE, WITH MY APOLLO GONE FOR A MIDWIFE.
A REAL ONE, A JAKE ONE.
SO IT WAS JUST ME AN' TH' FOOT.
AN' I WILL TELL YOU, I ALMOST BROKE. CALLED SOME HOSPITAL, GOT HIM CUT OUT.
PHONE WAS THERE. I COULDA DONE IT.
BUT I KEPT MY HEAD. I STAYED JAKE.
CUZ WHEN IT ALL FALLS IN, WON'T BE SOME DOCTOR T'RUN TO.
WON'T BE NUTHIN' LEFT.
YOU GET BORN YOUR NUMBER, BUT I BECAME THIRD MAN THAT NIGHT.
YOU CAN MUSIC!
ME AN' MY EUGENE BOTH.

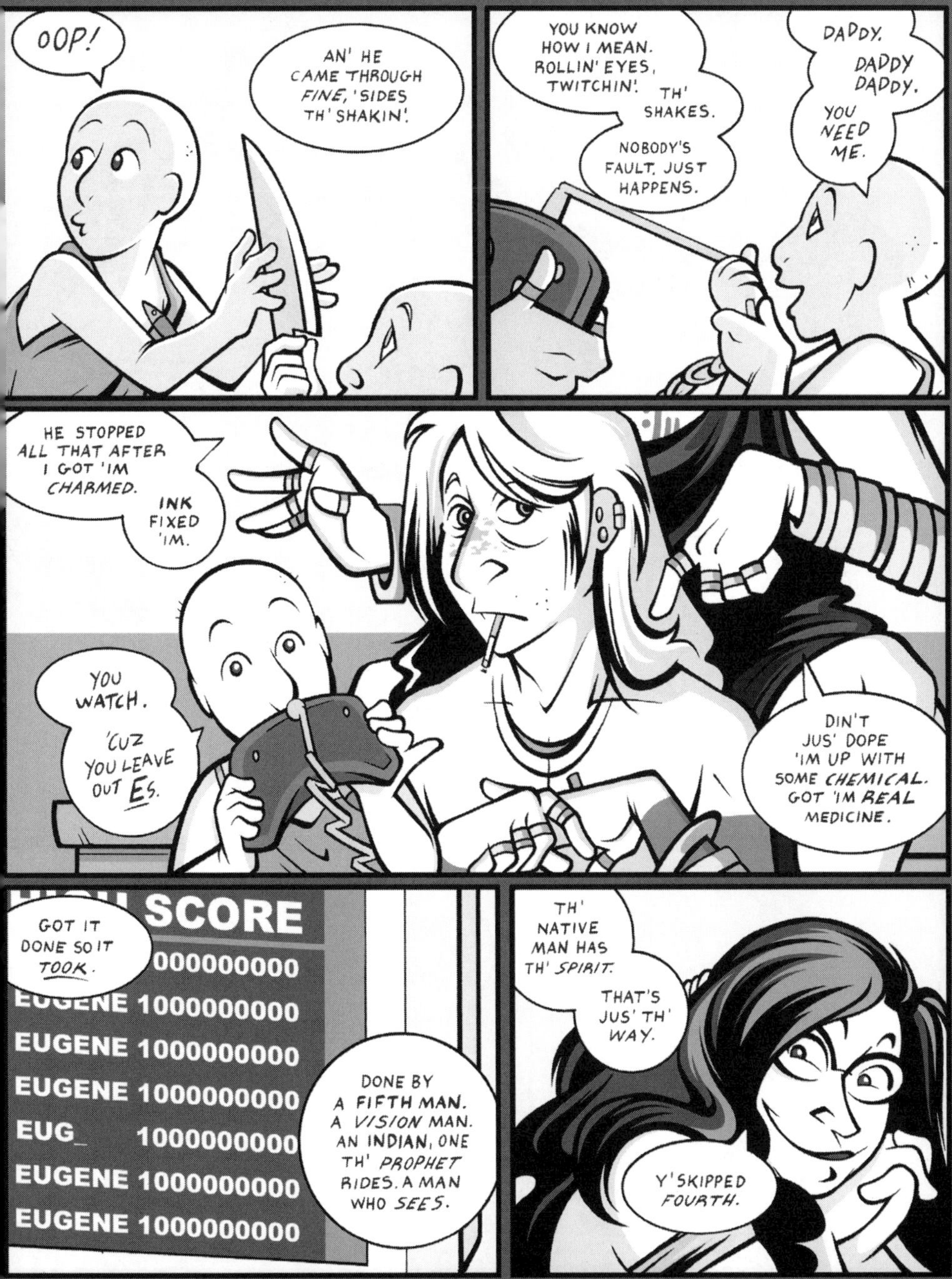

OOP!
AN' HE CAME THROUGH FINE, 'SIDES TH' SHAKIN'.
YOU KNOW HOW I MEAN. ROLLIN' EYES, TWITCHIN'.
TH' SHAKES.
NOBODY'S FAULT. JUST HAPPENS.
DADDY.
DADDY DADDY.
YOU NEED ME.
HE STOPPED ALL THAT AFTER I GOT 'IM CHARMED.
INK FIXED 'IM.
YOU WATCH.
'CUZ YOU LEAVE OUT Es.
DIN'T JUS' DOPE 'IM UP WITH SOME CHEMICAL. GOT 'IM REAL MEDICINE.
SCORE
GOT IT DONE SO IT TOOK.
0000000000
EUGENE 1000000000
EUGENE 1000000000
EUGENE 1000000000
EUG_ 1000000000
EUGENE 1000000000
EUGENE 1000000000
DONE BY A FIFTH MAN. A VISION MAN. AN INDIAN, ONE TH' PROPHET RIDES. A MAN WHO SEES.
TH' NATIVE MAN HAS TH' SPIRIT.
THAT'S JUS' TH' WAY.
Y'SKIPPED FOURTH.

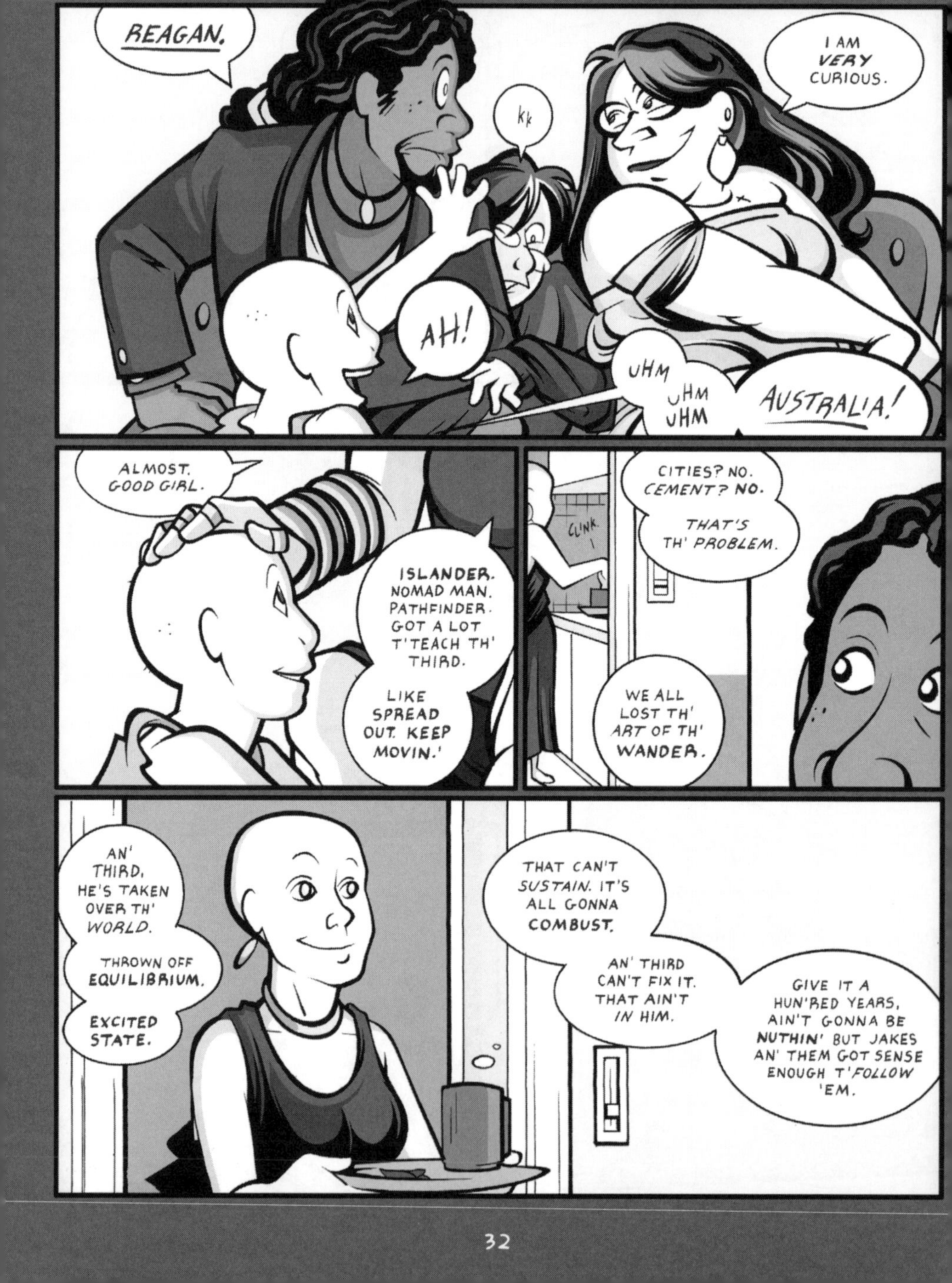
REAGAN.
I AM VERY CURIOUS.
Kk
AH!
UHM UHM UHM
AUSTRALIA!
ALMOST. GOOD GIRL.
ISLANDER. NOMAD MAN. PATHFINDER. GOT A LOT T'TEACH TH' THIRD.
LIKE SPREAD OUT. KEEP MOVIN.'
CLINK
CITIES? NO. CEMENT? NO.
THAT'S TH' PROBLEM.
WE ALL LOST TH' ART OF TH' WANDER.
AN' THIRD, HE'S TAKEN OVER TH' WORLD.
THROWN OFF EQUILIBRIUM.
EXCITED STATE.
THAT CAN'T SUSTAIN. IT'S ALL GONNA COMBUST.
AN' THIRD CAN'T FIX IT. THAT AIN'T IN HIM.
GIVE IT A HUN'RED YEARS, AIN'T GONNA BE NUTHIN' BUT JAKES AN' THEM GOT SENSE ENOUGH T'FOLLOW 'EM.

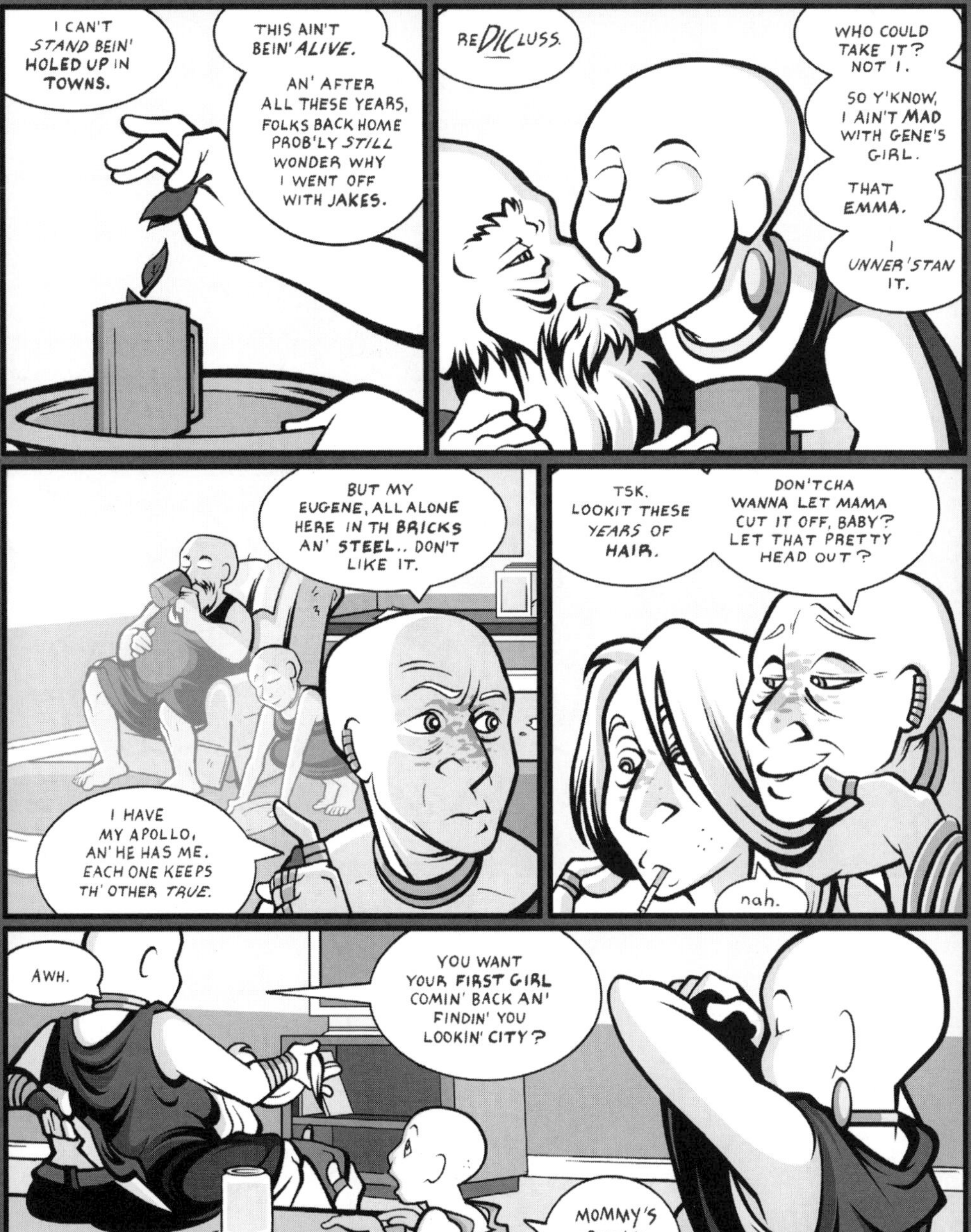
I CAN'T STAND BEIN' HOLED UP IN TOWNS.
THIS AIN'T BEIN' ALIVE.
AN' AFTER ALL THESE YEARS, FOLKS BACK HOME PROB'LY STILL WONDER WHY I WENT OFF WITH JAKES.
REDICLUSS.
WHO COULD TAKE IT? NOT I.
SO Y'KNOW, I AIN'T MAD WITH GENE'S GIRL.
THAT EMMA.
I UNNER'STAN IT.
BUT MY EUGENE, ALL ALONE HERE IN TH BRICKS AN' STEEL.. DON'T LIKE IT.
I HAVE MY APOLLO, AN' HE HAS ME. EACH ONE KEEPS TH' OTHER TRUE.
TSK. LOOKIT THESE YEARS OF HAIR.
DON'TCHA WANNA LET MAMA CUT IT OFF, BABY? LET THAT PRETTY HEAD OUT?
nah.
AWH.
YOU WANT YOUR FIRST GIRL COMIN' BACK AN' FINDIN' YOU LOOKIN' CITY?
MOMMY'S COMING HOME?

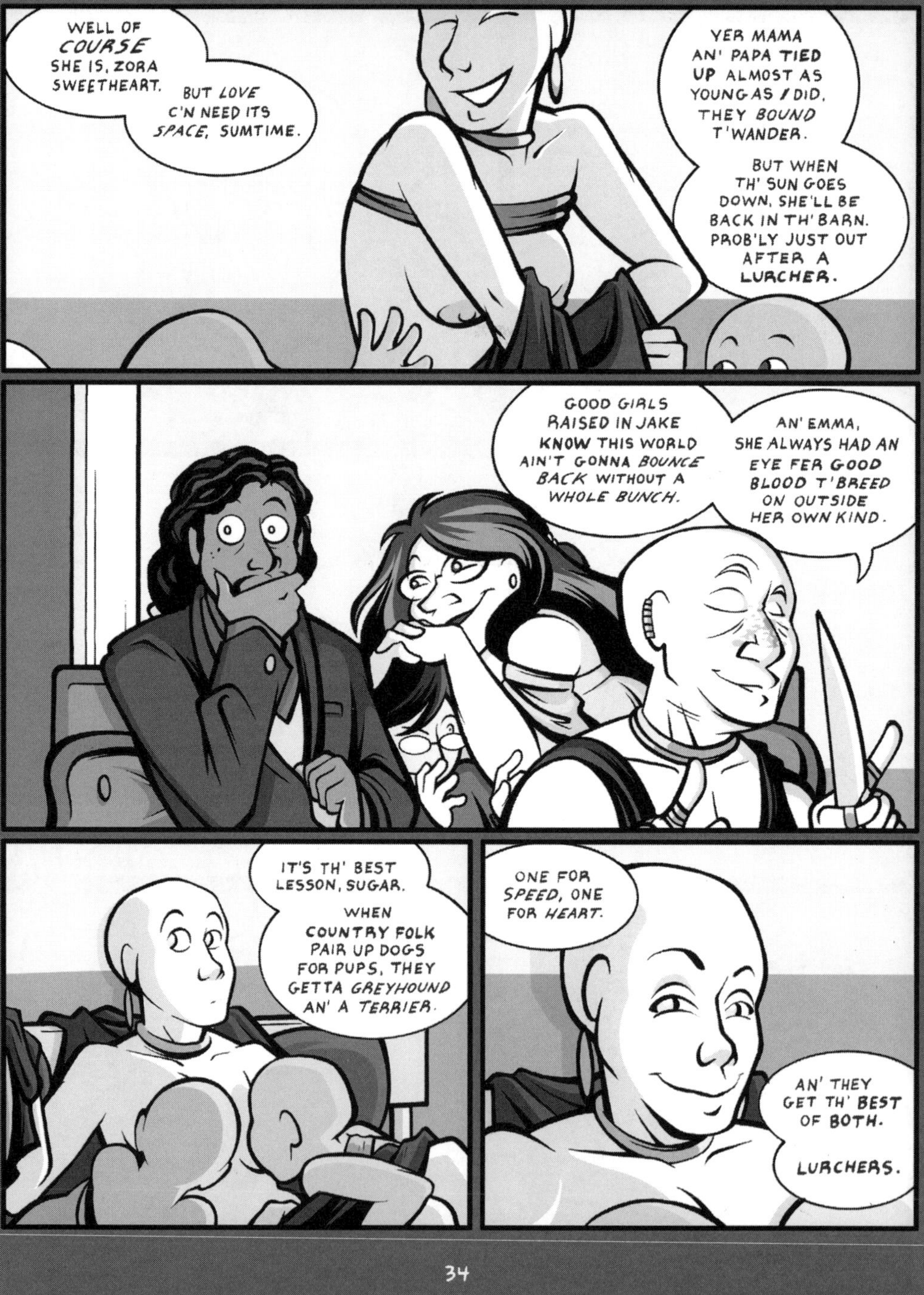
WELL OF COURSE SHE IS, ZORA SWEETHEART.
BUT LOVE C'N NEED ITS SPACE, SUMTIME.
YER MAMA AN' PAPA TIED UP ALMOST AS YOUNG AS I DID. THEY BOUND T'WANDER.
BUT WHEN TH' SUN GOES DOWN, SHE'LL BE BACK IN TH' BARN. PROB'LY JUST OUT AFTER A LURCHER.
GOOD GIRLS RAISED IN JAKE KNOW THIS WORLD AIN'T GONNA BOUNCE BACK WITHOUT A WHOLE BUNCH.
AN' EMMA, SHE ALWAYS HAD AN EYE FER GOOD BLOOD T'BREED ON OUTSIDE HER OWN KIND.
IT'S TH' BEST LESSON, SUGAR.
WHEN COUNTRY FOLK PAIR UP DOGS FOR PUPS, THEY GETTA GREYHOUND AN' A TERRIER.
ONE FOR SPEED, ONE FOR HEART.
AN' THEY GET TH' BEST OF BOTH.
LURCHERS.

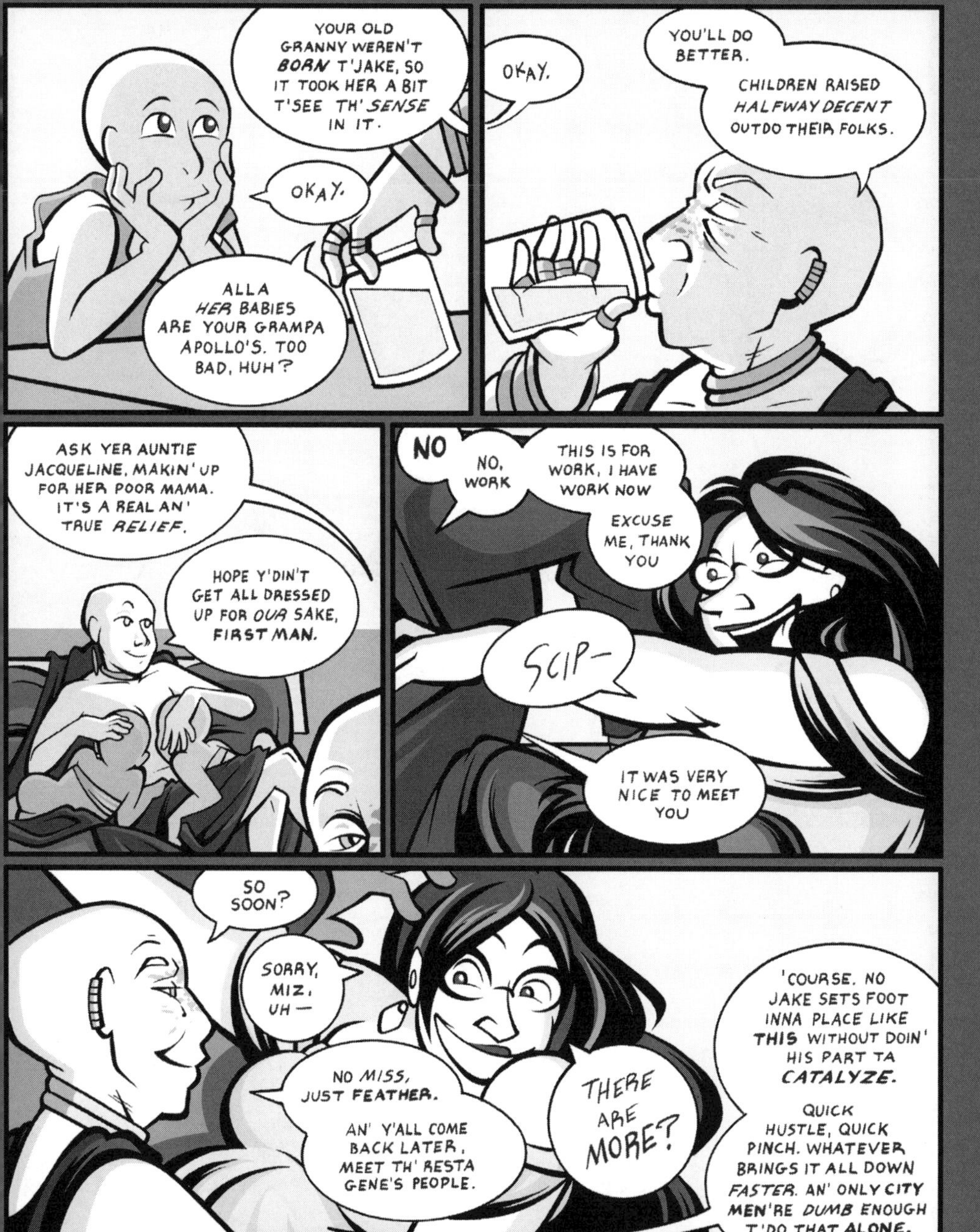
YOUR OLD GRANNY WEREN'T BORN T'JAKE, SO IT TOOK HER A BIT T'SEE TH' SENSE IN IT.
OKAY.
ALLA HER BABIES ARE YOUR GRAMPA APOLLO'S. TOO BAD, HUH?
OKAY.
YOU'LL DO BETTER.
CHILDREN RAISED HALFWAY DECENT OUTDO THEIR FOLKS.
ASK YER AUNTIE JACQUELINE, MAKIN' UP FOR HER POOR MAMA. IT'S A REAL AN' TRUE RELIEF.
HOPE Y'DIN'T GET ALL DRESSED UP FOR OUR SAKE, FIRST MAN.
NO
NO, WORK
THIS IS FOR WORK, I HAVE WORK NOW
EXCUSE ME, THANK YOU
SCIP—
IT WAS VERY NICE TO MEET YOU
SO SOON?
SORRY, MIZ. UH—
NO MISS, JUST FEATHER.
AN' Y'ALL COME BACK LATER, MEET TH' RESTA GENE'S PEOPLE.
THERE ARE MORE?
'COURSE. NO JAKE SETS FOOT INNA PLACE LIKE THIS WITHOUT DOIN' HIS PART TA CATALYZE.
QUICK HUSTLE, QUICK PINCH. WHATEVER BRINGS IT ALL DOWN FASTER. AN' ONLY CITY MEN'RE DUMB ENOUGH T'DO THAT ALONE.

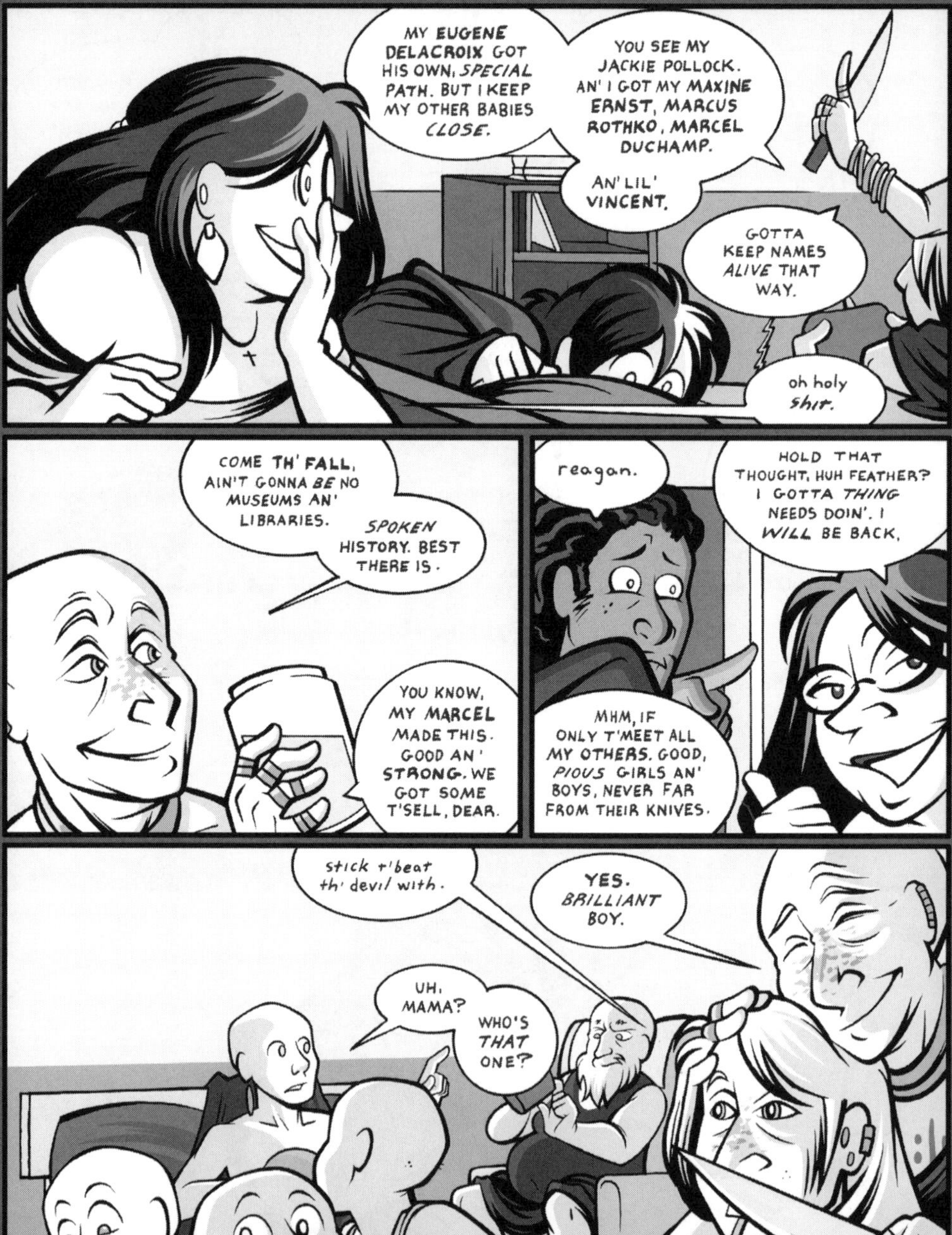
MY EUGENE DELACROIX GOT HIS OWN, SPECIAL PATH. BUT I KEEP MY OTHER BABIES CLOSE.
YOU SEE MY JACKIE POLLOCK. AN' I GOT MY MAXINE ERNST, MARCUS ROTHKO, MARCEL DUCHAMP.
AN' LIL' VINCENT.
GOTTA KEEP NAMES ALIVE THAT WAY.
oh holy shit.
COME TH' FALL, AIN'T GONNA BE NO MUSEUMS AN' LIBRARIES.
SPOKEN HISTORY. BEST THERE IS.
YOU KNOW, MY MARCEL MADE THIS. GOOD AN' STRONG. WE GOT SOME T'SELL, DEAR.
reagan.
HOLD THAT THOUGHT, HUH FEATHER? I GOTTA THING NEEDS DOIN'. I WILL BE BACK.
MHM, IF ONLY T'MEET ALL MY OTHERS. GOOD, PIOUS GIRLS AN' BOYS, NEVER FAR FROM THEIR KNIVES.
stick t'beat th' devil with.
YES. BRILLIANT BOY.
UH, MAMA?
WHO'S THAT ONE?

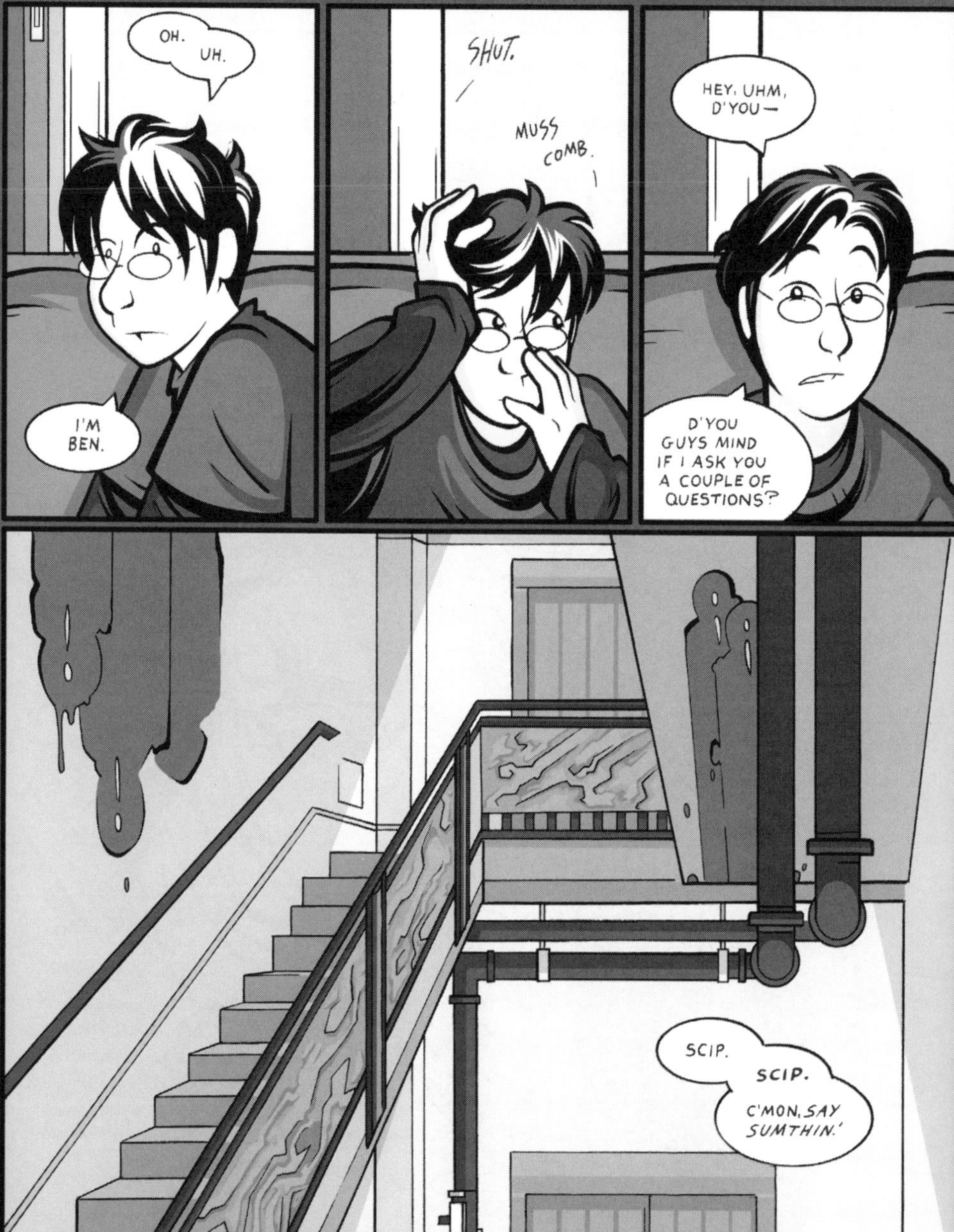
OH. UH.
I'M BEN.
SHUT.
MUSS COMB.
HEY, UHM, D'YOU—
D'YOU GUYS MIND IF I ASK YOU A COUPLE OF QUESTIONS?
SCIP.
SCIP.
C'MON, SAY SUMTHIN.'

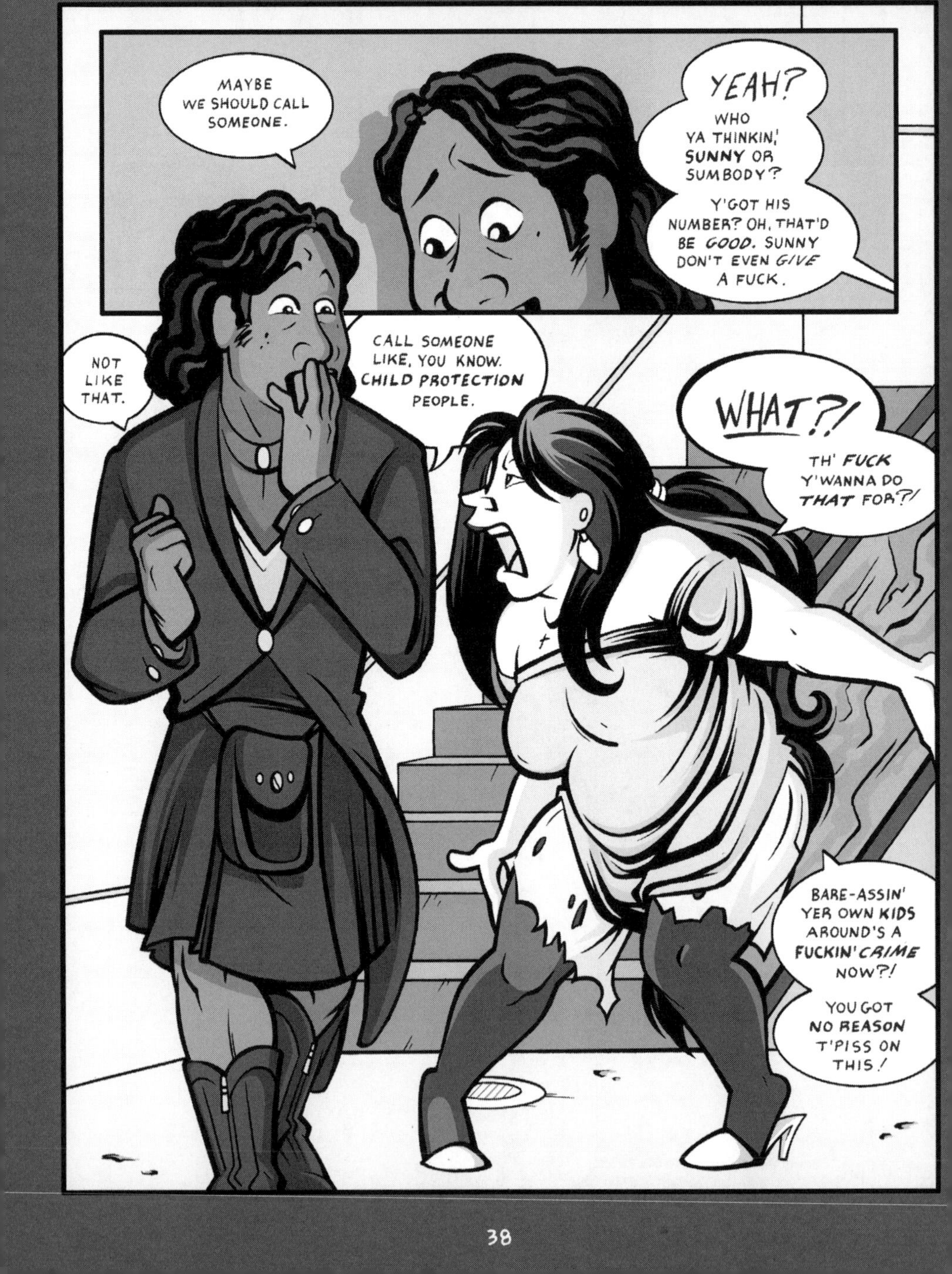
MAYBE WE SHOULD CALL SOMEONE.
YEAH?
WHO YA THINKIN,' SUNNY OR SUMBODY?
Y'GOT HIS NUMBER? OH, THAT'D BE GOOD. SUNNY DON'T EVEN GIVE A FUCK.
NOT LIKE THAT.
CALL SOMEONE LIKE, YOU KNOW. CHILD PROTECTION PEOPLE.
WHAT?!
TH' FUCK Y'WANNA DO THAT FOR?!
BARE-ASSIN' YER OWN KIDS AROUND'S A FUCKIN' CRIME NOW?!
YOU GOT NO REASON T'PISS ON THIS!

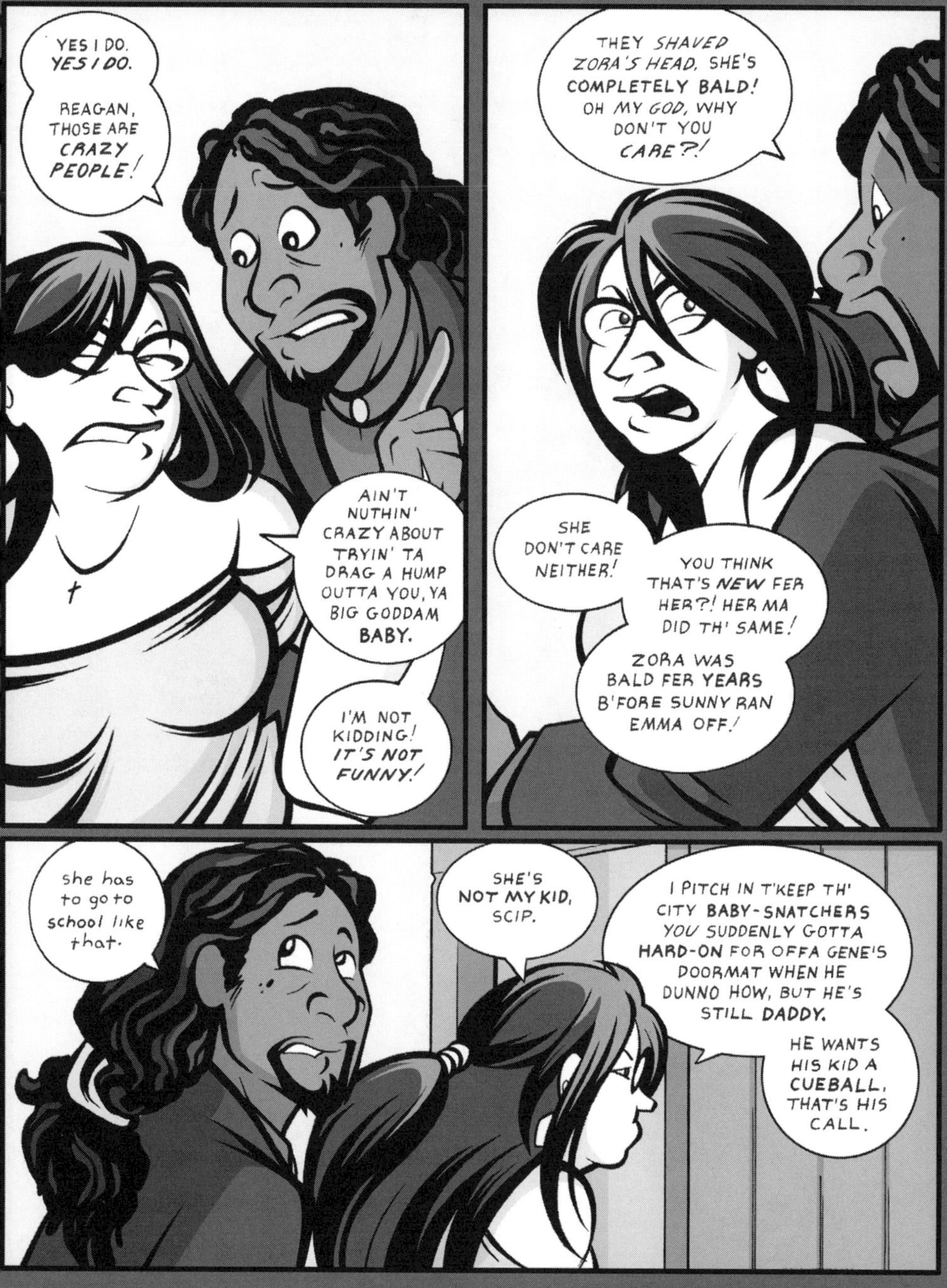

YES I DO. YES I DO.
REAGAN, THOSE ARE CRAZY PEOPLE!
AIN'T NUTHIN' CRAZY ABOUT TRYIN' TA DRAG A HUMP OUTTA YOU, YA BIG GODDAM BABY.
I'M NOT KIDDING! IT'S NOT FUNNY!
THEY SHAVED ZORA'S HEAD, SHE'S COMPLETELY BALD! OH MY GOD, WHY DON'T YOU CARE?!
SHE DON'T CARE NEITHER!
YOU THINK THAT'S NEW FER HER?! HER MA DID TH' SAME!
ZORA WAS BALD FER YEARS B'FORE SUNNY RAN EMMA OFF!
she has to go to school like that.
SHE'S NOT MY KID, SCIP.
I PITCH IN T'KEEP TH' CITY BABY-SNATCHERS YOU SUDDENLY GOTTA HARD-ON FOR OFFA GENE'S DOORMAT WHEN HE DUNNO HOW, BUT HE'S STILL DADDY.
HE WANTS HIS KID A CUEBALL. THAT'S HIS CALL.

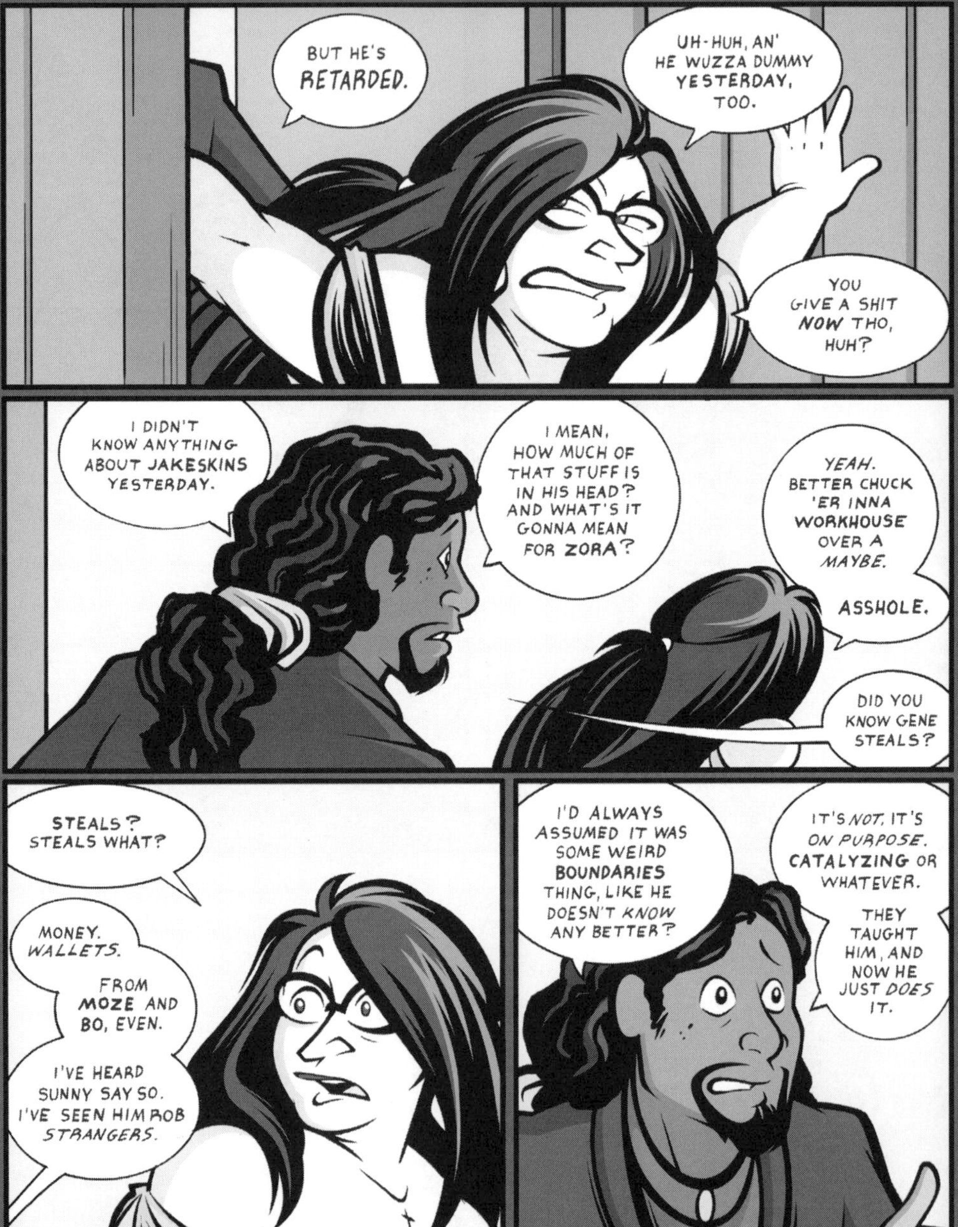
BUT HE'S RETARDED.
UH-HUH, AN' HE WUZZA DUMMY YESTERDAY, TOO.
YOU GIVE A SHIT NOW THO, HUH?
I DIDN'T KNOW ANYTHING ABOUT JAKESKINS YESTERDAY.
I MEAN, HOW MUCH OF THAT STUFF IS IN HIS HEAD? AND WHAT'S IT GONNA MEAN FOR ZORA?
YEAH. BETTER CHUCK 'ER INNA WORKHOUSE OVER A MAYBE.
ASSHOLE.
DID YOU KNOW GENE STEALS?
STEALS? STEALS WHAT?
MONEY. WALLETS.
FROM MOZE AND BO, EVEN.
I'VE HEARD SUNNY SAY SO. I'VE SEEN HIM ROB STRANGERS.
I'D ALWAYS ASSUMED IT WAS SOME WEIRD BOUNDARIES THING, LIKE HE DOESN'T KNOW ANY BETTER?
IT'S NOT, IT'S ON PURPOSE. CATALYZING OR WHATEVER.
THEY TAUGHT HIM, AND NOW HE JUST DOES IT.

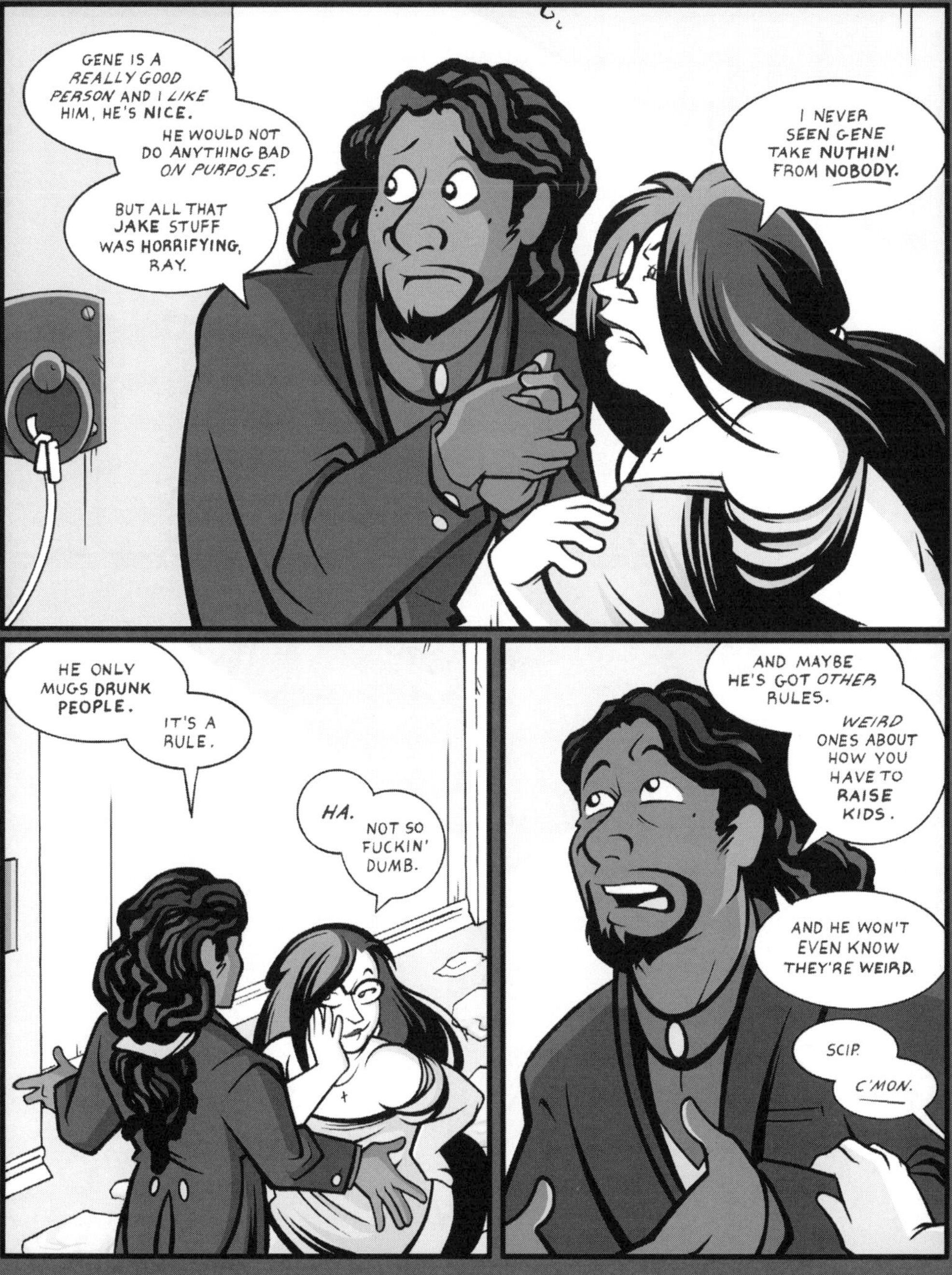
GENE IS A REALLY GOOD PERSON AND I LIKE HIM, HE'S NICE.
HE WOULD NOT DO ANYTHING BAD ON PURPOSE.
BUT ALL THAT JAKE STUFF WAS HORRIFYING, RAY.
I NEVER SEEN GENE TAKE NUTHIN' FROM NOBODY.
HE ONLY MUGS DRUNK PEOPLE.
IT'S A RULE.
HA.
NOT SO FUCKIN' DUMB.
AND MAYBE HE'S GOT OTHER RULES.
WEIRD ONES ABOUT HOW YOU HAVE TO RAISE KIDS.
AND HE WON'T EVEN KNOW THEY'RE WEIRD.
SCIP.
C'MON.

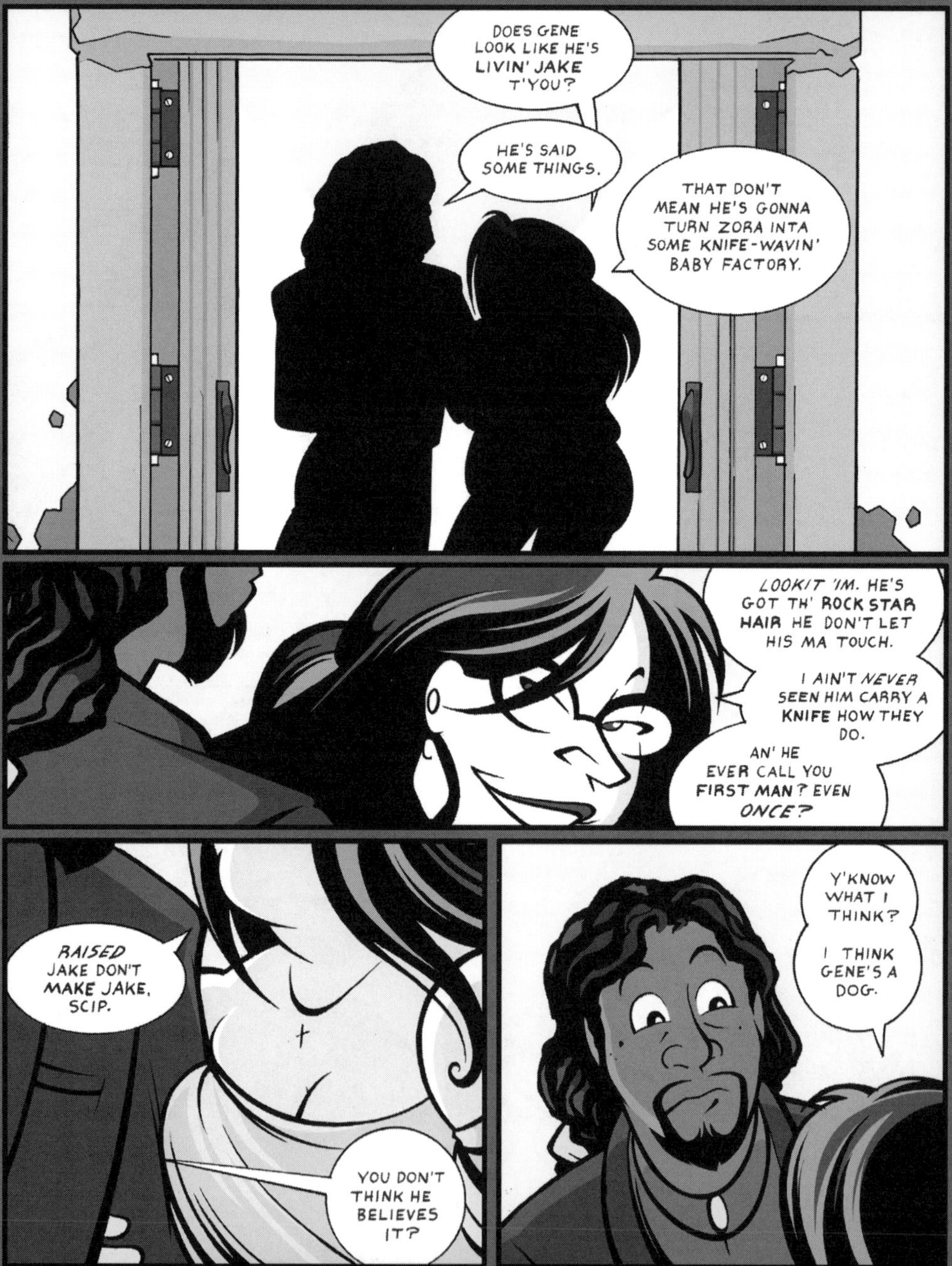
DOES GENE LOOK LIKE HE'S LIVIN' JAKE T'YOU?
HE'S SAID SOME THINGS.
THAT DON'T MEAN HE'S GONNA TURN ZORA INTA SOME KNIFE-WAVIN' BABY FACTORY.
LOOKIT 'IM. HE'S GOT TH' ROCK STAR HAIR HE DON'T LET HIS MA TOUCH.
I AIN'T NEVER SEEN HIM CARRY A KNIFE HOW THEY DO.
AN' HE EVER CALL YOU FIRST MAN? EVEN ONCE?
RAISED JAKE DON'T MAKE JAKE, SCIP.
YOU DON'T THINK HE BELIEVES IT?
Y'KNOW WHAT I THINK?
I THINK GENE'S A DOG.

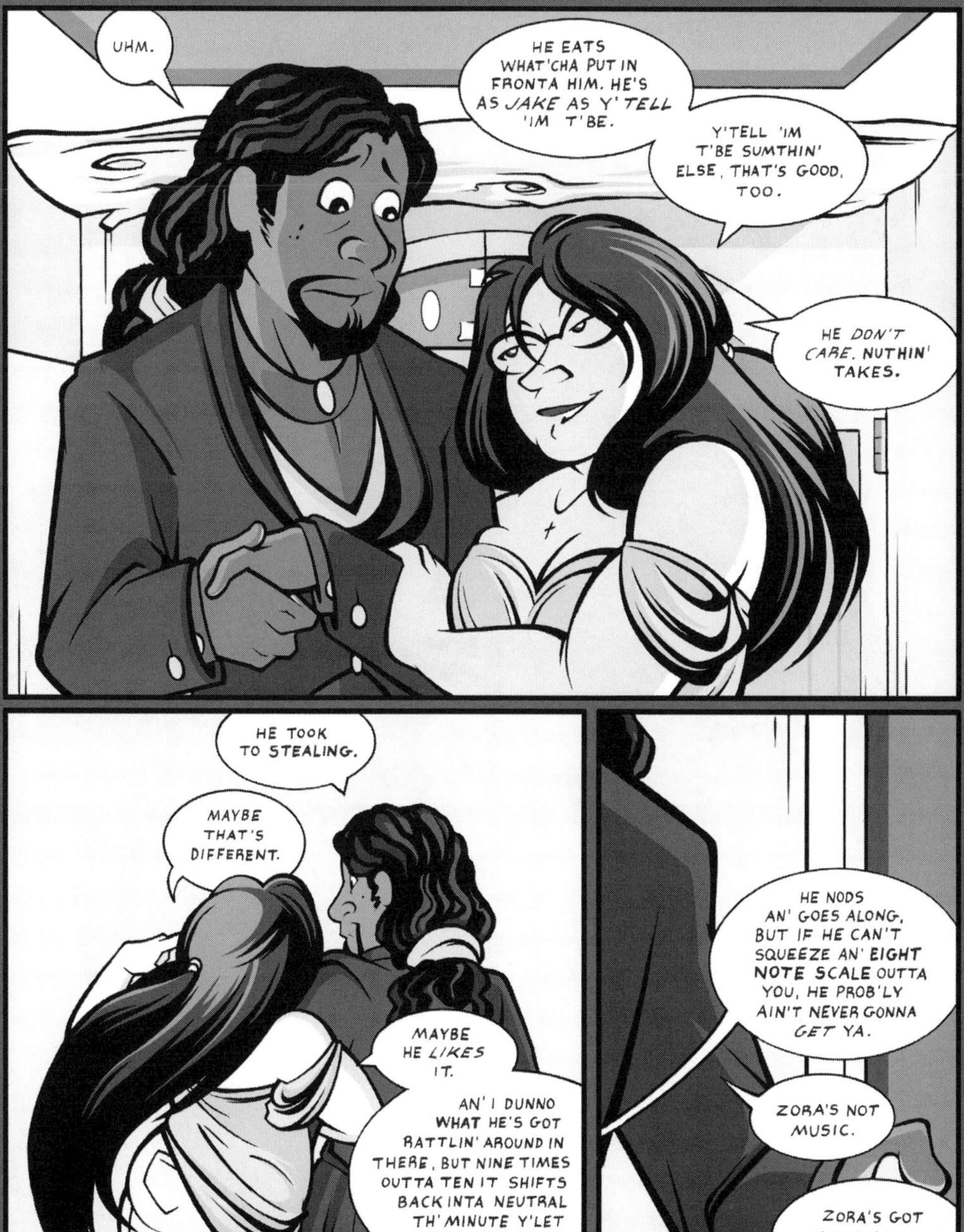
UHM.
HE EATS WHAT'CHA PUT IN FRONTA HIM. HE'S AS JAKE AS Y' TELL 'IM T'BE.
Y'TELL 'IM T'BE SUMTHIN' ELSE, THAT'S GOOD, TOO.
HE DON'T CARE. NUTHIN' TAKES.
HE TOOK TO STEALING.
MAYBE THAT'S DIFFERENT.
MAYBE HE LIKES IT.
AN' I DUNNO WHAT HE'S GOT RATTLIN' AROUND IN THERE, BUT NINE TIMES OUTTA TEN IT SHIFTS BACK INTA NEUTRAL TH' MINUTE Y'LET GO OF TH' STICK.
HE NODS AN' GOES ALONG, BUT IF HE CAN'T SQUEEZE AN' EIGHT NOTE SCALE OUTTA YOU, HE PROB'LY AIN'T NEVER GONNA GET YA.
ZORA'S NOT MUSIC.
ZORA'S GOT ME. AN' SUNNY AN' MOZE.

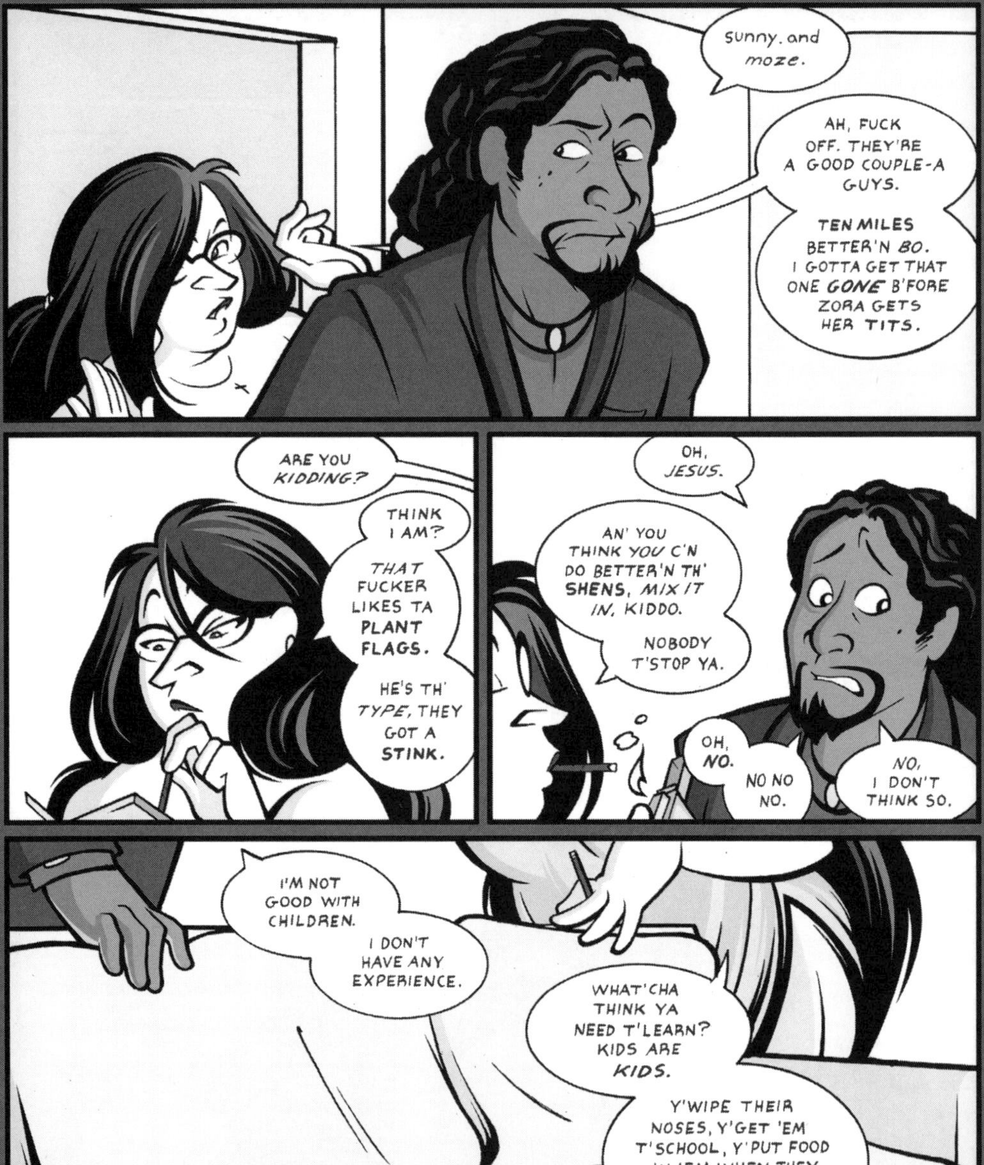
sunny. and moze.
AH, FUCK OFF. THEY'RE A GOOD COUPLE-A GUYS.
TEN MILES BETTER'N BO. I GOTTA GET THAT ONE GONE B'FORE ZORA GETS HER TITS.
ARE YOU KIDDING?
THINK I AM?
THAT FUCKER LIKES TA PLANT FLAGS.
HE'S TH' TYPE, THEY GOT A STINK.
OH, JESUS.
AN' YOU THINK YOU C'N DO BETTER'N TH' SHENS, MIX IT IN, KIDDO.
NOBODY T'STOP YA.
OH, NO.
NO NO NO.
NO, I DON'T THINK SO.
I'M NOT GOOD WITH CHILDREN.
I DON'T HAVE ANY EXPERIENCE.
WHAT'CHA THINK YA NEED T'LEARN? KIDS ARE KIDS.
Y'WIPE THEIR NOSES, Y'GET 'EM T'SCHOOL, Y'PUT FOOD IN 'EM WHEN THEY ASK, Y'MAKE 'EM PISS B'FORE BED.

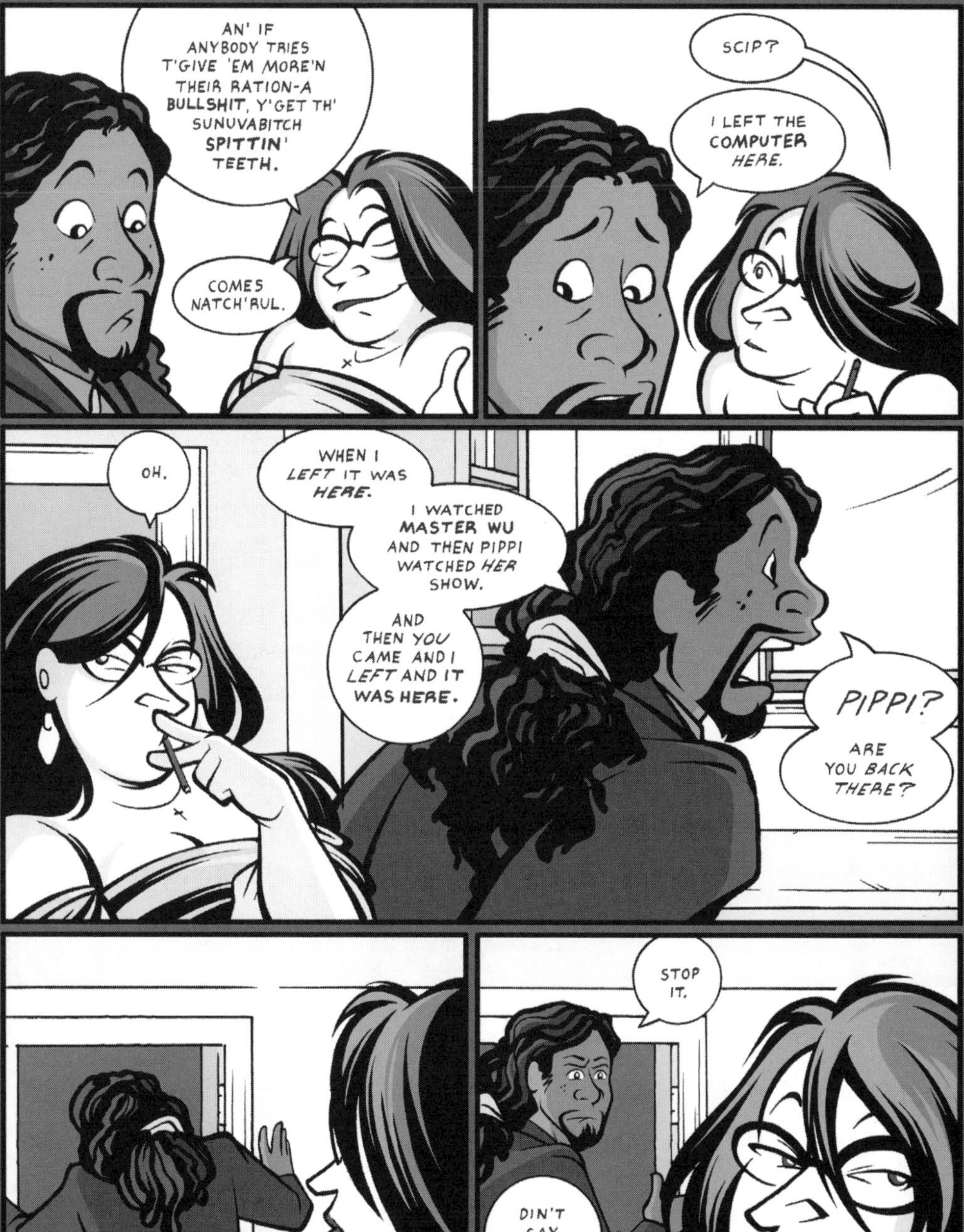
AN' IF ANYBODY TRIES T'GIVE 'EM MORE'N THEIR RATION-A BULLSHIT, Y'GET TH' SUNUVABITCH SPITTIN' TEETH.
COMES NATCH'RUL.
SCIP?
I LEFT THE COMPUTER HERE.
OH.
WHEN I LEFT IT WAS HERE.
I WATCHED MASTER WU AND THEN PIPPI WATCHED HER SHOW.
AND THEN YOU CAME AND I LEFT AND IT WAS HERE.
PIPPI?
ARE YOU BACK THERE?
STOP IT.
DIN'T SAY NUTHIN'.

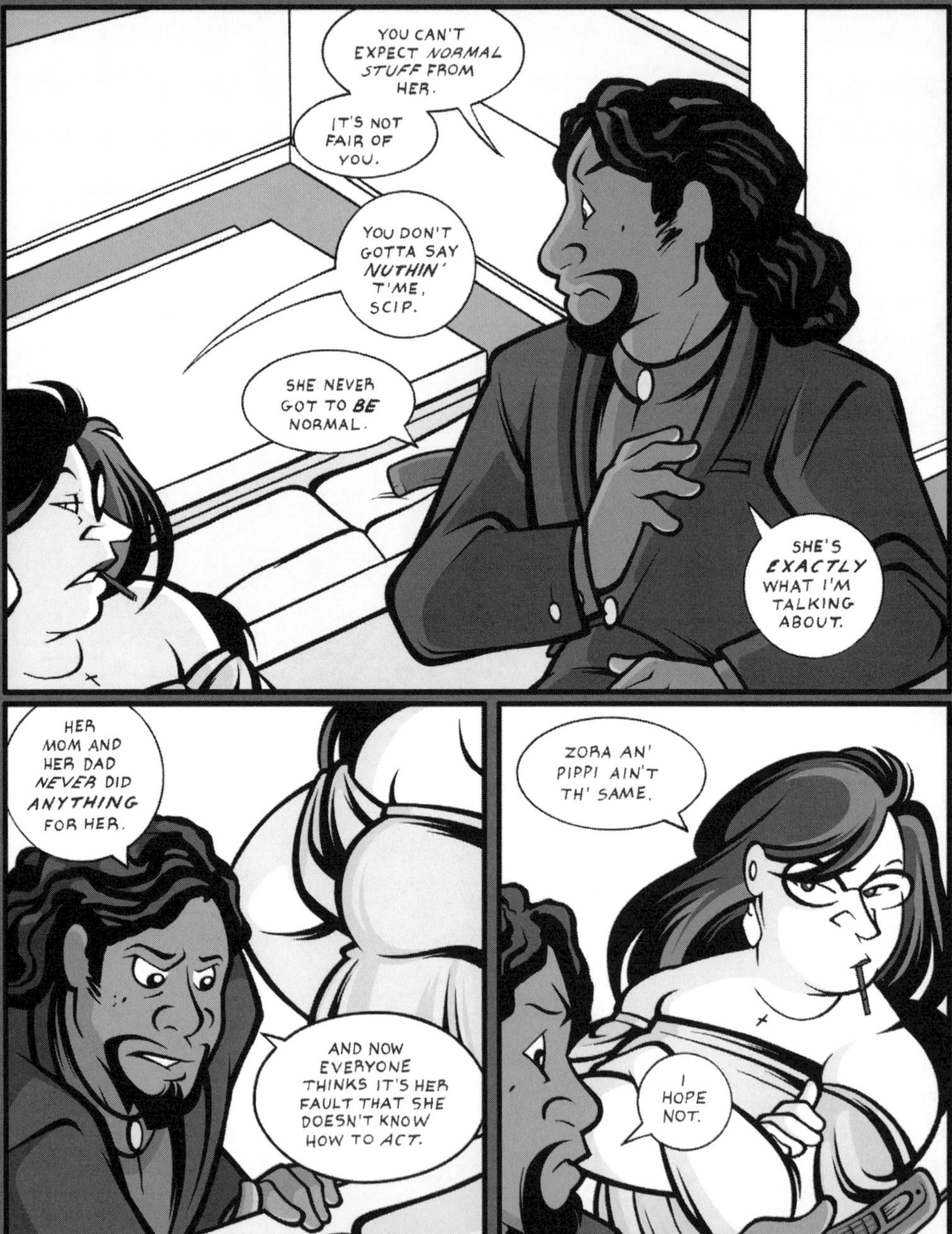
YOU CAN'T EXPECT *NORMAL STUFF* FROM HER.
IT'S NOT FAIR OF YOU.
YOU DON'T GOTTA SAY *NUTHIN'* T'ME, SCIP.
SHE NEVER GOT TO *BE* NORMAL.
SHE'S *EXACTLY* WHAT I'M TALKING ABOUT.
HER MOM AND HER DAD *NEVER* DID *ANYTHING* FOR HER.
AND NOW EVERYONE THINKS IT'S HER FAULT THAT SHE DOESN'T KNOW HOW TO *ACT*.
ZORA AN' PIPPI AIN'T TH' SAME.
I HOPE NOT.

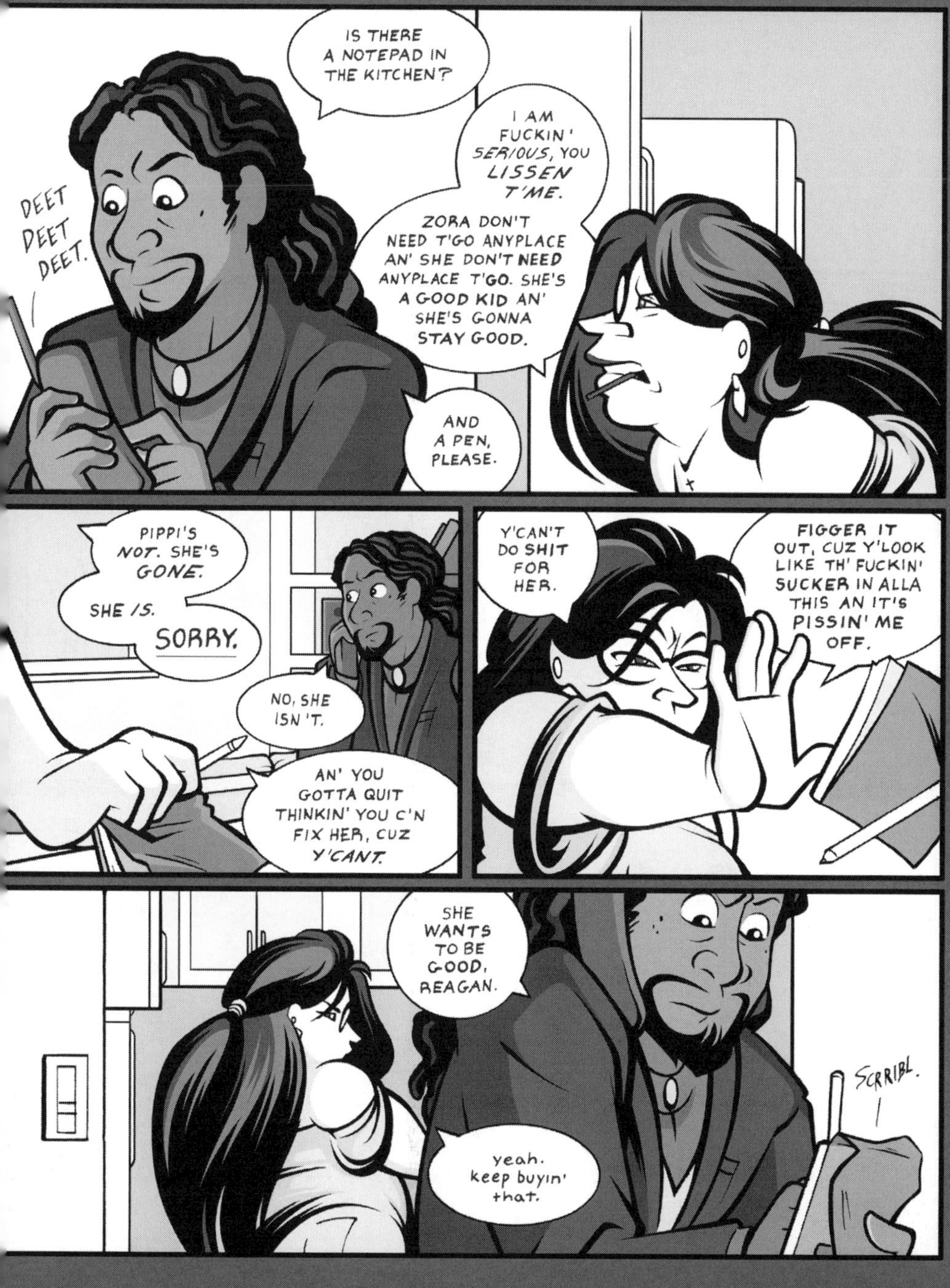
IS THERE A NOTEPAD IN THE KITCHEN?
DEET DEET DEET.
I AM FUCKIN' SERIOUS, YOU LISSEN T'ME.
ZORA DON'T NEED T'GO ANYPLACE AN' SHE DON'T NEED ANYPLACE T'GO. SHE'S A GOOD KID AN' SHE'S GONNA STAY GOOD.
AND A PEN, PLEASE.
PIPPI'S NOT. SHE'S GONE.
SHE IS.
SORRY.
NO, SHE ISN'T.
AN' YOU GOTTA QUIT THINKIN' YOU C'N FIX HER, CUZ Y'CANT.
Y'CAN'T DO SHIT FOR HER.
FIGGER IT OUT, CUZ Y'LOOK LIKE TH' FUCKIN' SUCKER IN ALLA THIS AN IT'S PISSIN' ME OFF.
SHE WANTS TO BE GOOD, REAGAN.
yeah. keep buyin' that.
SCRRIBL.

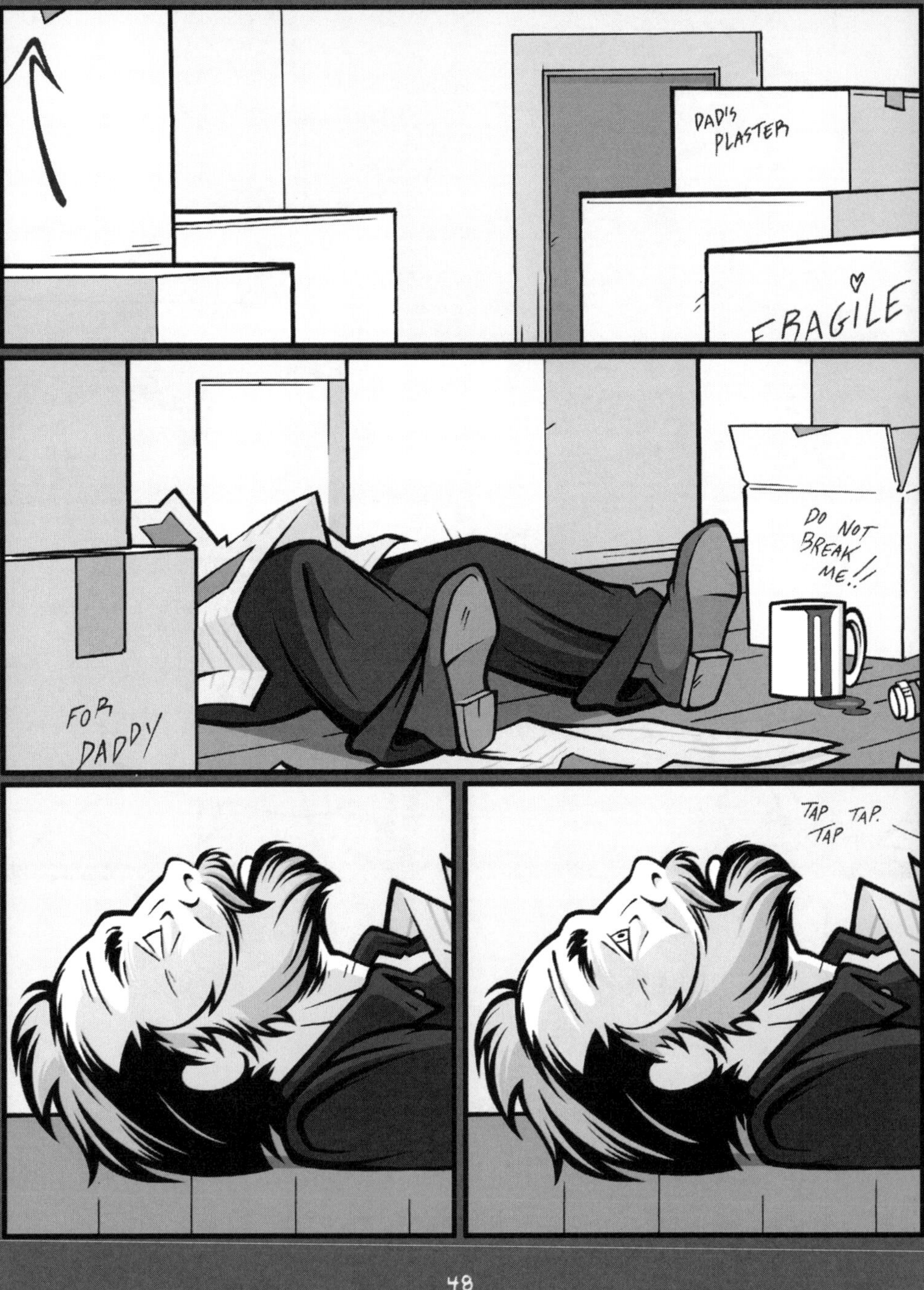
DAD'S PLASTER
FRAGILE
DO NOT BREAK ME!!
FOR DADDY
TAP TAP TAP.

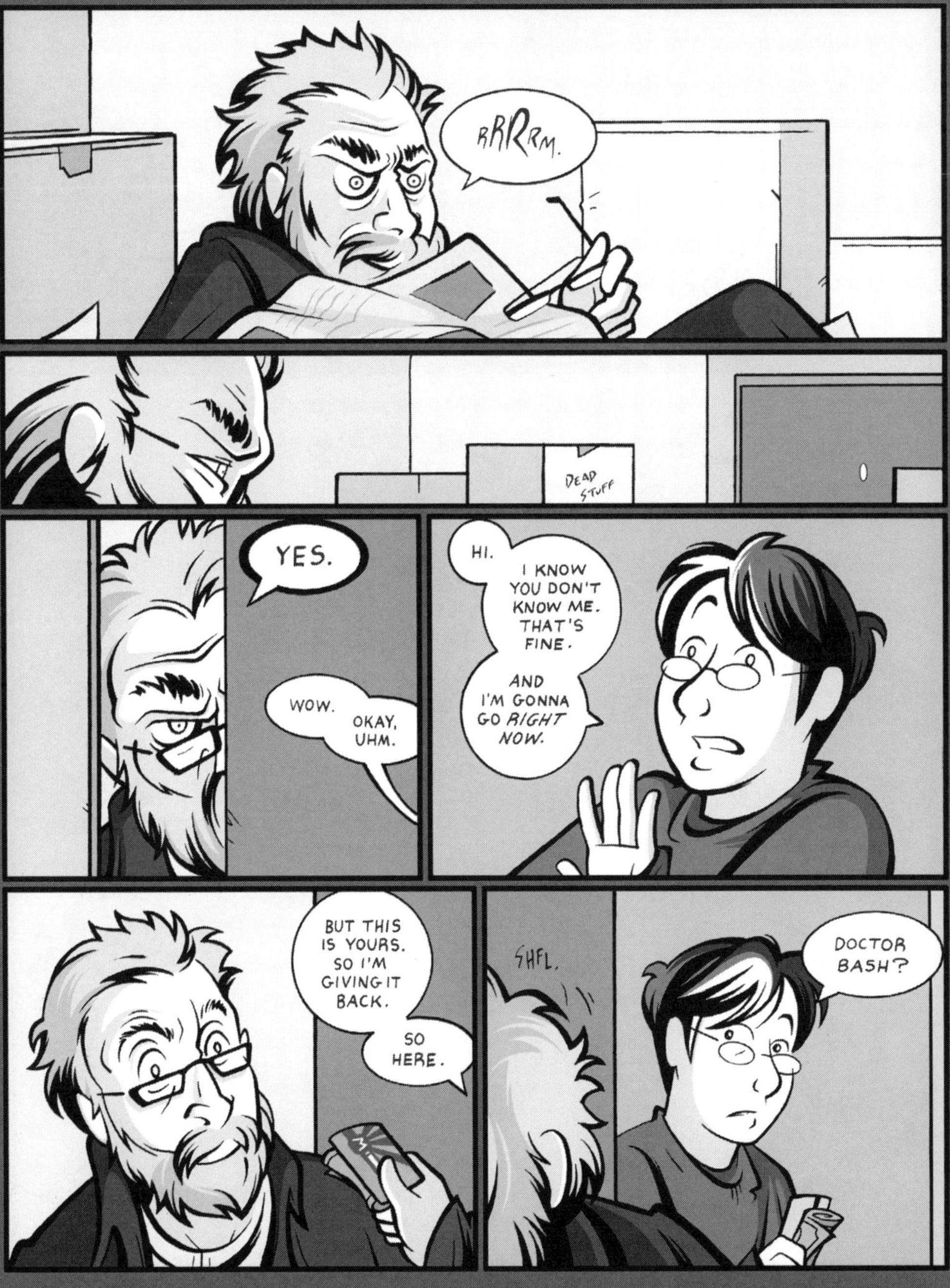
RRRRRM.
DEAD STUFF
YES.
WOW.
OKAY, UHM.
HI.
I KNOW YOU DON'T KNOW ME. THAT'S FINE.
AND I'M GONNA GO *RIGHT NOW.*
BUT THIS IS YOURS. SO I'M GIVING IT BACK.
SO HERE.
SHFL.
DOCTOR BASH?

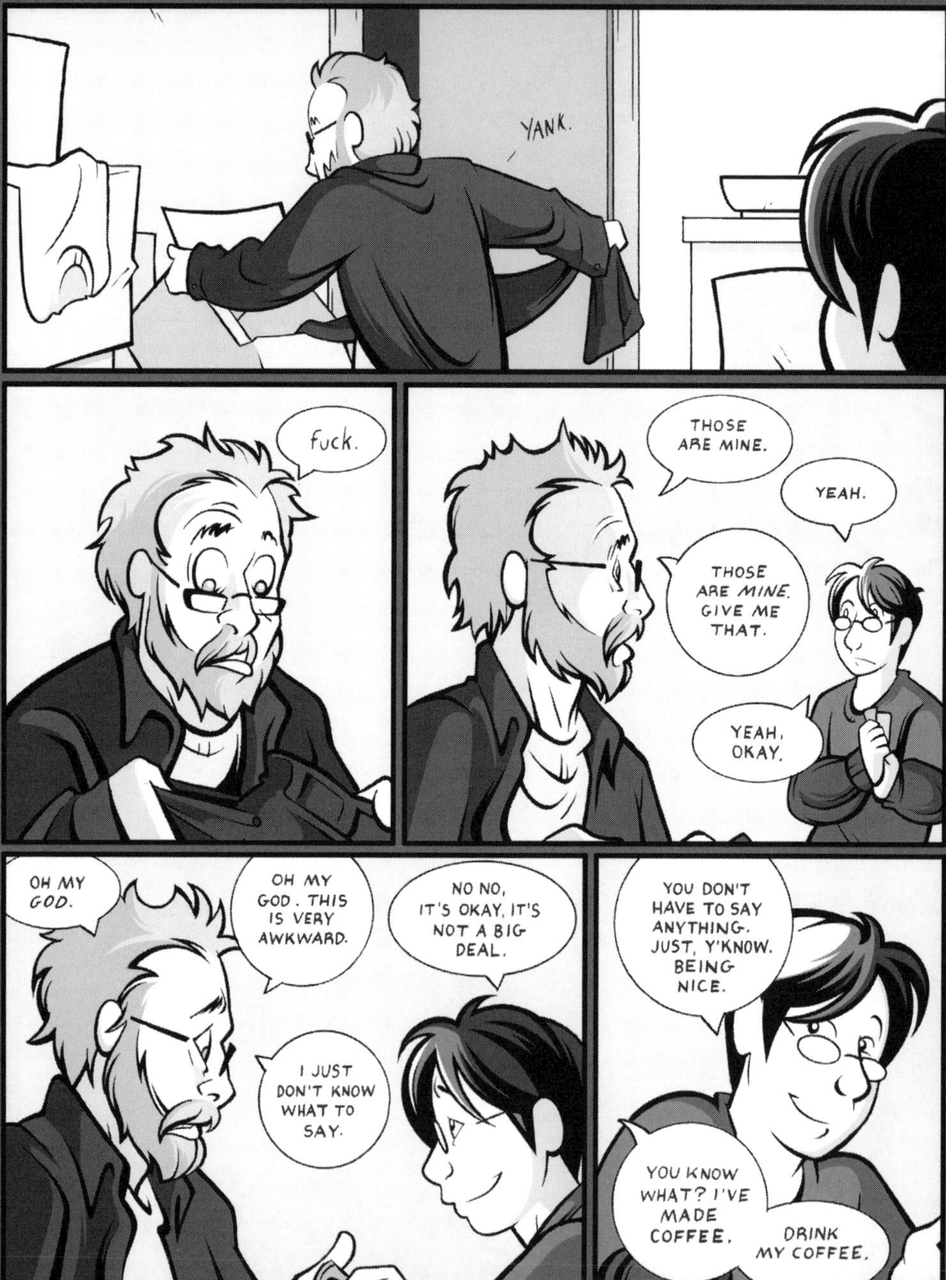
YANK.
fuck.
THOSE ARE MINE.
YEAH.
THOSE ARE *MINE*. GIVE ME THAT.
YEAH, OKAY.
OH MY *GOD*.
OH MY GOD. THIS IS VERY AWKWARD.
NO NO, IT'S OKAY, IT'S NOT A BIG DEAL.
I JUST DON'T KNOW WHAT TO SAY.
YOU DON'T HAVE TO SAY ANYTHING. JUST, Y'KNOW. BEING NICE.
YOU KNOW WHAT? I'VE MADE COFFEE.
DRINK MY COFFEE.

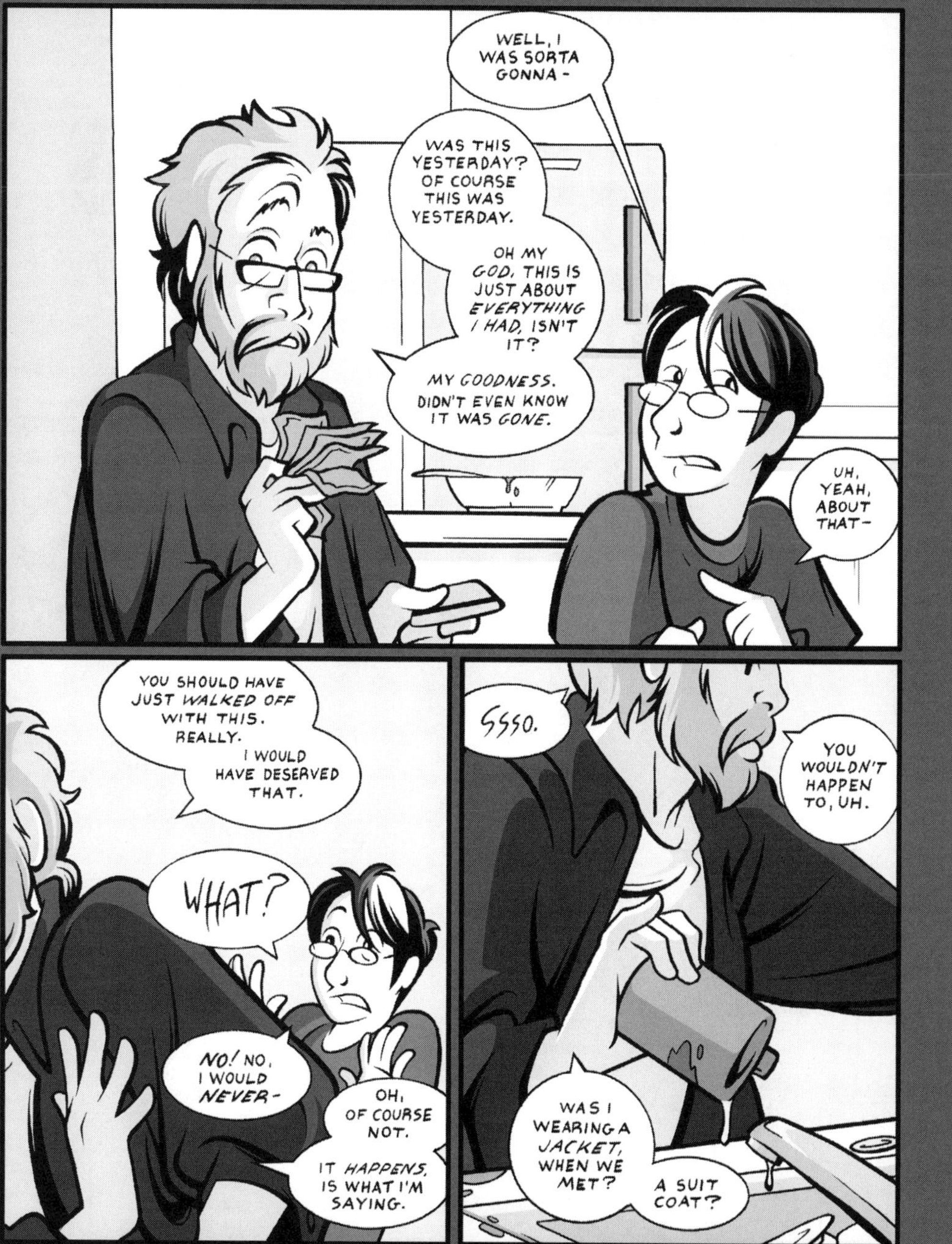
WELL, I WAS SORTA GONNA -
WAS THIS YESTERDAY? OF COURSE THIS WAS YESTERDAY.
OH MY *GOD*, THIS IS JUST ABOUT *EVERYTHING I HAD*, ISN'T IT?
MY *GOODNESS*. DIDN'T EVEN KNOW IT WAS *GONE*.
UH, YEAH, ABOUT THAT-
YOU SHOULD HAVE JUST *WALKED OFF* WITH THIS. REALLY.
I WOULD HAVE DESERVED THAT.
WHAT?
NO! NO, I WOULD *NEVER*-
OH, OF COURSE NOT.
IT *HAPPENS*, IS WHAT I'M SAYING.
SSSO.
YOU *WOULDN'T* HAPPEN TO, UH.
WAS I WEARING A *JACKET*, WHEN WE MET?
A SUIT COAT?

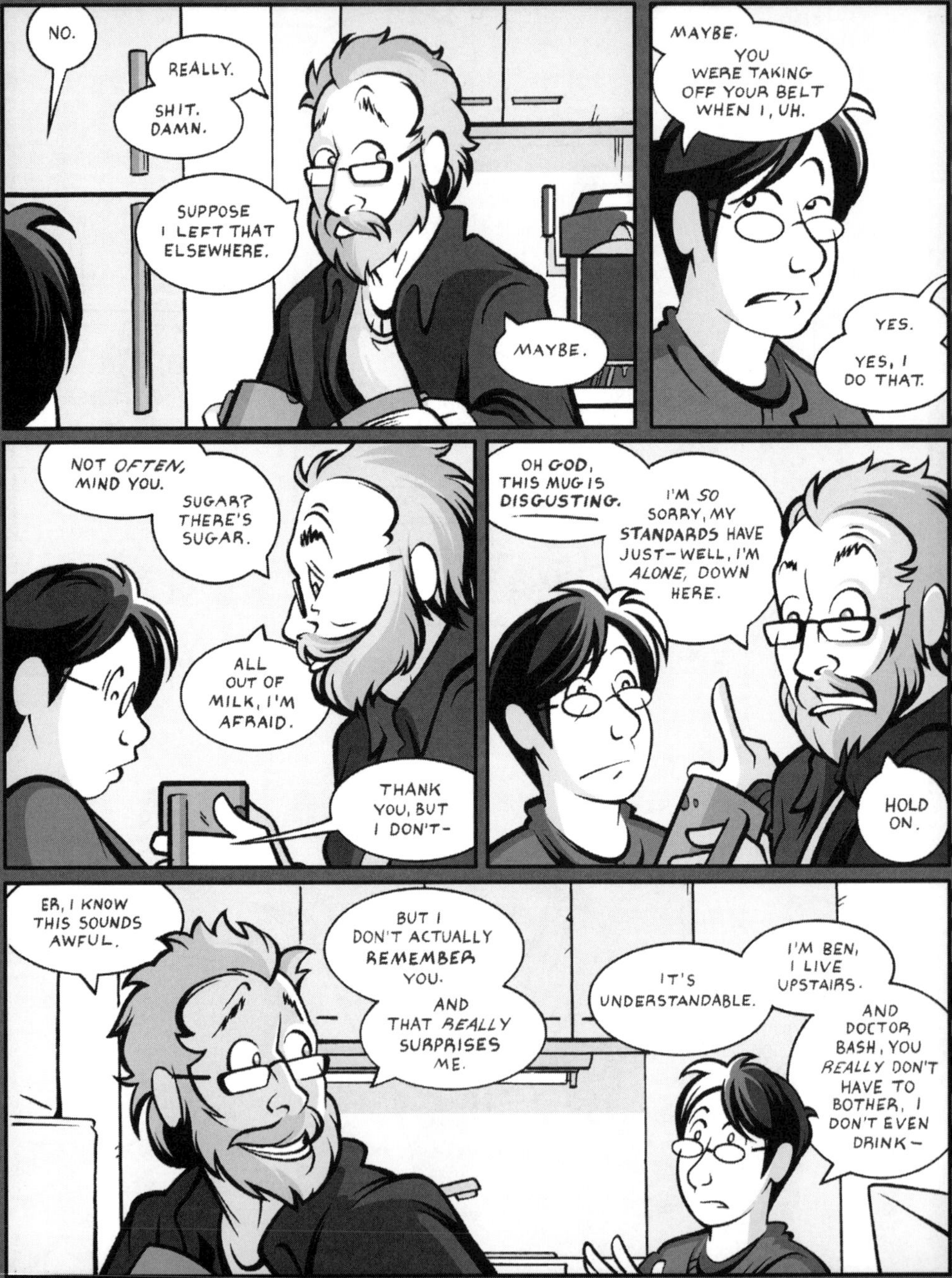
NO.
REALLY.
SHIT. DAMN.
SUPPOSE I LEFT THAT ELSEWHERE.
MAYBE.
MAYBE. YOU WERE TAKING OFF YOUR BELT WHEN I, UH.
YES.
YES, I DO THAT.
NOT OFTEN, MIND YOU.
SUGAR? THERE'S SUGAR.
ALL OUT OF MILK, I'M AFRAID.
THANK YOU, BUT I DON'T-
OH GOD, THIS MUG IS DISGUSTING.
I'M SO SORRY, MY STANDARDS HAVE JUST—WELL, I'M ALONE, DOWN HERE.
HOLD ON.
ER, I KNOW THIS SOUNDS AWFUL.
BUT I DON'T ACTUALLY REMEMBER YOU.
AND THAT REALLY SURPRISES ME.
IT'S UNDERSTANDABLE.
I'M BEN, I LIVE UPSTAIRS.
AND DOCTOR BASH, YOU REALLY DON'T HAVE TO BOTHER, I DON'T EVEN DRINK—

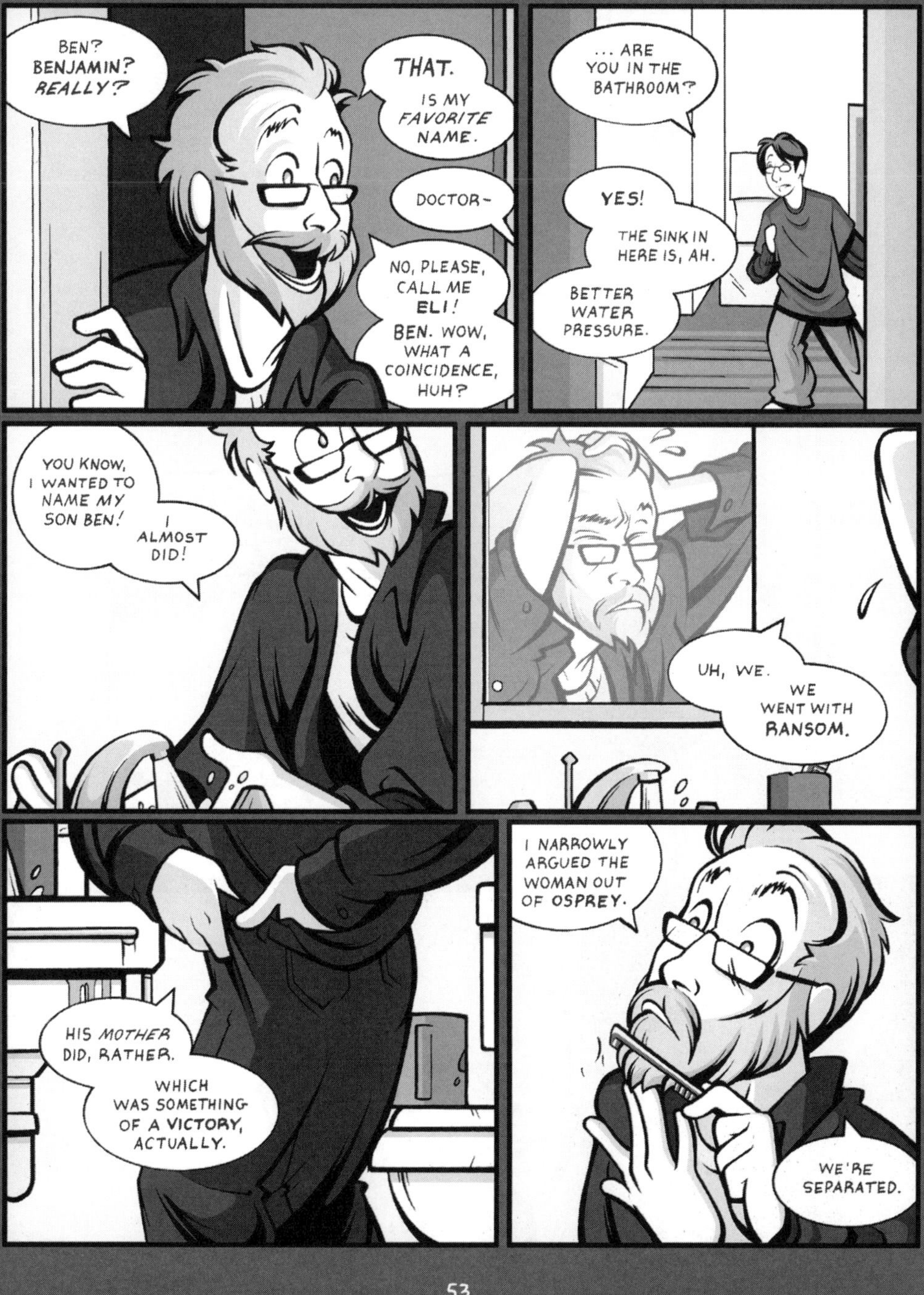
BEN? BENJAMIN? *REALLY?*
THAT.
IS MY *FAVORITE* NAME.
DOCTOR–
NO, PLEASE, CALL ME **ELI**!
BEN. WOW, WHAT A COINCIDENCE, HUH?
... ARE YOU IN THE BATHROOM?
YES!
THE SINK IN HERE IS, AH.
BETTER WATER PRESSURE.
YOU KNOW, I WANTED TO NAME *MY* SON BEN!
I ALMOST DID!
UH, WE.
WE WENT WITH **RANSOM**.
HIS *MOTHER* DID, RATHER.
WHICH WAS SOMETHING OF A **VICTORY**, ACTUALLY.
I NARROWLY ARGUED THE WOMAN OUT OF **OSPREY**.
WE'RE SEPARATED.

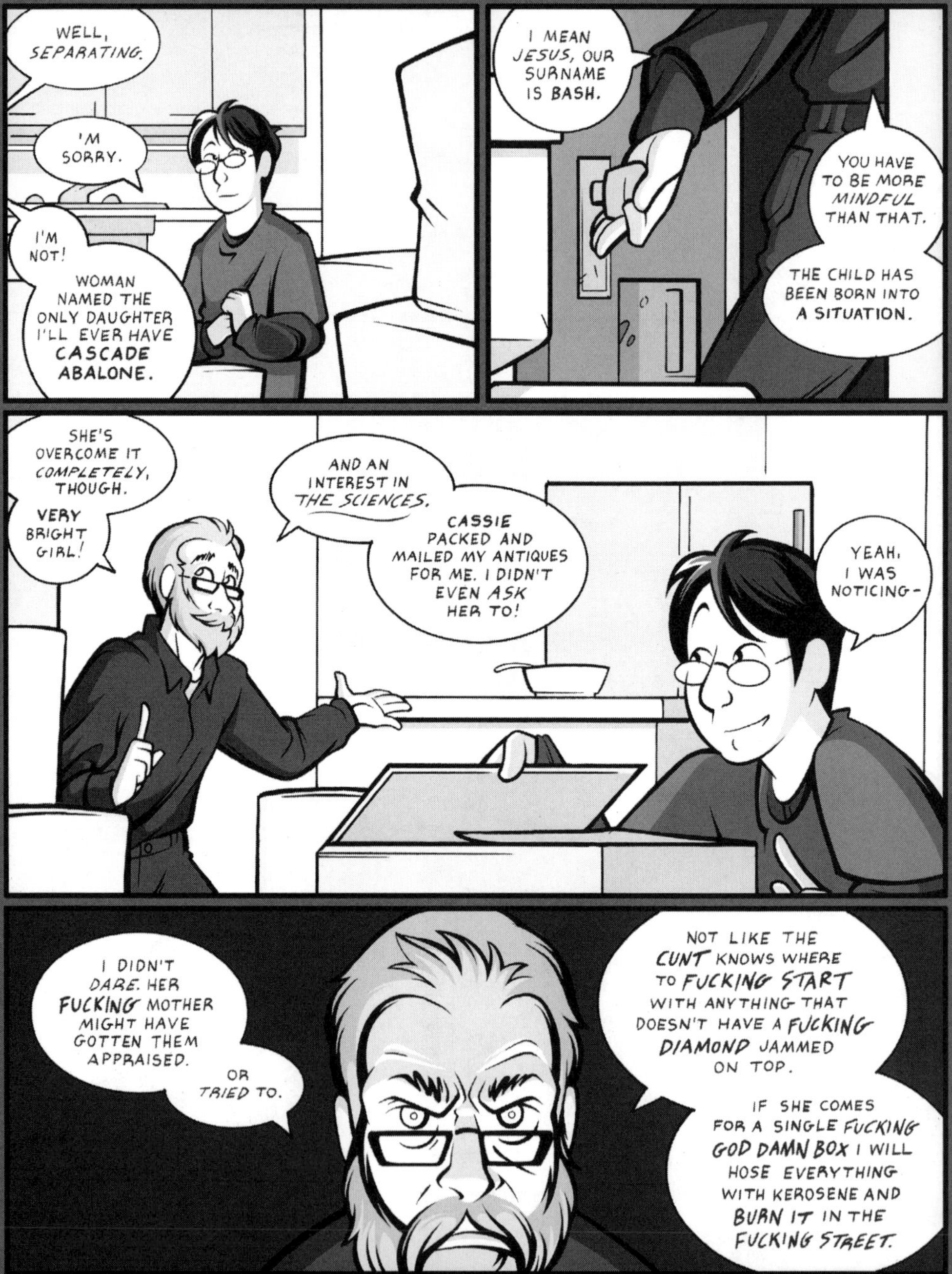
WELL, SEPARATING.
'M SORRY.
I'M NOT!
WOMAN NAMED THE ONLY DAUGHTER I'LL EVER HAVE CASCADE ABALONE.
I MEAN JESUS, OUR SURNAME IS BASH.
YOU HAVE TO BE MORE MINDFUL THAN THAT.
THE CHILD HAS BEEN BORN INTO A SITUATION.
SHE'S OVERCOME IT COMPLETELY, THOUGH.
VERY BRIGHT GIRL!
AND AN INTEREST IN THE SCIENCES.
CASSIE PACKED AND MAILED MY ANTIQUES FOR ME. I DIDN'T EVEN ASK HER TO!
YEAH, I WAS NOTICING-
I DIDN'T DARE. HER FUCKING MOTHER MIGHT HAVE GOTTEN THEM APPRAISED.
OR TRIED TO.
NOT LIKE THE CUNT KNOWS WHERE TO FUCKING START WITH ANYTHING THAT DOESN'T HAVE A FUCKING DIAMOND JAMMED ON TOP.
IF SHE COMES FOR A SINGLE FUCKING GOD DAMN BOX I WILL HOSE EVERYTHING WITH KEROSENE AND BURN IT IN THE FUCKING STREET.

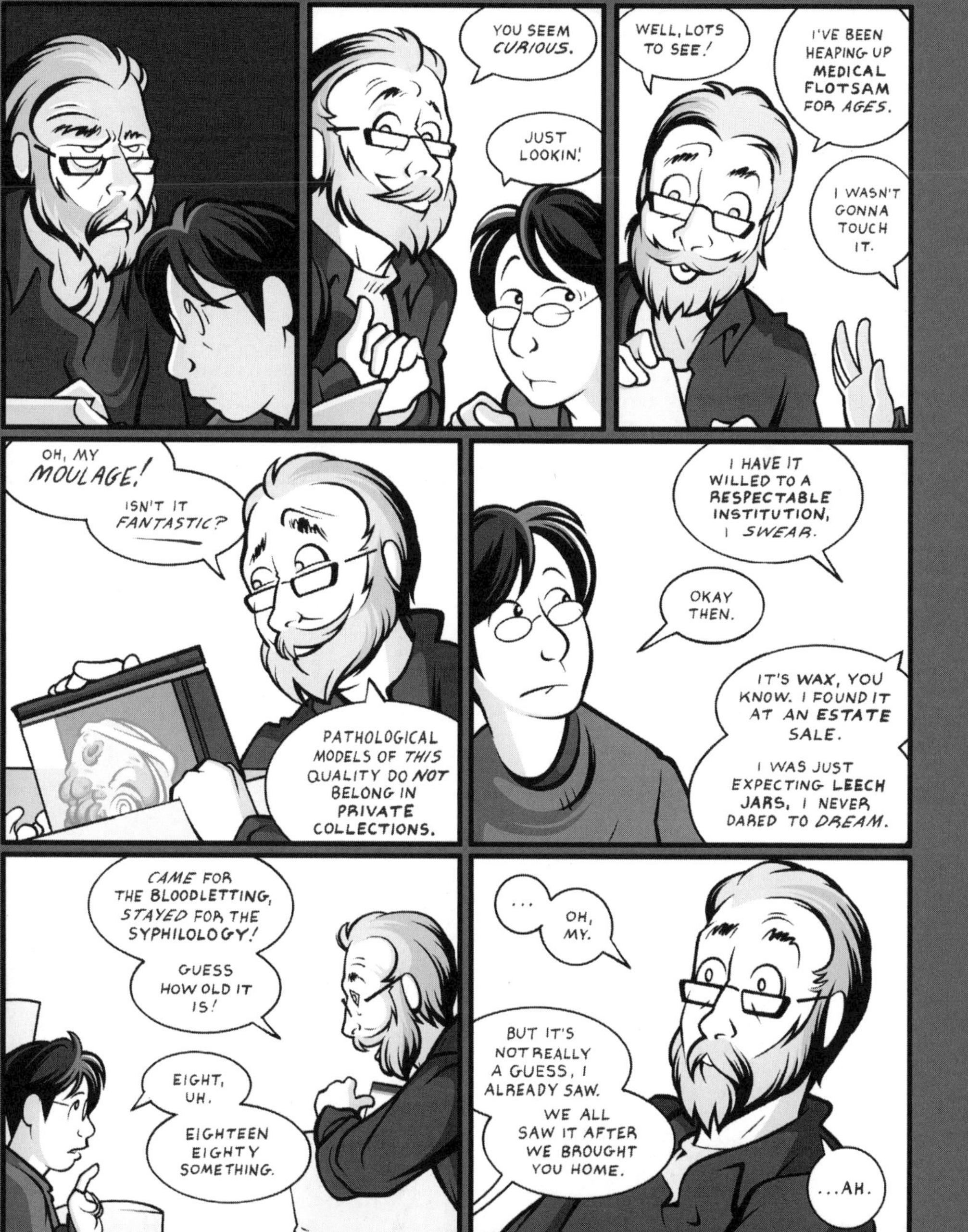
YOU SEEM CURIOUS.
JUST LOOKIN!
WELL, LOTS TO SEE!
I'VE BEEN HEAPING UP MEDICAL FLOTSAM FOR AGES.
I WASN'T GONNA TOUCH IT.
OH, MY MOULAGE!
ISN'T IT FANTASTIC?
PATHOLOGICAL MODELS OF THIS QUALITY DO NOT BELONG IN PRIVATE COLLECTIONS.
I HAVE IT WILLED TO A RESPECTABLE INSTITUTION, I SWEAR.
OKAY THEN.
IT'S WAX, YOU KNOW. I FOUND IT AT AN ESTATE SALE.
I WAS JUST EXPECTING LEECH JARS, I NEVER DARED TO DREAM.
CAME FOR THE BLOODLETTING, STAYED FOR THE SYPHILOLOGY!
GUESS HOW OLD IT IS!
EIGHT, UH.
EIGHTEEN EIGHTY SOMETHING.
...
OH, MY.
BUT IT'S NOT REALLY A GUESS, I ALREADY SAW.
WE ALL SAW IT AFTER WE BROUGHT YOU HOME.
...AH.

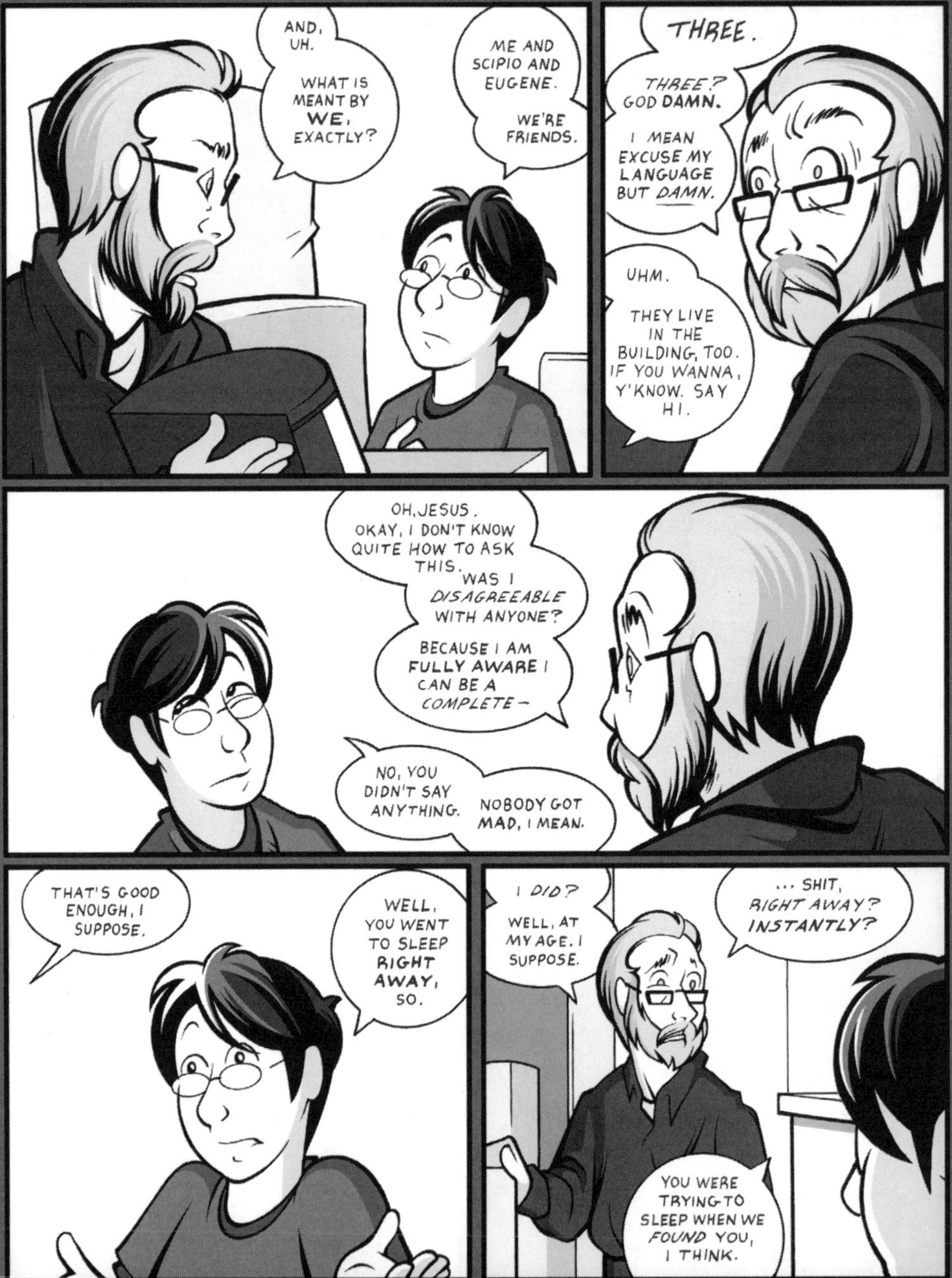
AND, UH.
WHAT IS MEANT BY **WE**, EXACTLY?
ME AND SCIPIO AND EUGENE.
WE'RE FRIENDS.
THREE.
THREE? GOD **DAMN.**
I MEAN EXCUSE MY LANGUAGE BUT *DAMN.*
UHM.
THEY LIVE IN THE BUILDING, TOO. IF YOU WANNA, Y'KNOW. SAY HI.
OH, JESUS. OKAY, I DON'T KNOW QUITE HOW TO ASK THIS.
WAS I *DISAGREEABLE* WITH ANYONE?
BECAUSE I AM **FULLY AWARE** I CAN BE A *COMPLETE* –
NO, YOU DIDN'T SAY ANYTHING.
NOBODY GOT MAD, I MEAN.
THAT'S GOOD ENOUGH, I SUPPOSE.
WELL, YOU WENT TO SLEEP **RIGHT AWAY**, SO.
I *DID?*
WELL, AT MY AGE, I SUPPOSE.
... SHIT, *RIGHT AWAY?* ***INSTANTLY?***
YOU WERE TRYING TO SLEEP WHEN WE *FOUND* YOU, I THINK.

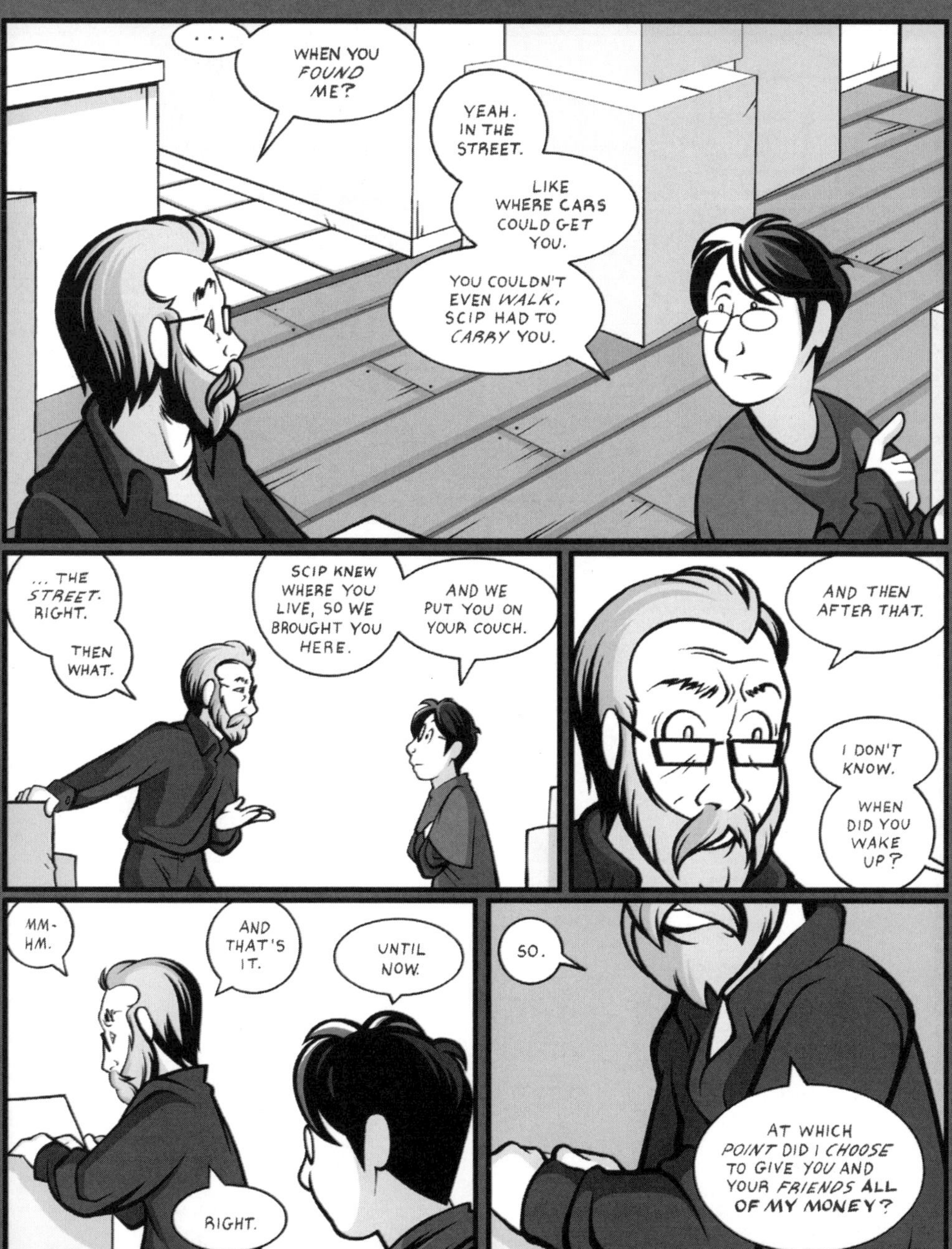
...
WHEN YOU FOUND ME?
YEAH. IN THE STREET.
LIKE WHERE CARS COULD GET YOU.
YOU COULDN'T EVEN WALK, SCIP HAD TO CARRY YOU.
... THE STREET. RIGHT.
THEN WHAT.
SCIP KNEW WHERE YOU LIVE, SO WE BROUGHT YOU HERE.
AND WE PUT YOU ON YOUR COUCH.
AND THEN AFTER THAT.
I DON'T KNOW.
WHEN DID YOU WAKE UP?
MM-HM.
AND THAT'S IT.
UNTIL NOW.
RIGHT.
SO.
AT WHICH POINT DID I CHOOSE TO GIVE YOU AND YOUR FRIENDS ALL OF MY MONEY?

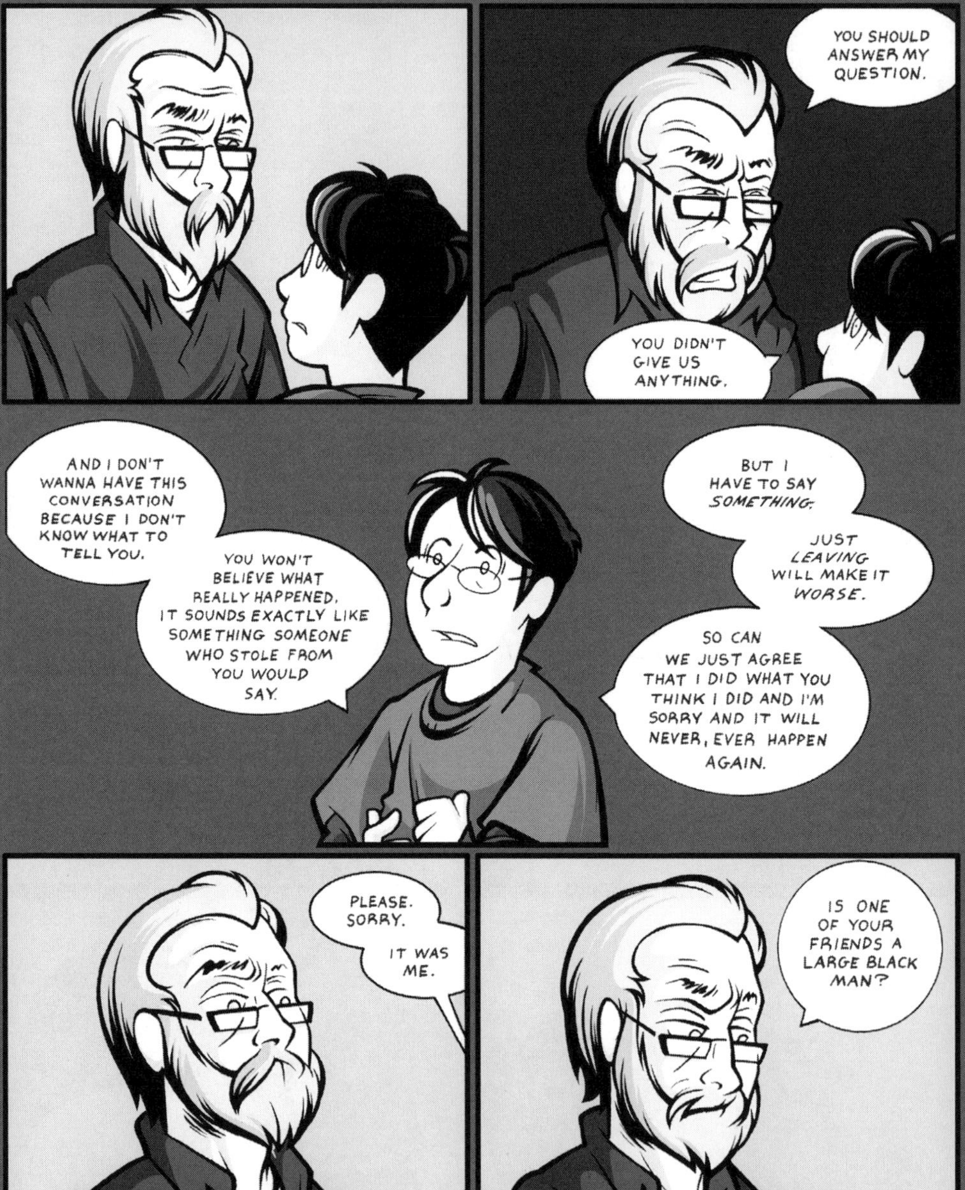
YOU SHOULD ANSWER MY QUESTION.
YOU DIDN'T GIVE US ANYTHING.
AND I DON'T WANNA HAVE THIS CONVERSATION BECAUSE I DON'T KNOW WHAT TO TELL YOU.
YOU WON'T BELIEVE WHAT REALLY HAPPENED. IT SOUNDS EXACTLY LIKE SOMETHING SOMEONE WHO STOLE FROM YOU WOULD SAY.
BUT I HAVE TO SAY *SOMETHING.*
JUST *LEAVING* WILL MAKE IT *WORSE.*
SO CAN WE JUST AGREE THAT I DID WHAT YOU THINK I DID AND I'M SORRY AND IT WILL NEVER, EVER HAPPEN AGAIN.
PLEASE. SORRY.
IT WAS ME.
IS ONE OF YOUR FRIENDS A LARGE BLACK MAN?

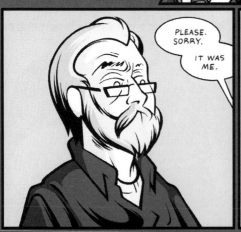

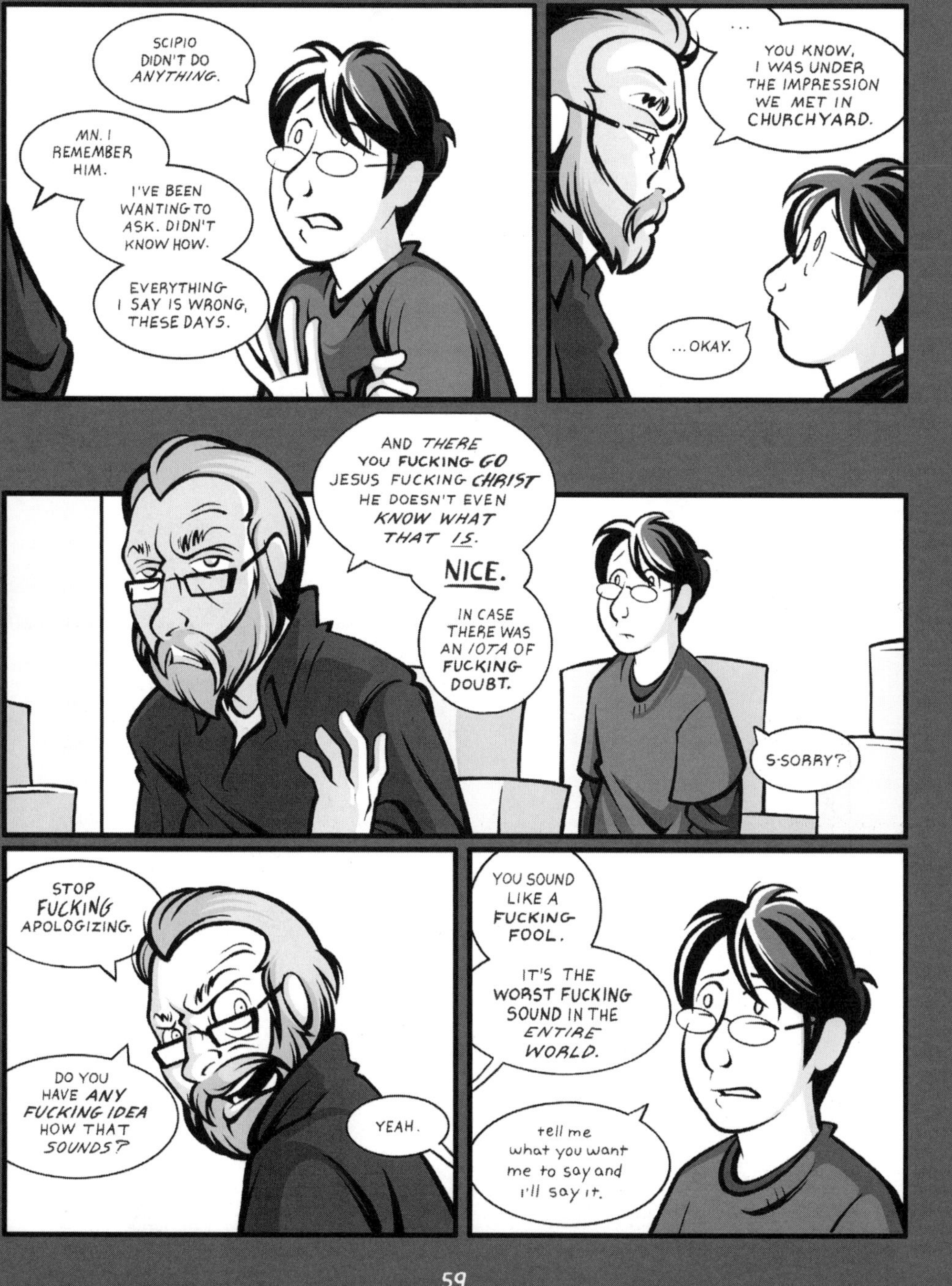

SCIPIO DIDN'T DO ANYTHING.
MN. I REMEMBER HIM.
I'VE BEEN WANTING TO ASK. DIDN'T KNOW HOW.
EVERYTHING I SAY IS WRONG, THESE DAYS.
...
YOU KNOW, I WAS UNDER THE IMPRESSION WE MET IN CHURCHYARD.
...OKAY.
AND THERE YOU FUCKING GO JESUS FUCKING CHRIST HE DOESN'T EVEN KNOW WHAT THAT IS.
NICE.
IN CASE THERE WAS AN IOTA OF FUCKING DOUBT.
S-SORRY?
STOP FUCKING APOLOGIZING.
DO YOU HAVE ANY FUCKING IDEA HOW THAT SOUNDS?
YEAH.
YOU SOUND LIKE A FUCKING FOOL.
IT'S THE WORST FUCKING SOUND IN THE ENTIRE WORLD.
tell me what you want me to say and i'll say it.

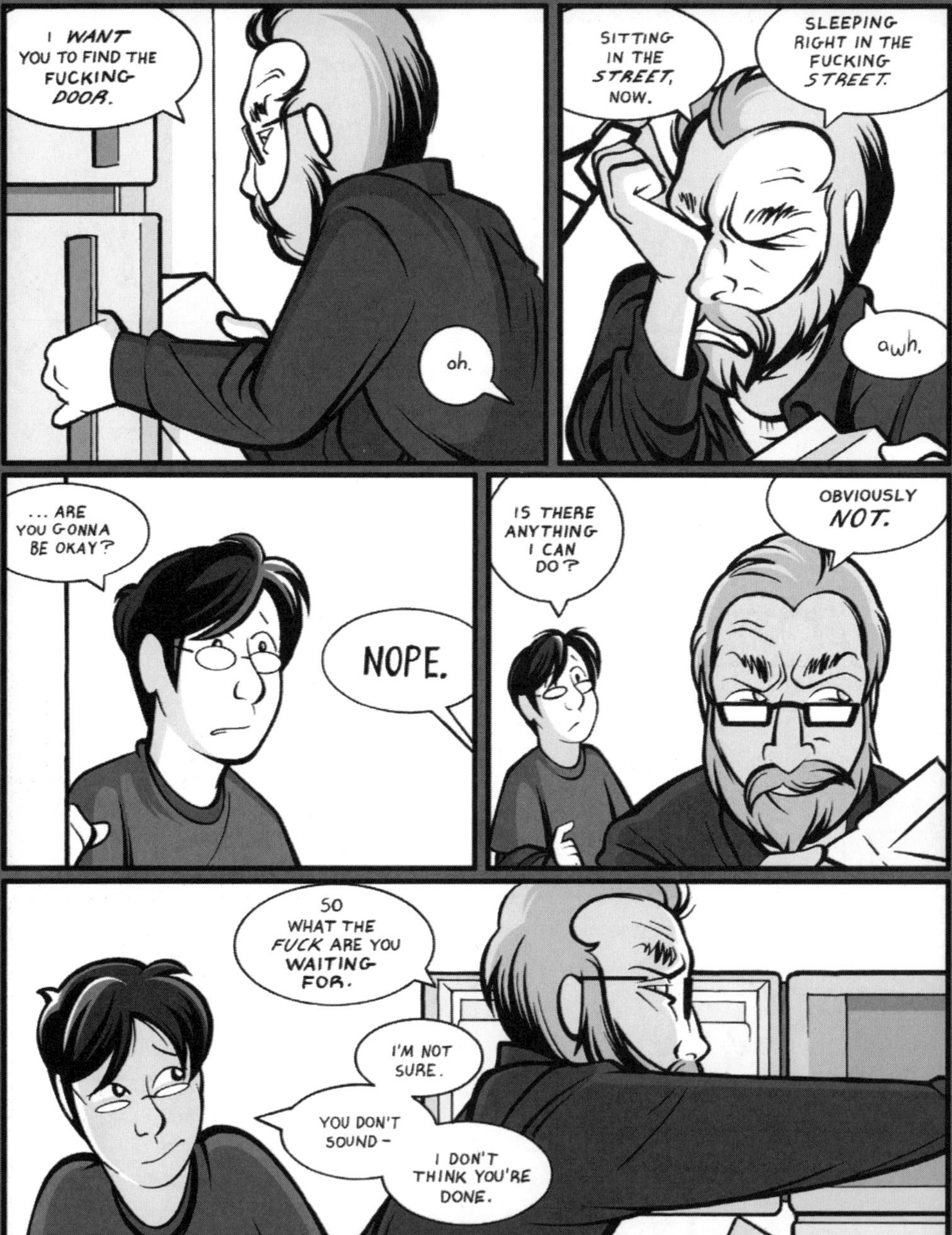
I WANT YOU TO FIND THE FUCKING DOOR.
oh.
SITTING IN THE STREET, NOW.
SLEEPING RIGHT IN THE FUCKING STREET.
awh.
... ARE YOU GONNA BE OKAY?
NOPE.
IS THERE ANYTHING I CAN DO?
OBVIOUSLY NOT.
SO WHAT THE FUCK ARE YOU WAITING FOR.
I'M NOT SURE.
YOU DON'T SOUND-
I DON'T THINK YOU'RE DONE.

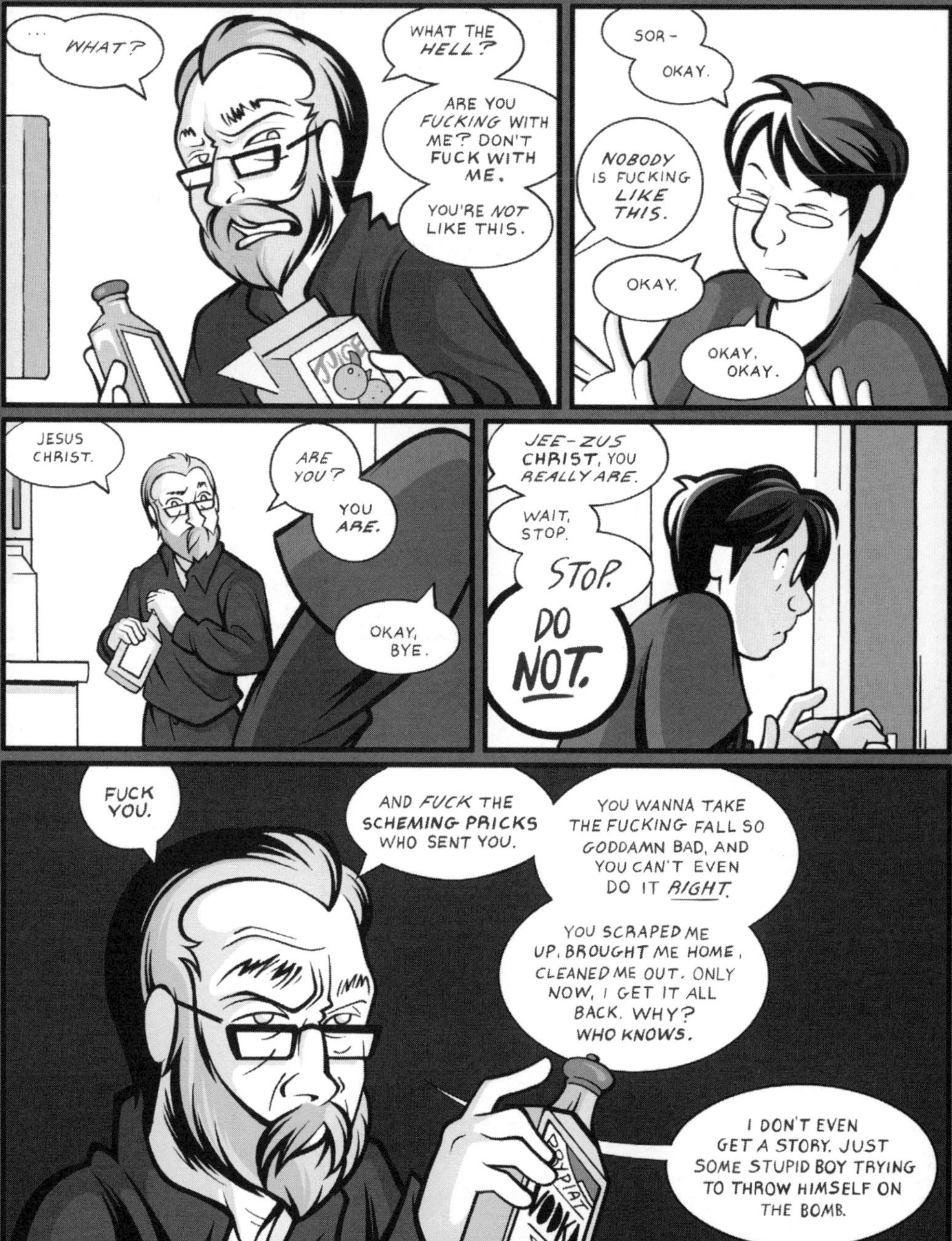
... WHAT?
WHAT THE HELL?
ARE YOU FUCKING WITH ME? DON'T FUCK WITH ME.
YOU'RE NOT LIKE THIS.
JUICE
SOR -
OKAY.
NOBODY IS FUCKING LIKE THIS.
OKAY.
OKAY, OKAY.
JESUS CHRIST.
ARE YOU?
YOU ARE.
OKAY, BYE.
JEE-ZUS CHRIST, YOU REALLY ARE.
WAIT, STOP.
STOP.
DO NOT.
FUCK YOU.
AND FUCK THE SCHEMING PRICKS WHO SENT YOU.
YOU WANNA TAKE THE FUCKING FALL SO GODDAMN BAD, AND YOU CAN'T EVEN DO IT RIGHT.
YOU SCRAPED ME UP, BROUGHT ME HOME, CLEANED ME OUT. ONLY NOW, I GET IT ALL BACK. WHY? WHO KNOWS.
I DON'T EVEN GET A STORY. JUST SOME STUPID BOY TRYING TO THROW HIMSELF ON THE BOMB.
VODKA

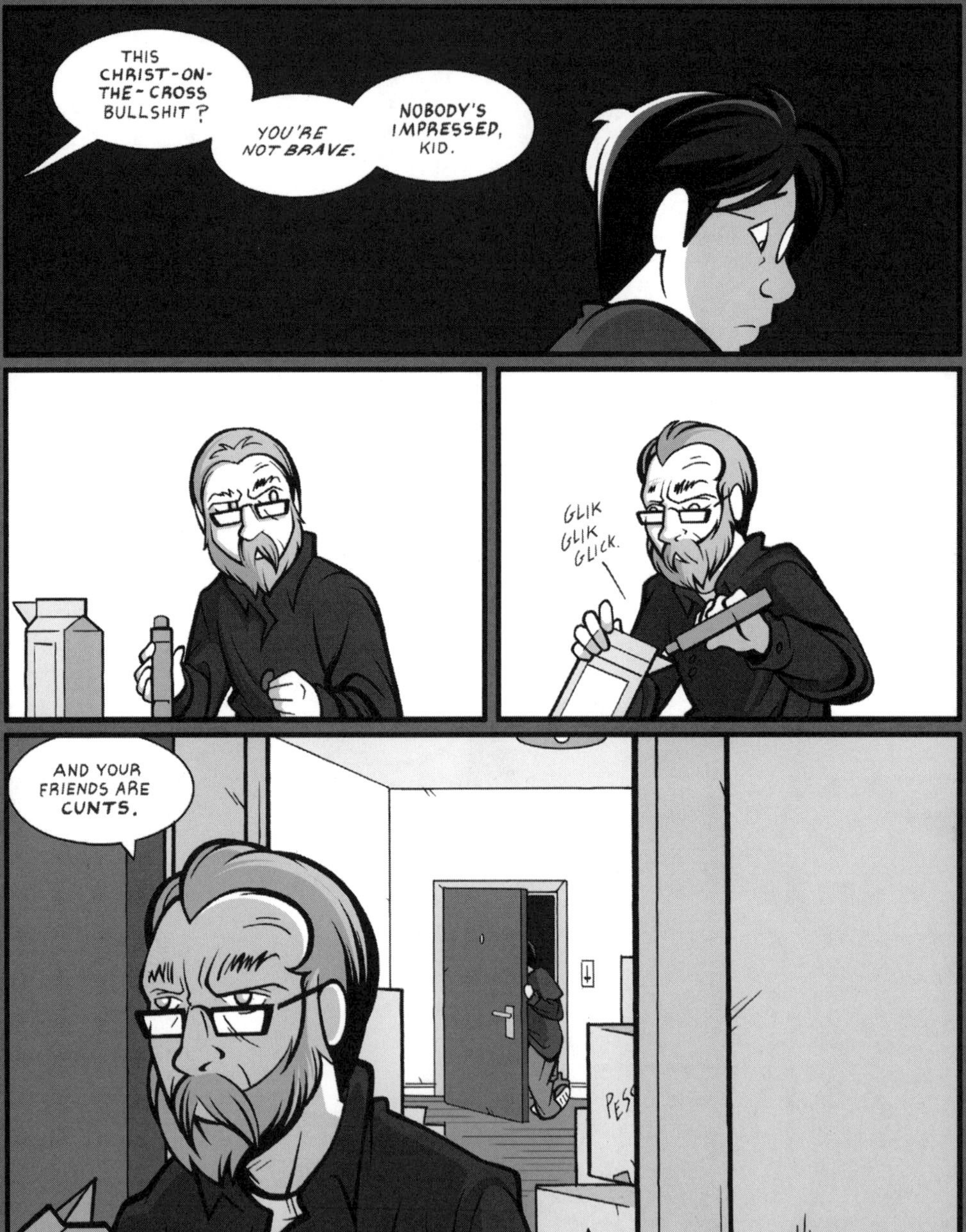
THIS CHRIST-ON-THE-CROSS BULLSHIT?
YOU'RE NOT BRAVE.
NOBODY'S IMPRESSED, KID.
GLIK GLIK GLICK.
AND YOUR FRIENDS ARE CUNTS.

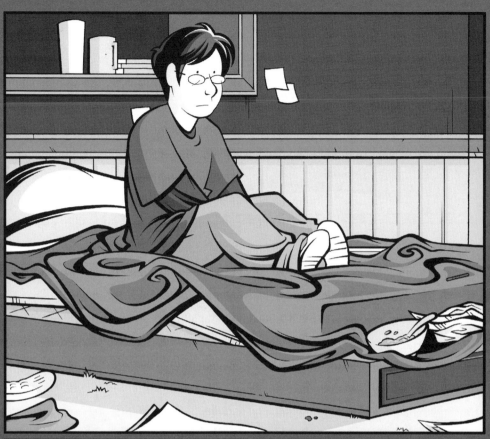

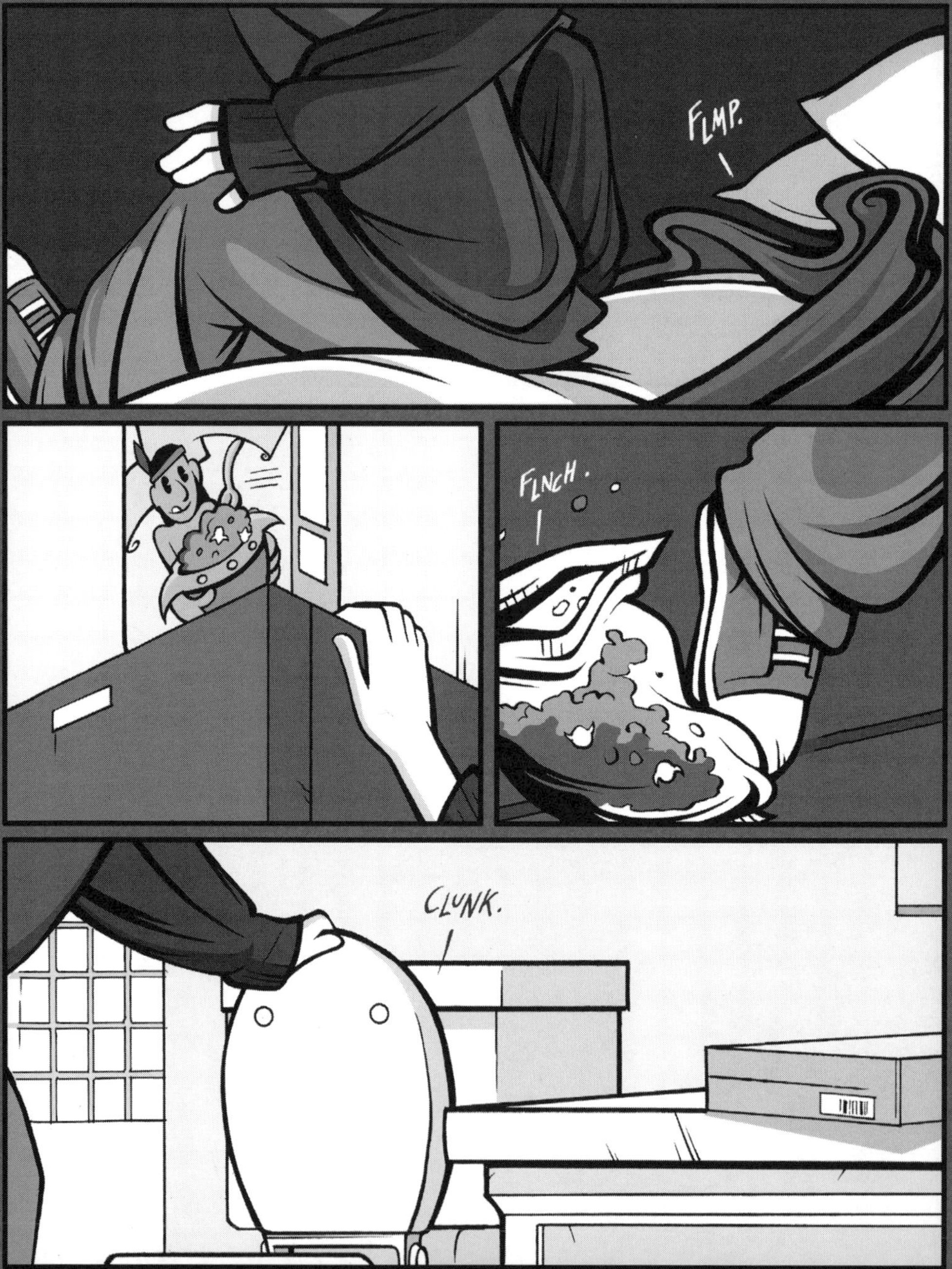
FLMP.
FLNCH.
CLUNK.

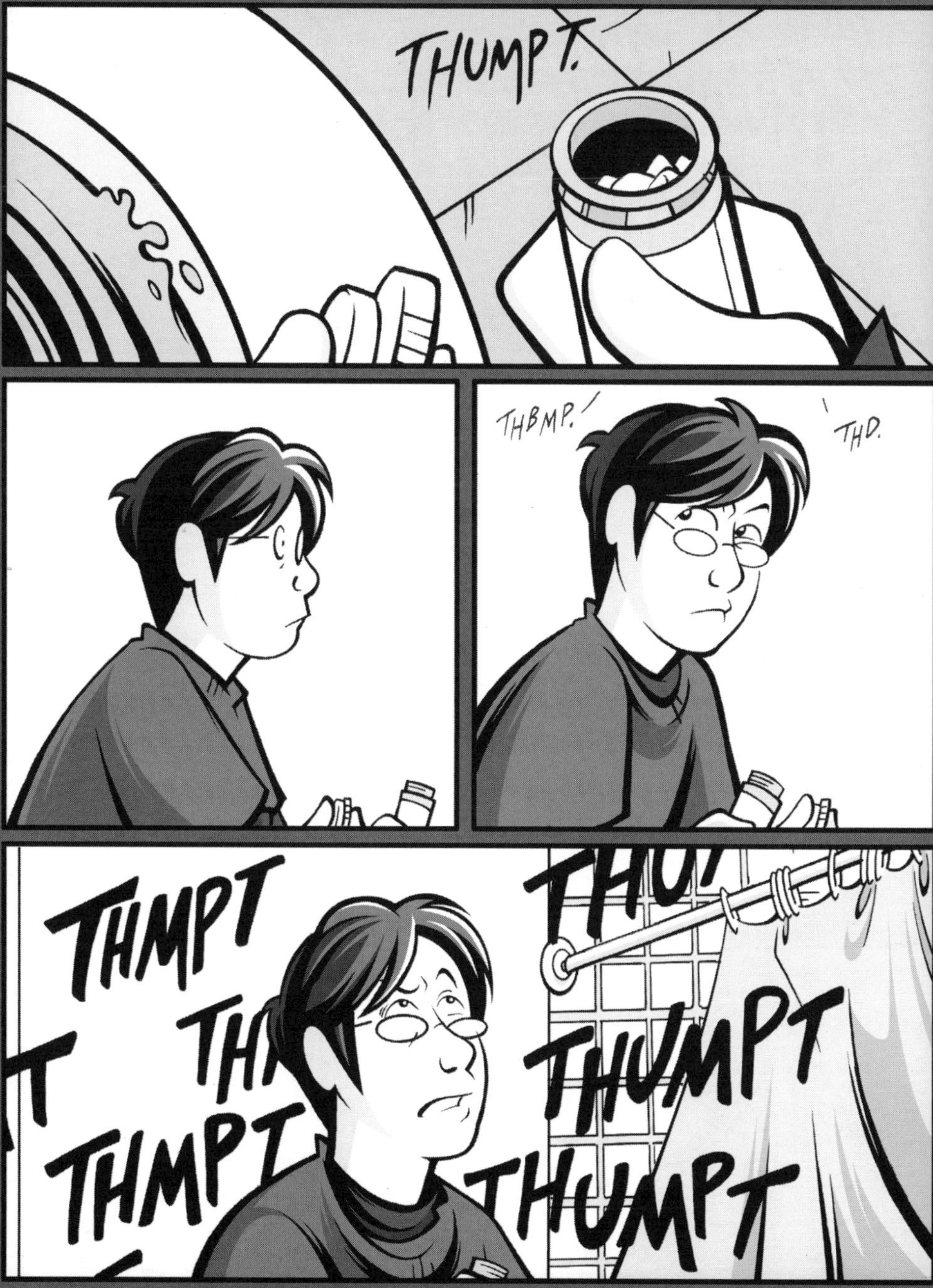
THUMPT.
THBMP!
THD.
THMPT
THUMPT
THMPT
THUMPT
THUMPT

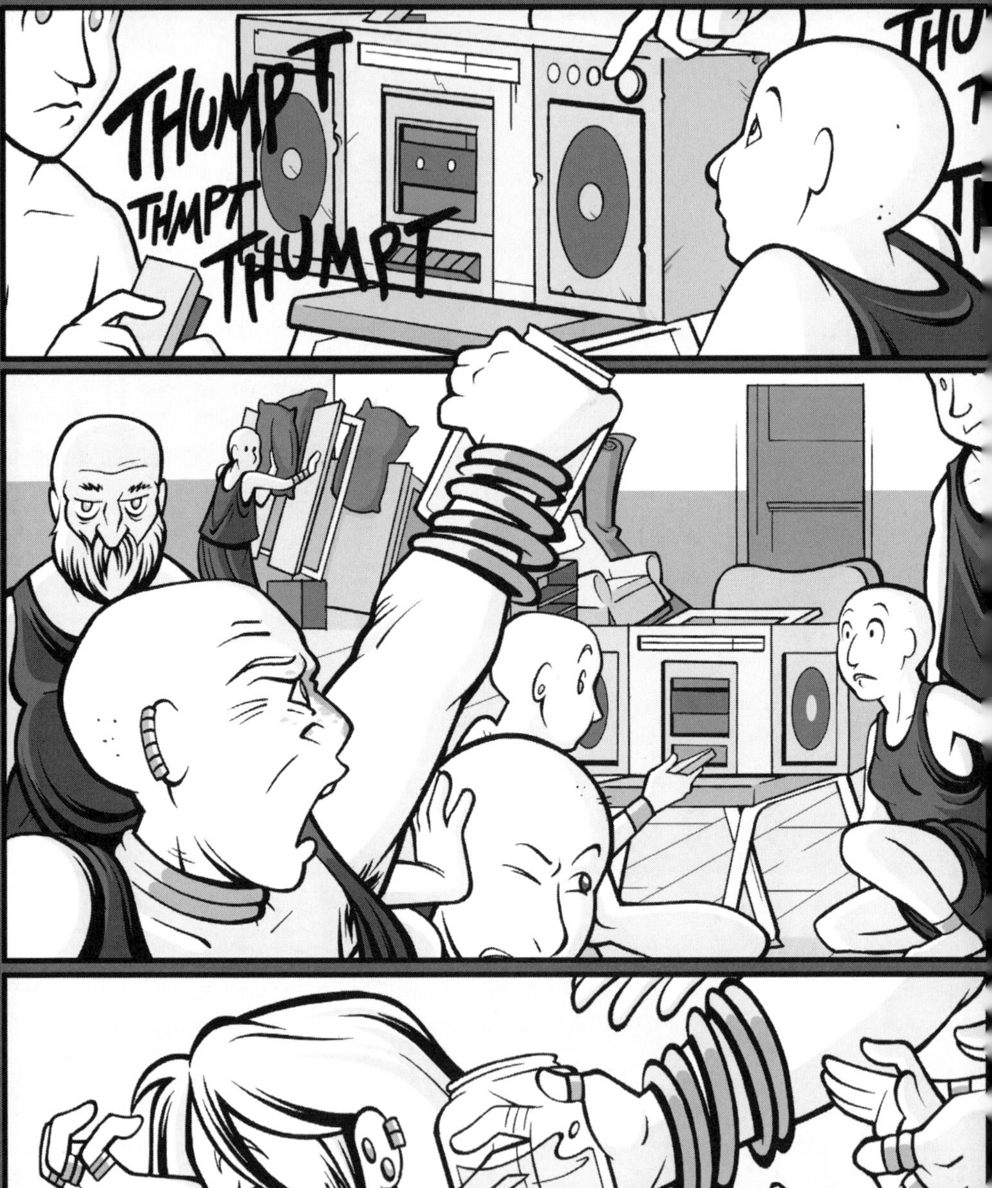
THUMPT
THMPT
THUMPT

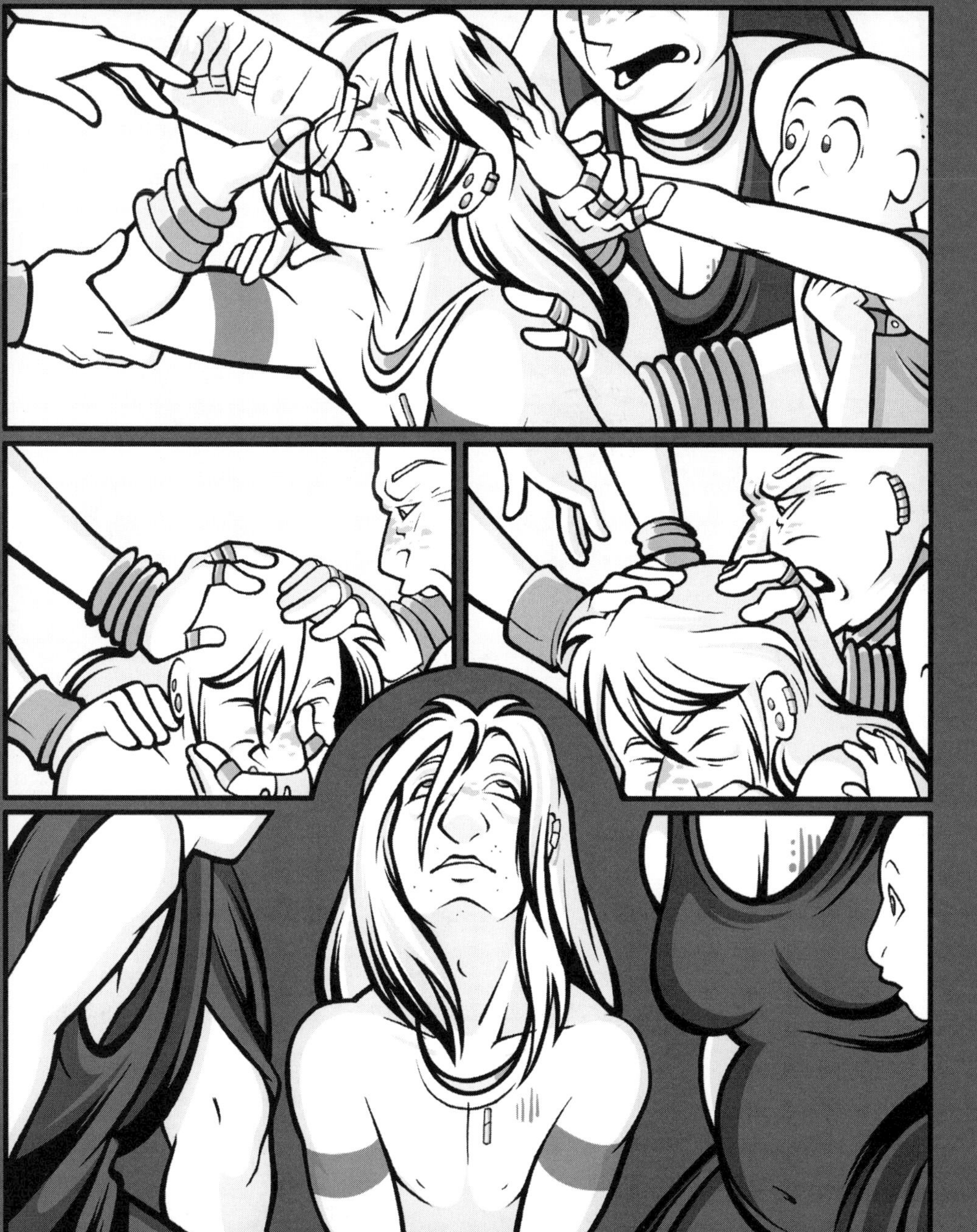

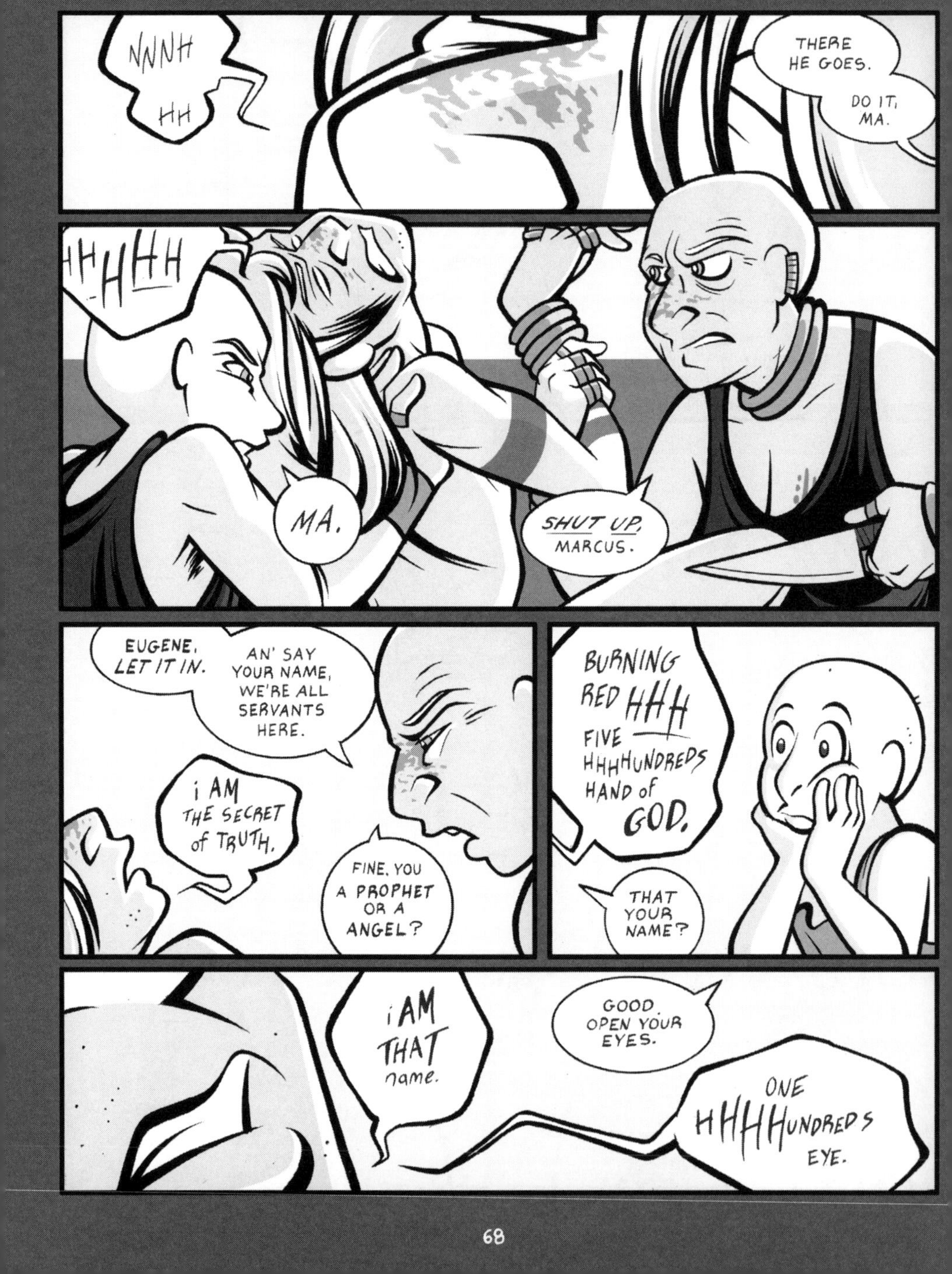
NNNH HH
THERE HE GOES.
DO IT, MA.
HHHHHH
MA.
SHUT UP, MARCUS.
EUGENE, LET IT IN.
AN' SAY YOUR NAME, WE'RE ALL SERVANTS HERE.
i AM THE SECRET of TRUTH.
FINE. YOU A PROPHET OR A ANGEL?
BURNING RED HHH FIVE HHHHUNDREDS HAND of GOD.
THAT YOUR NAME?
i AM THAT name.
GOOD. OPEN YOUR EYES.
ONE HHHHUNDREDS EYE.

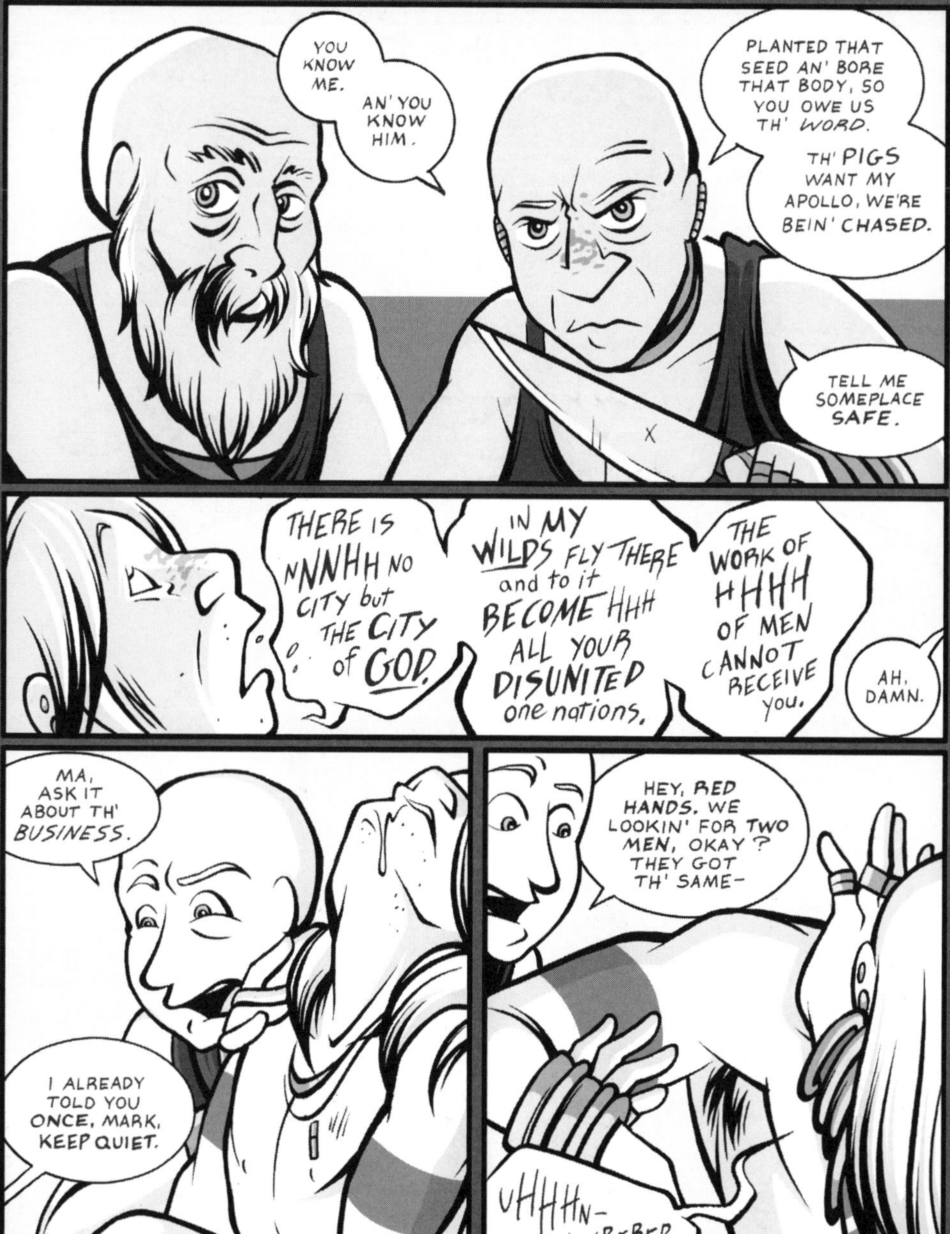

YOU KNOW ME.
AN' YOU KNOW HIM.
PLANTED THAT SEED AN' BORE THAT BODY, SO YOU OWE US TH' WORD.
TH' PIGS WANT MY APOLLO, WE'RE BEIN' CHASED.
TELL ME SOMEPLACE SAFE.
THERE IS NNNHH NO CITY but THE CITY of GOD.
IN MY WILDS FLY THERE and to it BECOME HHH ALL YOUR DISUNITED one nations,
THE WORK OF HHHH OF MEN CANNOT RECEIVE YOU.
AH, DAMN.
MA, ASK IT ABOUT TH' BUSINESS.
I ALREADY TOLD YOU ONCE, MARK, KEEP QUIET.
HEY, RED HANDS. WE LOOKIN' FOR TWO MEN, OKAY? THEY GOT TH' SAME-
UHHHN-NUMBERED.

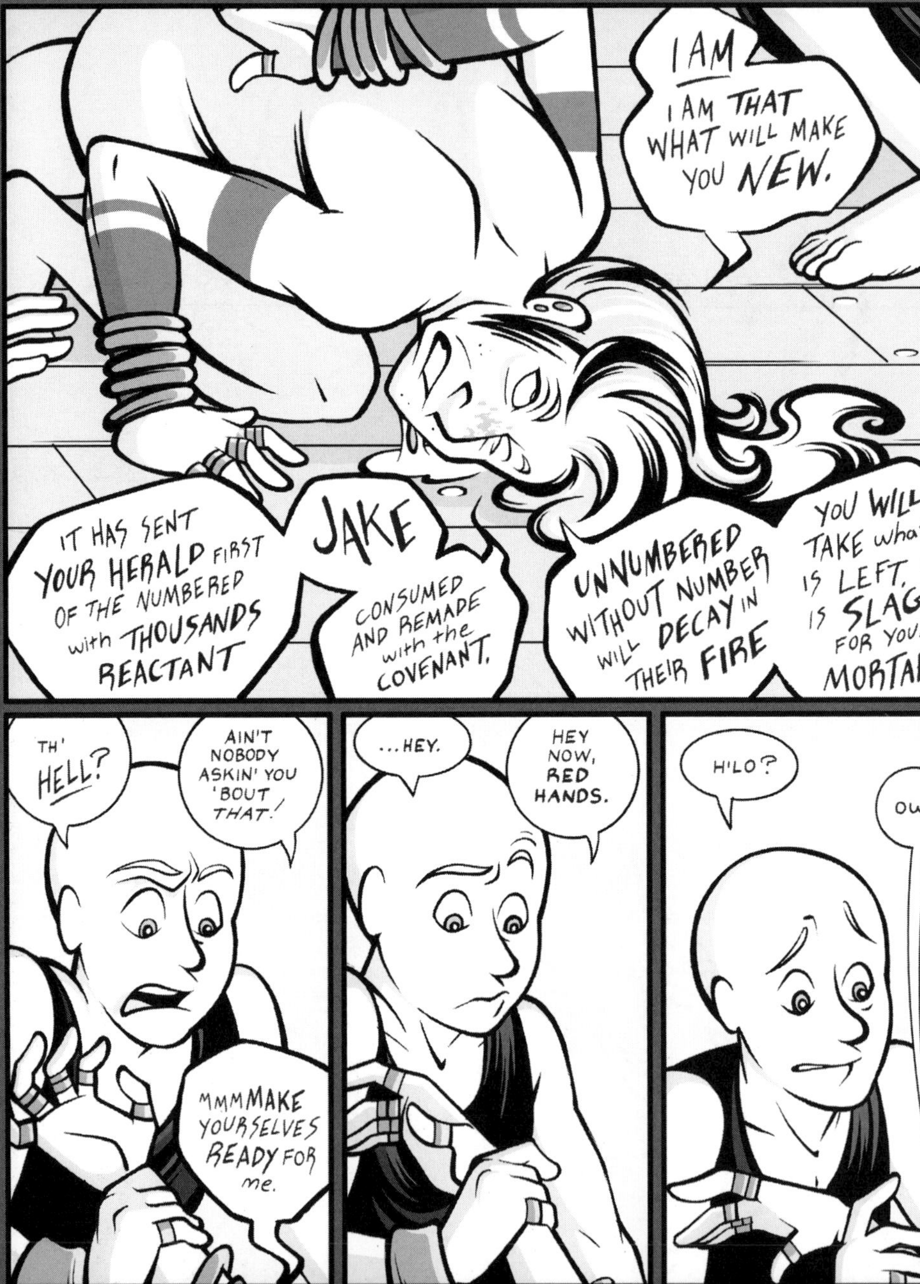
I AM
I AM THAT WHAT WILL MAKE YOU NEW.
IT HAS SENT YOUR HERALD FIRST OF THE NUMBERED with THOUSANDS REACTANT
JAKE
CONSUMED AND REMADE with the COVENANT.
UNNUMBERED WITHOUT NUMBER WILL DECAY IN THEIR FIRE
YOU WILL TAKE what IS LEFT. IT IS SLAG FOR YOUR MORTAR.
TH' HELL?
AIN'T NOBODY ASKIN' YOU 'BOUT THAT!
MMMMAKE YOURSELVES READY FOR me.
...HEY.
HEY NOW, RED HANDS.
H'LO?
OW.

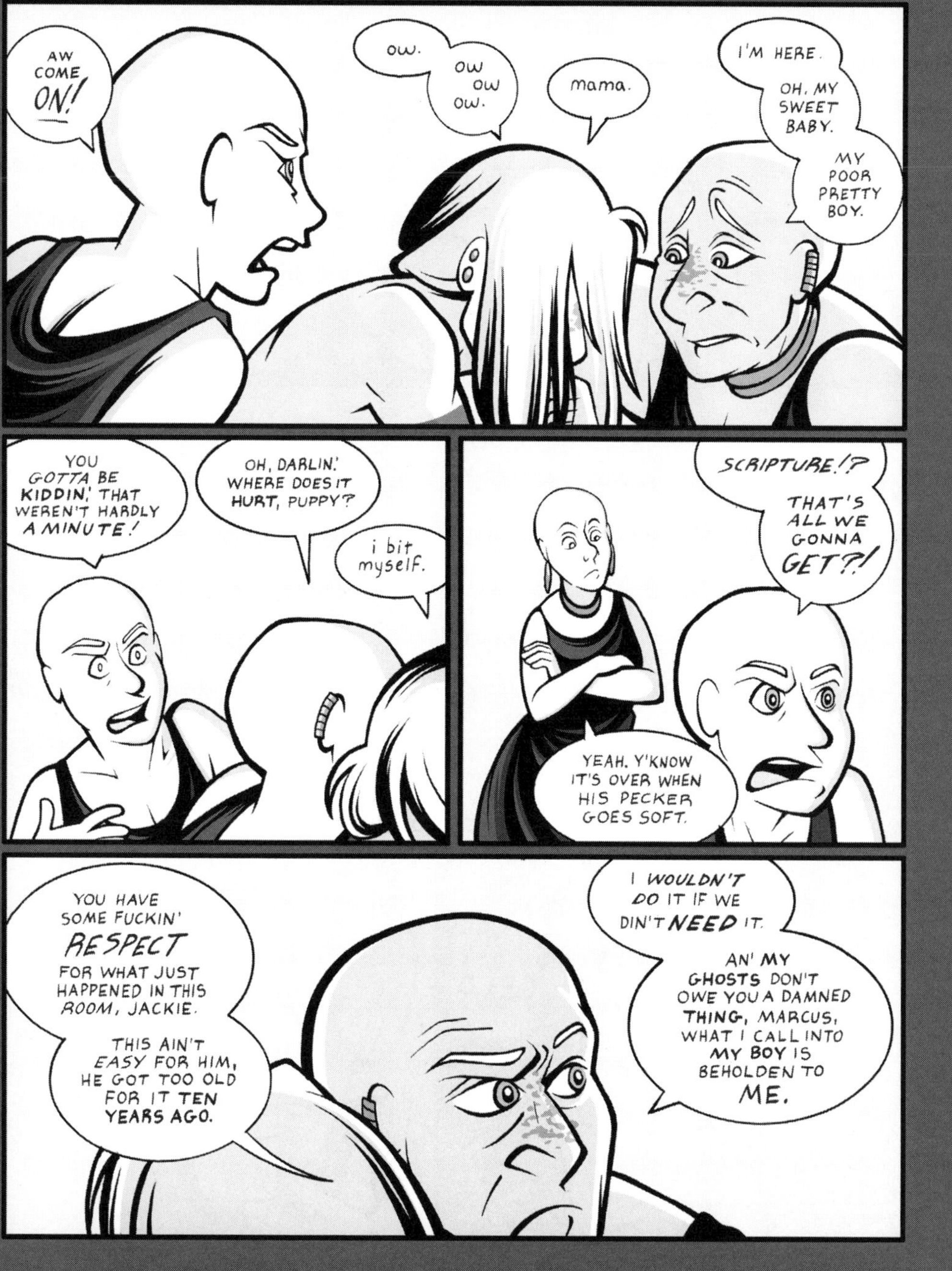
AW COME ON!
ow.
OW OW OW.
mama.
I'M HERE.
OH, MY SWEET BABY.
MY POOR PRETTY BOY.
YOU GOTTA BE KIDDIN', THAT WEREN'T HARDLY A MINUTE!
OH, DARLIN'! WHERE DOES IT HURT, PUPPY?
i bit myself.
SCRIPTURE!?
THAT'S ALL WE GONNA GET?!
YEAH. Y'KNOW IT'S OVER WHEN HIS PECKER GOES SOFT.
YOU HAVE SOME FUCKIN' RESPECT FOR WHAT JUST HAPPENED IN THIS ROOM, JACKIE.
THIS AIN'T EASY FOR HIM, HE GOT TOO OLD FOR IT TEN YEARS AGO.
I WOULDN'T DO IT IF WE DIN'T NEED IT.
AN' MY GHOSTS DON'T OWE YOU A DAMNED THING, MARCUS, WHAT I CALL INTO MY BOY IS BEHOLDEN TO ME.

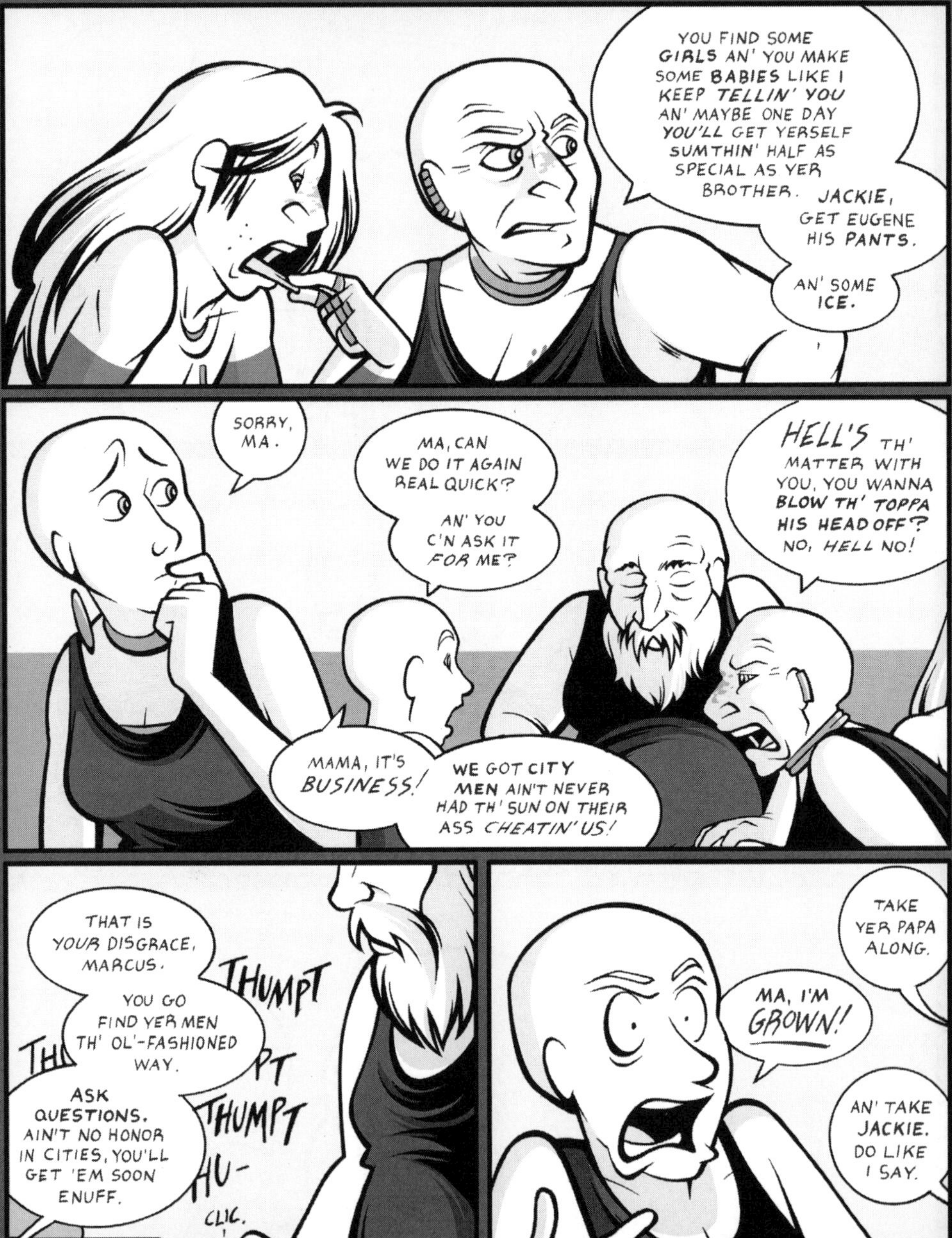
YOU FIND SOME GIRLS AN' YOU MAKE SOME BABIES LIKE I KEEP TELLIN' YOU AN' MAYBE ONE DAY YOU'LL GET YERSELF SUMTHIN' HALF AS SPECIAL AS YER BROTHER.
JACKIE, GET EUGENE HIS PANTS.
AN' SOME ICE.
SORRY, MA.
MA, CAN WE DO IT AGAIN REAL QUICK?
AN' YOU C'N ASK IT FOR ME?
HELL'S TH' MATTER WITH YOU, YOU WANNA BLOW TH' TOPPA HIS HEAD OFF? NO, HELL NO!
MAMA, IT'S BUSINESS!
WE GOT CITY MEN AIN'T NEVER HAD TH' SUN ON THEIR ASS CHEATIN' US!
THAT IS YOUR DISGRACE, MARCUS.
YOU GO FIND YER MEN TH' OL'-FASHIONED WAY.
ASK QUESTIONS. AIN'T NO HONOR IN CITIES, YOU'LL GET 'EM SOON ENUFF.
THUMPT
THUMPT
THUMPT
CLIC.
TAKE YER PAPA ALONG.
MA, I'M GROWN!
AN' TAKE JACKIE. DO LIKE I SAY.

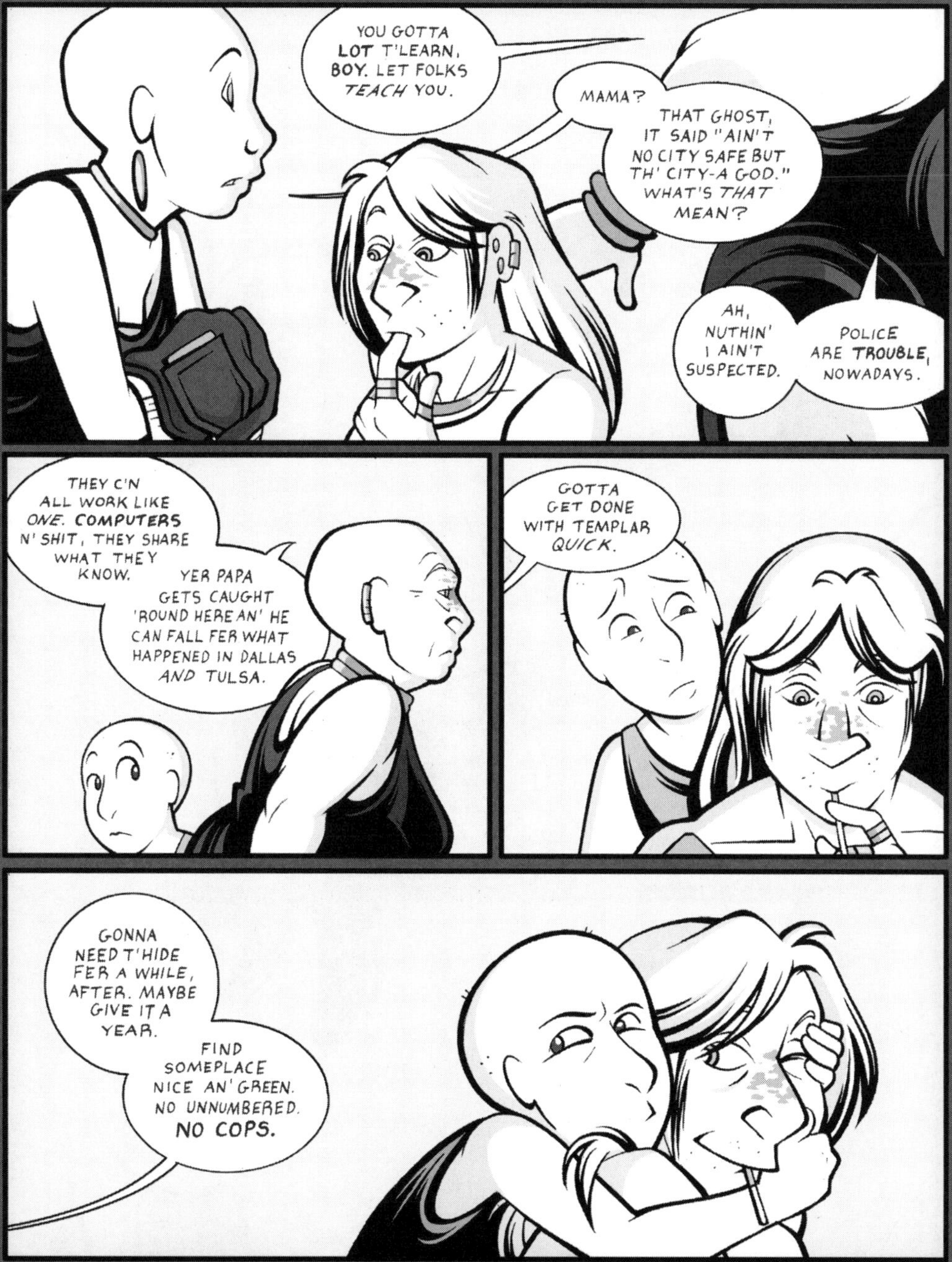
YOU GOTTA LOT T'LEARN, BOY. LET FOLKS TEACH YOU.
MAMA?
THAT GHOST, IT SAID "AIN'T NO CITY SAFE BUT TH' CITY-A GOD." WHAT'S THAT MEAN?
AH, NUTHIN' I AIN'T SUSPECTED.
POLICE ARE TROUBLE, NOWADAYS.
THEY C'N ALL WORK LIKE ONE. COMPUTERS N' SHIT, THEY SHARE WHAT THEY KNOW.
YER PAPA GETS CAUGHT 'ROUND HERE AN' HE CAN FALL FER WHAT HAPPENED IN DALLAS AND TULSA.
GOTTA GET DONE WITH TEMPLAR QUICK.
GONNA NEED T'HIDE FER A WHILE, AFTER. MAYBE GIVE IT A YEAR.
FIND SOMEPLACE NICE AN' GREEN. NO UNNUMBERED. NO COPS.

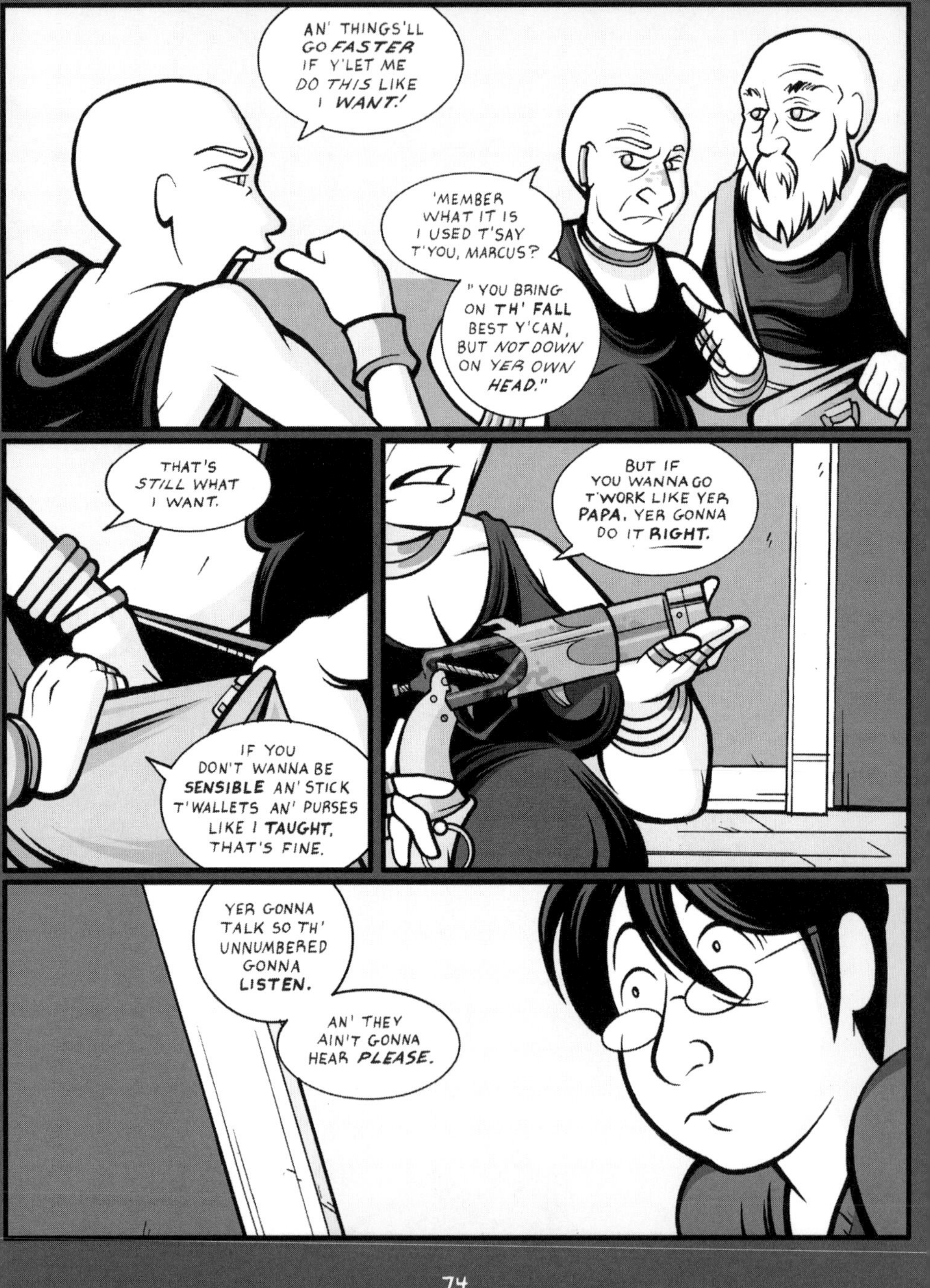
AN' THINGS'LL GO FASTER IF Y'LET ME DO THIS LIKE I WANT!
'MEMBER WHAT IT IS I USED T'SAY T'YOU, MARCUS?
"YOU BRING ON TH' FALL BEST Y'CAN, BUT NOT DOWN ON YER OWN HEAD."
THAT'S STILL WHAT I WANT.
IF YOU DON'T WANNA BE SENSIBLE AN' STICK T'WALLETS AN' PURSES LIKE I TAUGHT, THAT'S FINE.
BUT IF YOU WANNA GO T'WORK LIKE YER PAPA, YER GONNA DO IT RIGHT.
YER GONNA TALK SO TH' UNNUMBERED GONNA LISTEN.
AN' THEY AIN'T GONNA HEAR PLEASE.

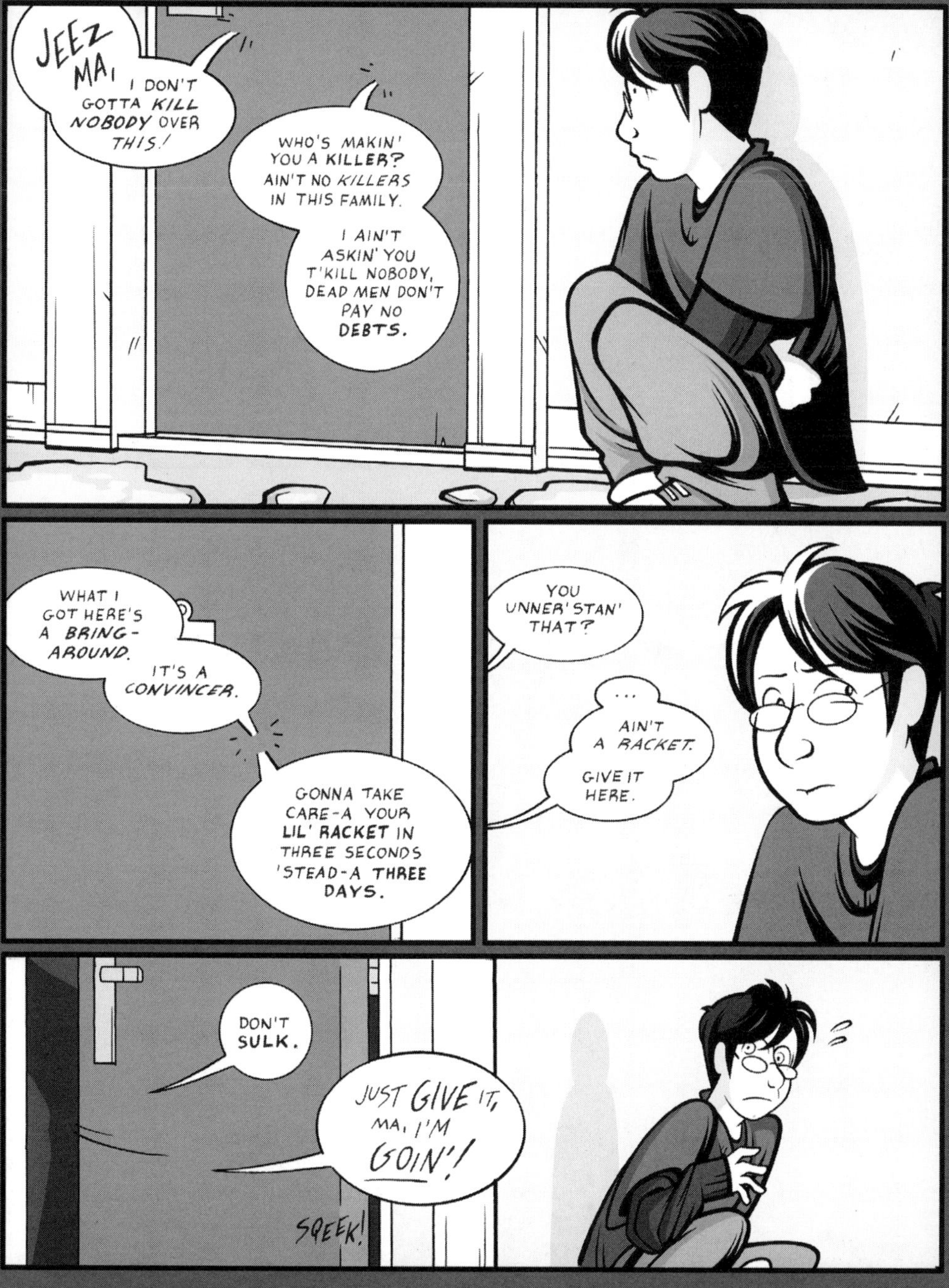
JEEZ MA, I DON'T GOTTA KILL NOBODY OVER THIS!
WHO'S MAKIN' YOU A KILLER? AIN'T NO KILLERS IN THIS FAMILY.
I AIN'T ASKIN' YOU T'KILL NOBODY, DEAD MEN DON'T PAY NO DEBTS.
WHAT I GOT HERE'S A BRING-AROUND.
IT'S A CONVINCER.
GONNA TAKE CARE-A YOUR LIL' RACKET IN THREE SECONDS 'STEAD-A THREE DAYS.
YOU UNNER'STAN' THAT?
...
AIN'T A RACKET.
GIVE IT HERE.
DON'T SULK.
JUST GIVE IT, MA, I'M GOIN'!
SQEEK!

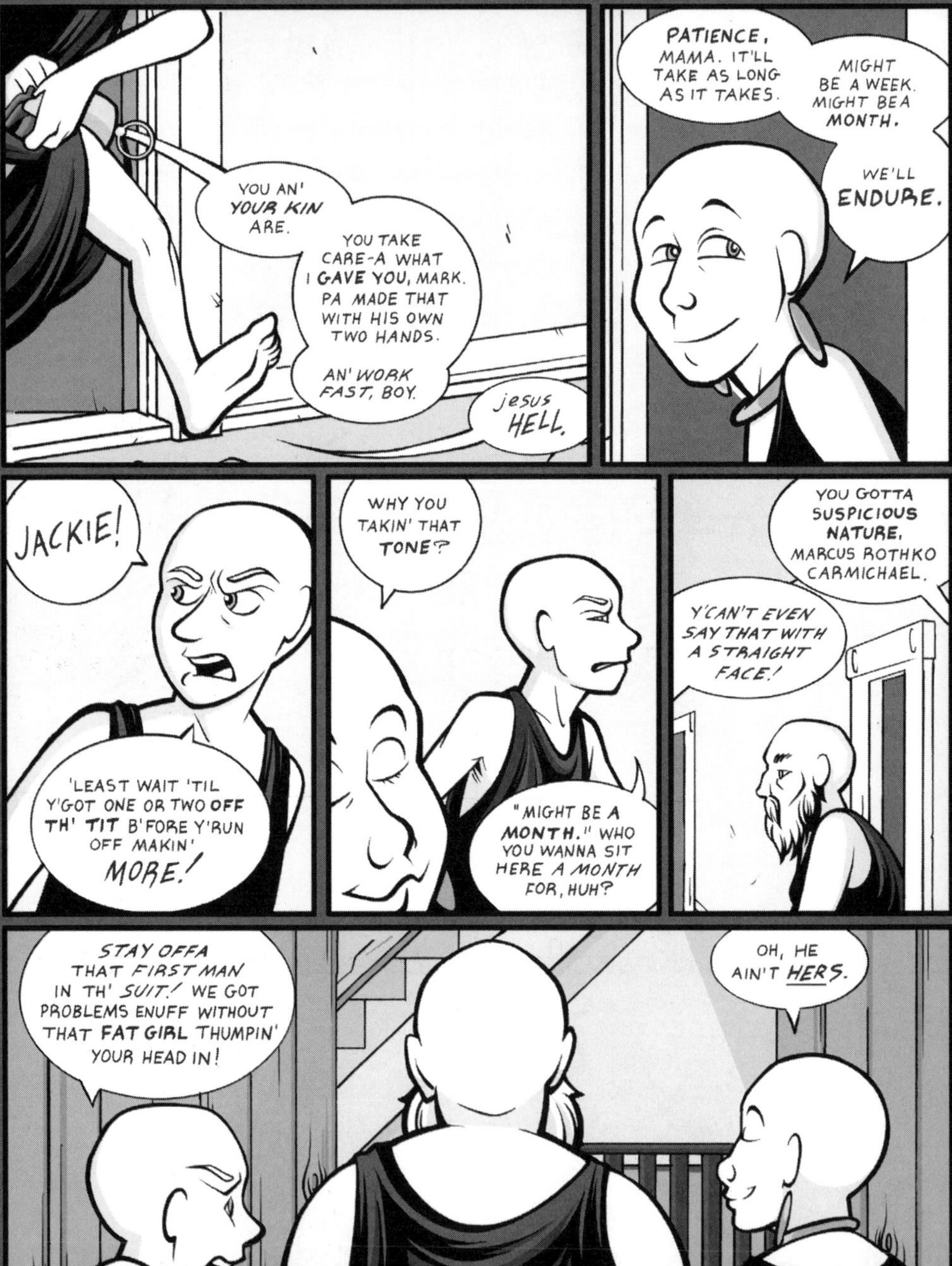
YOU AN' YOUR KIN ARE.
YOU TAKE CARE-A WHAT I GAVE YOU, MARK. PA MADE THAT WITH HIS OWN TWO HANDS.
AN' WORK FAST, BOY.
jesus HELL.
PATIENCE, MAMA. IT'LL TAKE AS LONG AS IT TAKES.
MIGHT BE A WEEK. MIGHT BE A MONTH.
WE'LL ENDURE.
JACKIE!
'LEAST WAIT 'TIL Y'GOT ONE OR TWO OFF TH' TIT B'FORE Y'RUN OFF MAKIN' MORE!
WHY YOU TAKIN' THAT TONE?
"MIGHT BE A MONTH." WHO YOU WANNA SIT HERE A MONTH FOR, HUH?
YOU GOTTA SUSPICIOUS NATURE, MARCUS ROTHKO CARMICHAEL.
Y'CAN'T EVEN SAY THAT WITH A STRAIGHT FACE!
STAY OFFA THAT FIRST MAN IN TH' SUIT! WE GOT PROBLEMS ENUFF WITHOUT THAT FAT GIRL THUMPIN' YOUR HEAD IN!
OH, HE AIN'T HERS.

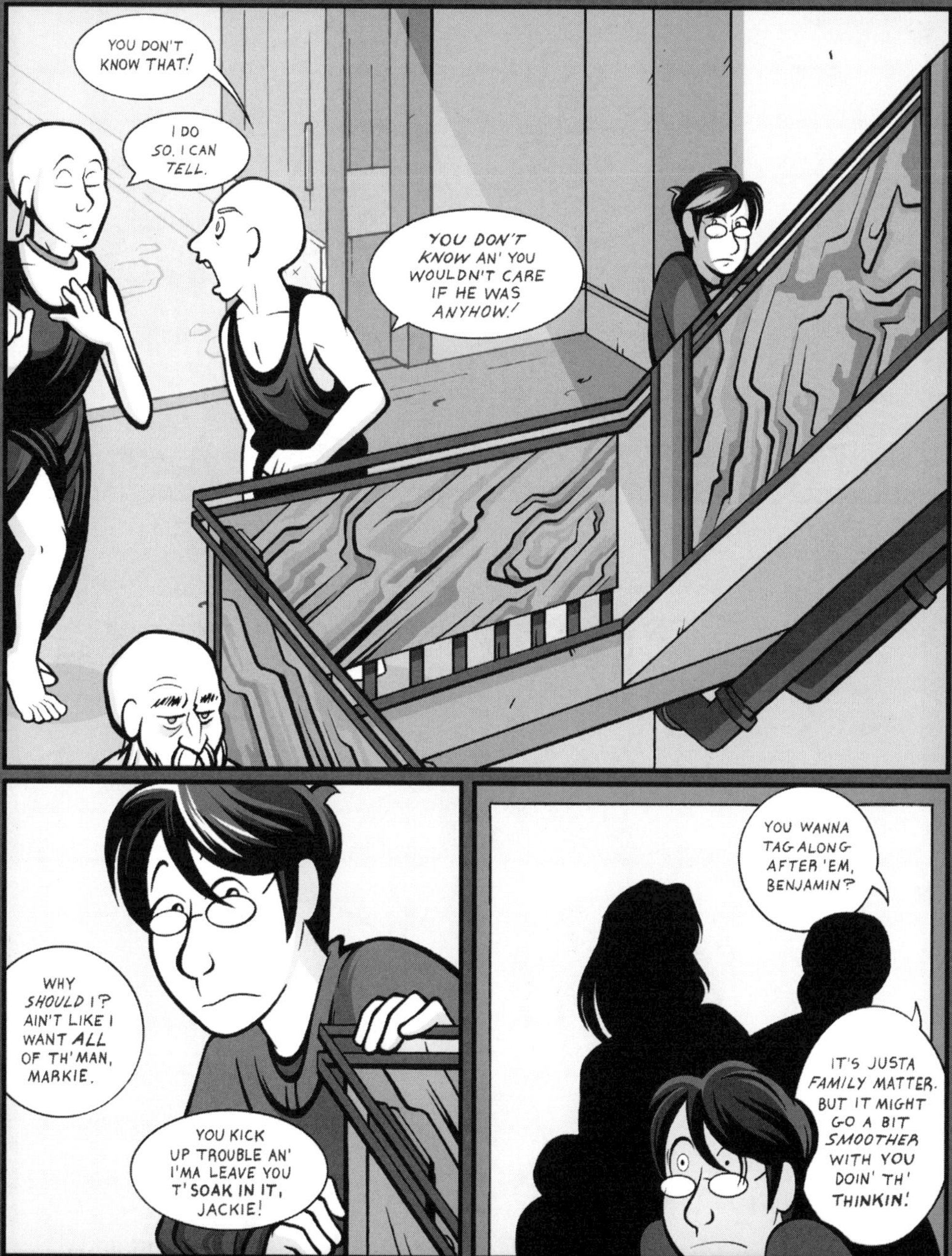
YOU DON'T KNOW THAT!
I DO SO. I CAN TELL.
YOU DON'T KNOW AN' YOU WOULDN'T CARE IF HE WAS ANYHOW!
WHY SHOULD I? AIN'T LIKE I WANT ALL OF TH' MAN, MARKIE.
YOU KICK UP TROUBLE AN' I'MA LEAVE YOU T' SOAK IN IT, JACKIE!
YOU WANNA TAG ALONG AFTER 'EM, BENJAMIN?
IT'S JUSTA FAMILY MATTER. BUT IT MIGHT GO A BIT SMOOTHER WITH YOU DOIN' TH' THINKIN!

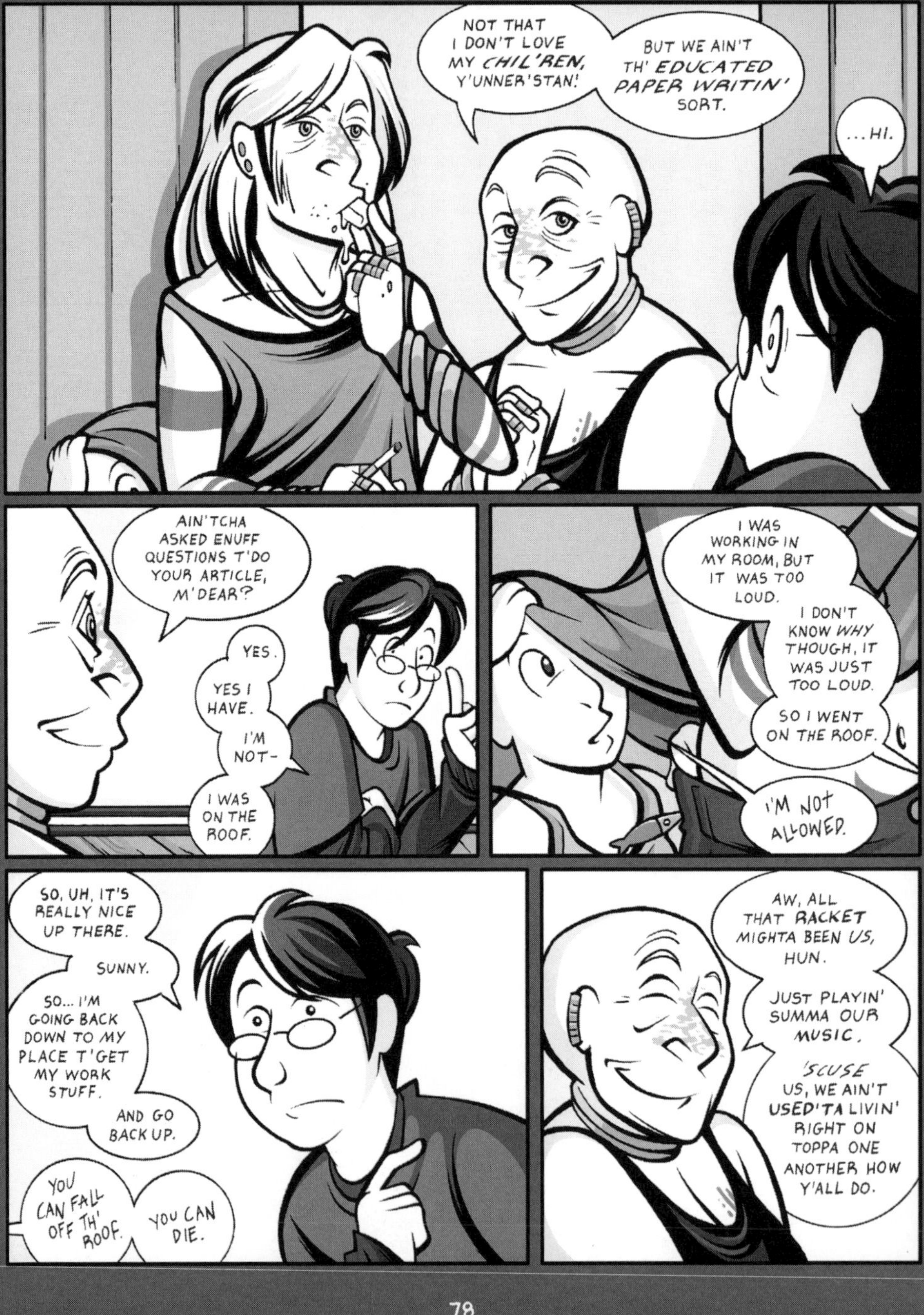

NOT THAT I DON'T LOVE MY CHIL'REN, Y'UNNER'STAN!
BUT WE AIN'T TH' EDUCATED PAPER WRITIN' SORT.
...HI.
AIN'TCHA ASKED ENUFF QUESTIONS T'DO YOUR ARTICLE, M'DEAR?
YES.
YES I HAVE.
I'M NOT-
I WAS ON THE ROOF.
I WAS WORKING IN MY ROOM, BUT IT WAS TOO LOUD.
I DON'T KNOW WHY THOUGH, IT WAS JUST TOO LOUD.
SO I WENT ON THE ROOF.
I'M NOT ALLOWED.
SO, UH, IT'S REALLY NICE UP THERE.
SUNNY.
SO... I'M GOING BACK DOWN TO MY PLACE T'GET MY WORK STUFF.
AND GO BACK UP.
YOU CAN FALL OFF TH' ROOF.
YOU CAN DIE.
AW, ALL THAT RACKET MIGHTA BEEN US, HUN.
JUST PLAYIN' SUMMA OUR MUSIC.
'SCUSE US, WE AIN'T USED'TA LIVIN' RIGHT ON TOPPA ONE ANOTHER HOW Y'ALL DO.

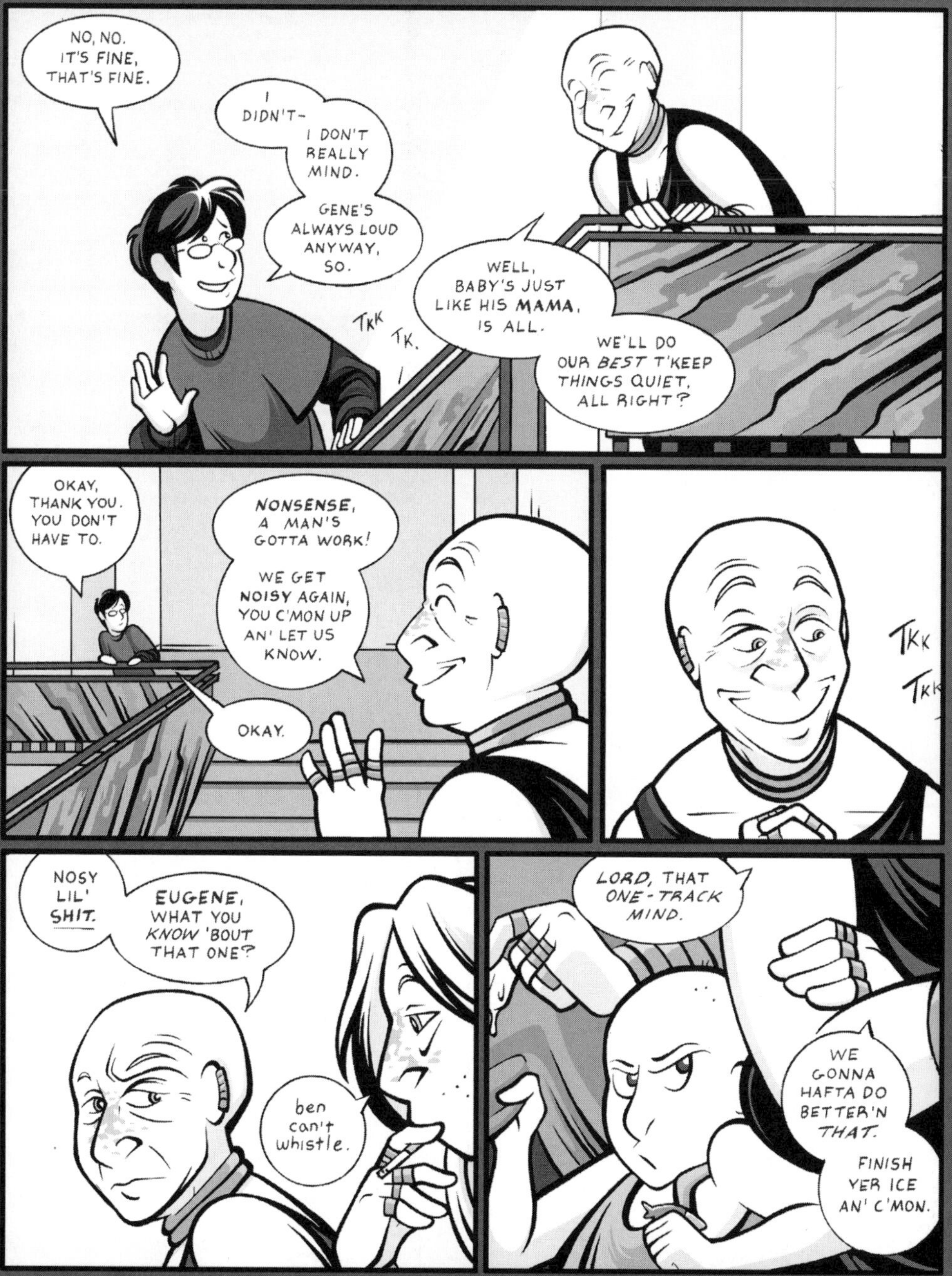
NO, NO. IT'S FINE, THAT'S FINE.
I DIDN'T- I DON'T REALLY MIND.
GENE'S ALWAYS LOUD ANYWAY, SO.
TKK TK.
WELL, BABY'S JUST LIKE HIS MAMA, IS ALL.
WE'LL DO OUR BEST T'KEEP THINGS QUIET, ALL RIGHT?
OKAY, THANK YOU. YOU DON'T HAVE TO.
NONSENSE, A MAN'S GOTTA WORK!
WE GET NOISY AGAIN, YOU C'MON UP AN' LET US KNOW.
OKAY.
TKK
TKK
NOSY LIL' SHIT.
EUGENE, WHAT YOU KNOW 'BOUT THAT ONE?
ben can't whistle.
LORD, THAT ONE-TRACK MIND.
WE GONNA HAFTA DO BETTER'N THAT.
FINISH YER ICE AN' C'MON.

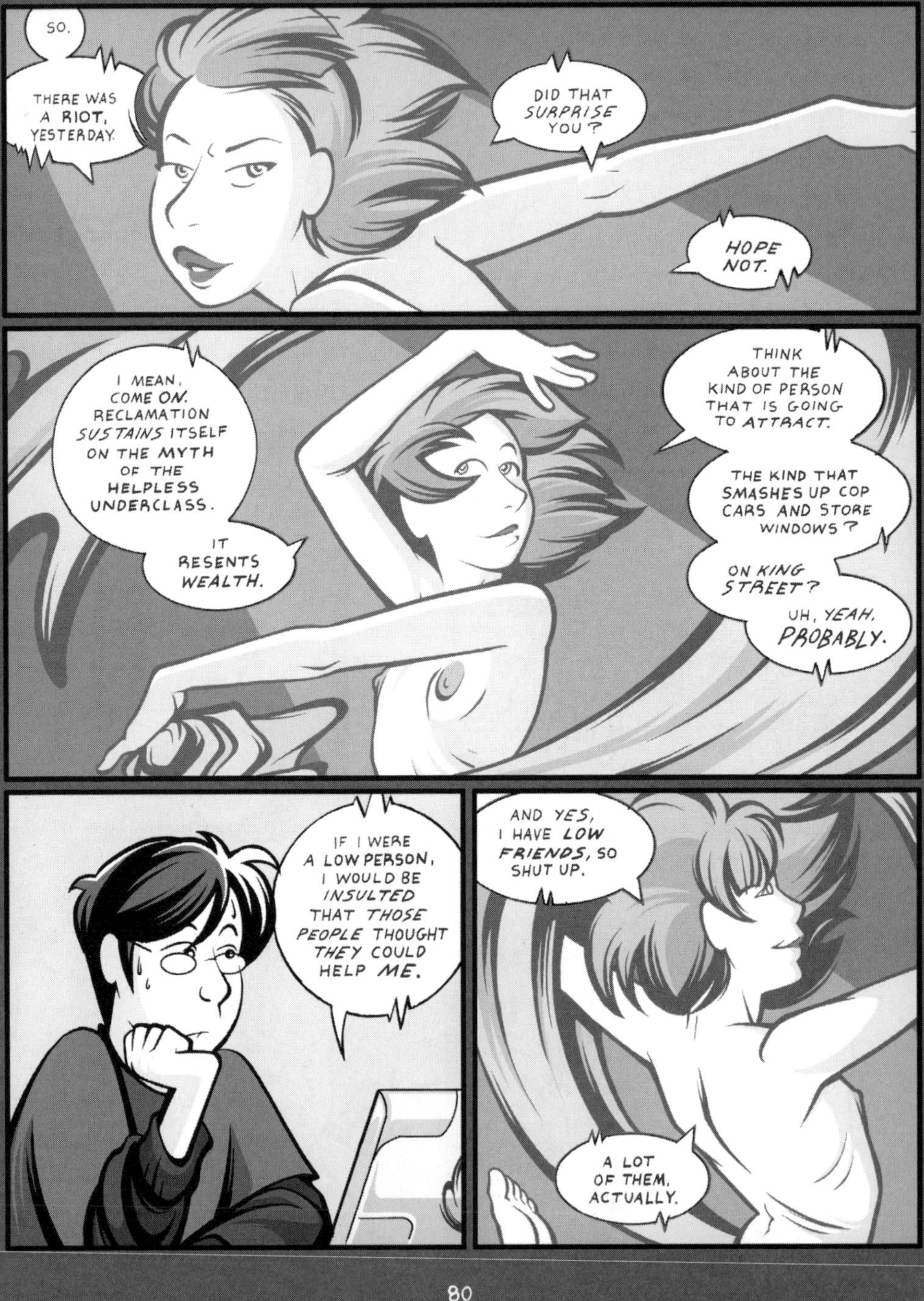
SO.
THERE WAS A RIOT, YESTERDAY.
DID THAT SURPRISE YOU?
HOPE NOT.
I MEAN, COME ON. RECLAMATION SUSTAINS ITSELF ON THE MYTH OF THE HELPLESS UNDERCLASS.
IT RESENTS WEALTH.
THINK ABOUT THE KIND OF PERSON THAT IS GOING TO ATTRACT.
THE KIND THAT SMASHES UP COP CARS AND STORE WINDOWS?
ON KING STREET?
UH, YEAH, PROBABLY.
IF I WERE A LOW PERSON, I WOULD BE INSULTED THAT THOSE PEOPLE THOUGHT THEY COULD HELP ME.
AND YES, I HAVE LOW FRIENDS, SO SHUT UP.
A LOT OF THEM, ACTUALLY.

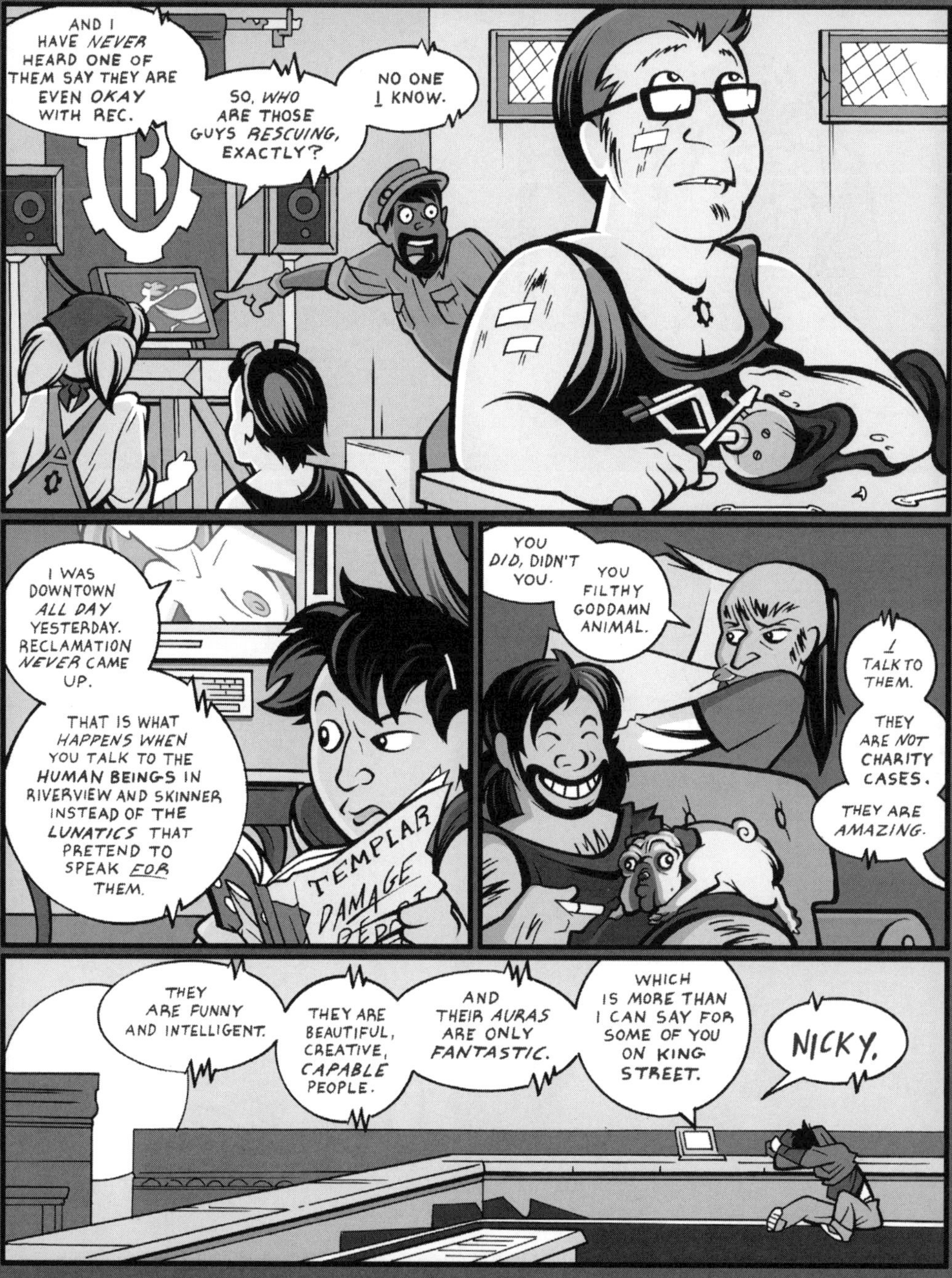
AND I HAVE NEVER HEARD ONE OF THEM SAY THEY ARE EVEN OKAY WITH REC.
SO, WHO ARE THOSE GUYS RESCUING, EXACTLY?
NO ONE I KNOW.
I WAS DOWNTOWN ALL DAY YESTERDAY. RECLAMATION NEVER CAME UP.
THAT IS WHAT HAPPENS WHEN YOU TALK TO THE HUMAN BEINGS IN RIVERVIEW AND SKINNER INSTEAD OF THE LUNATICS THAT PRETEND TO SPEAK FOR THEM.
TEMPLAR DAMAGE
YOU DID, DIDN'T YOU.
YOU FILTHY GODDAMN ANIMAL.
I TALK TO THEM.
THEY ARE NOT CHARITY CASES.
THEY ARE AMAZING.
THEY ARE FUNNY AND INTELLIGENT.
THEY ARE BEAUTIFUL, CREATIVE, CAPABLE PEOPLE.
AND THEIR AURAS ARE ONLY FANTASTIC.
WHICH IS MORE THAN I CAN SAY FOR SOME OF YOU ON KING STREET.
NICKY.

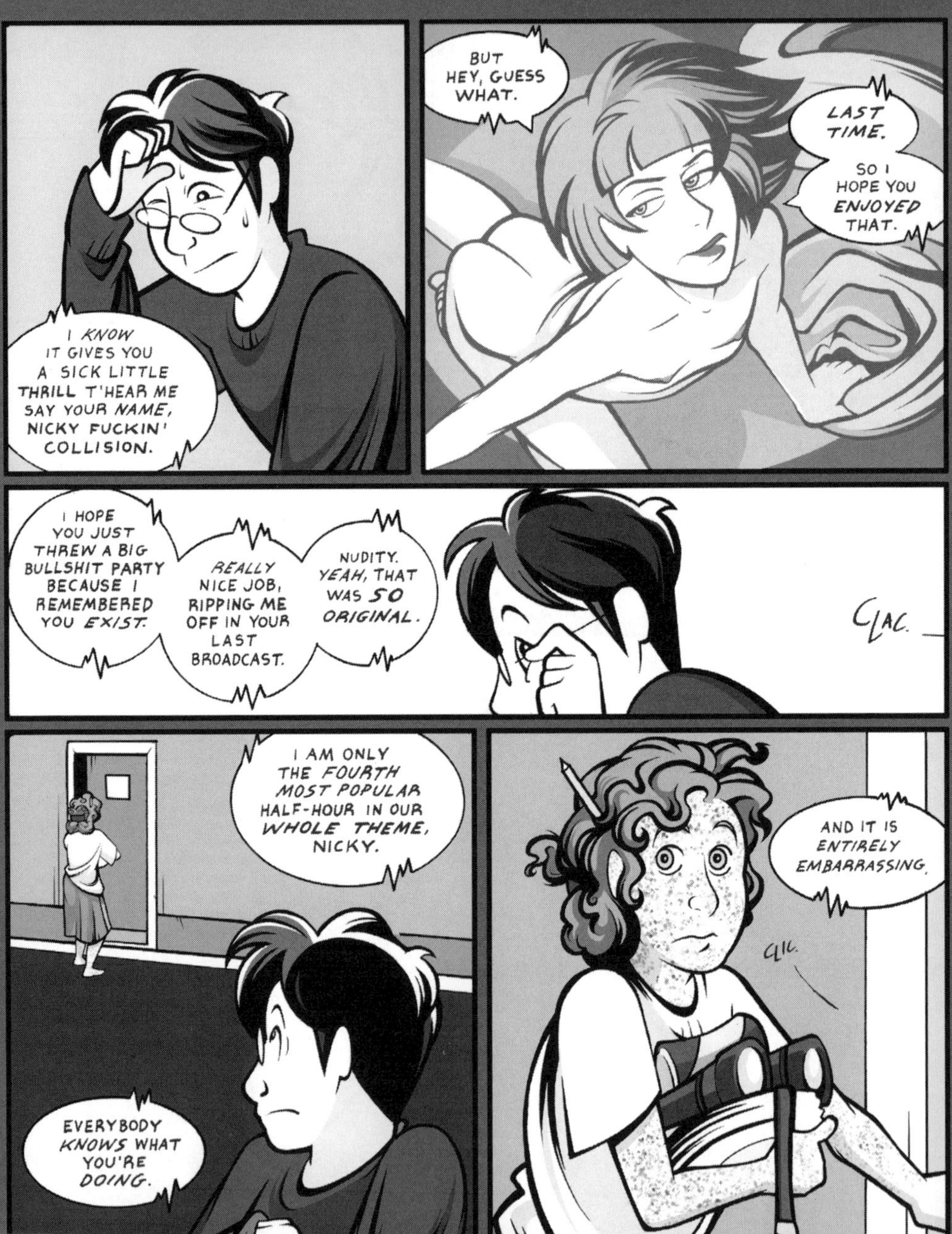
I KNOW IT GIVES YOU A SICK LITTLE THRILL T'HEAR ME SAY YOUR NAME, NICKY FUCKIN' COLLISION.
BUT HEY, GUESS WHAT.
LAST TIME.
SO I HOPE YOU ENJOYED THAT.
I HOPE YOU JUST THREW A BIG BULLSHIT PARTY BECAUSE I REMEMBERED YOU EXIST.
REALLY NICE JOB, RIPPING ME OFF IN YOUR LAST BROADCAST.
NUDITY. YEAH, THAT WAS SO ORIGINAL.
CLAC.
I AM ONLY THE FOURTH MOST POPULAR HALF-HOUR IN OUR WHOLE THEME, NICKY.
EVERYBODY KNOWS WHAT YOU'RE DOING.
AND IT IS ENTIRELY EMBARRASSING.
CLIC.

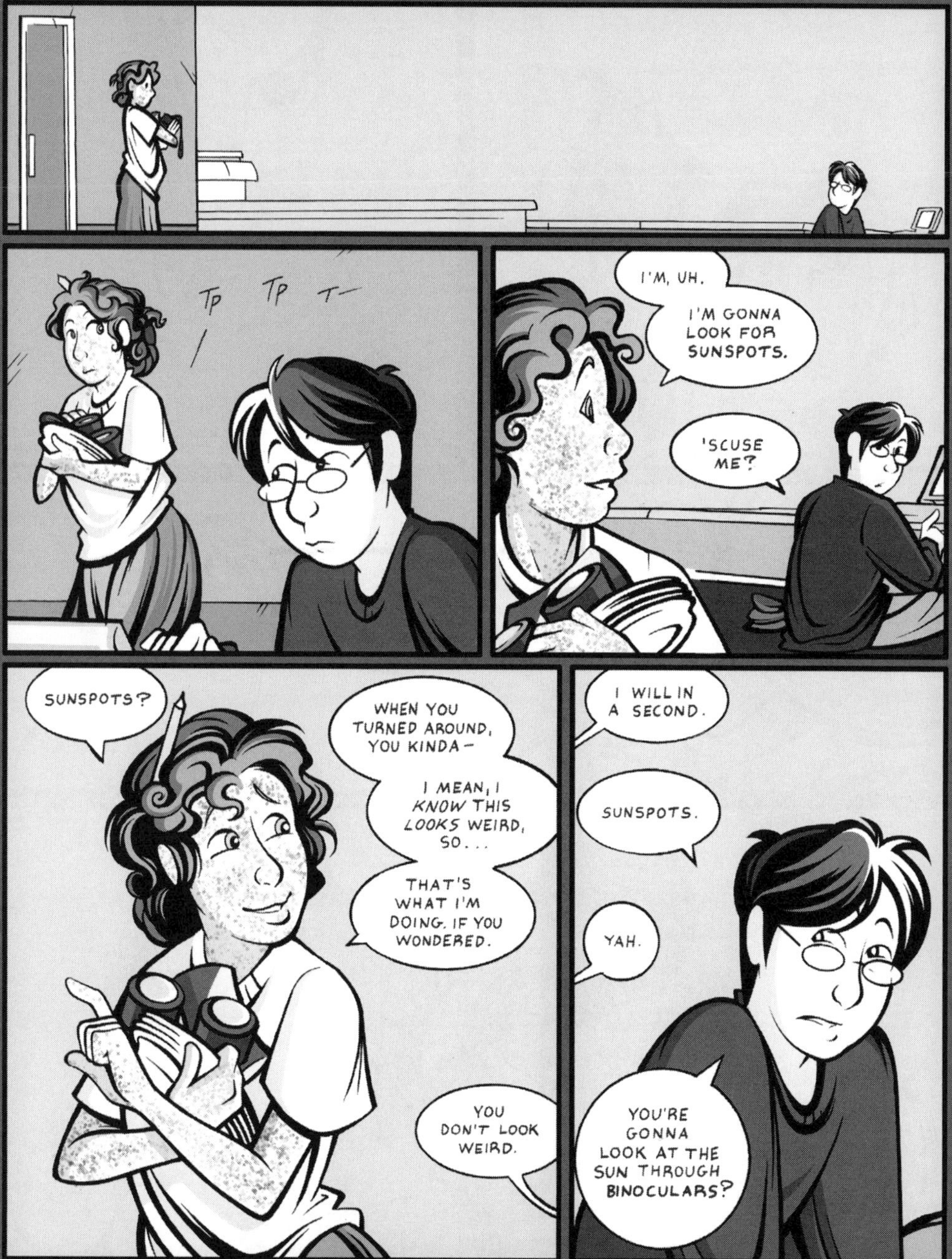
TP TP T—
I'M, UH.
I'M GONNA LOOK FOR SUNSPOTS.
'SCUSE ME?
SUNSPOTS?
WHEN YOU TURNED AROUND, YOU KINDA—
I MEAN, I *KNOW* THIS *LOOKS* WEIRD, SO...
THAT'S WHAT I'M DOING. IF YOU WONDERED.
YOU DON'T LOOK WEIRD.
I WILL IN A SECOND.
SUNSPOTS.
YAH.
YOU'RE GONNA LOOK AT THE SUN THROUGH BINOCULARS?

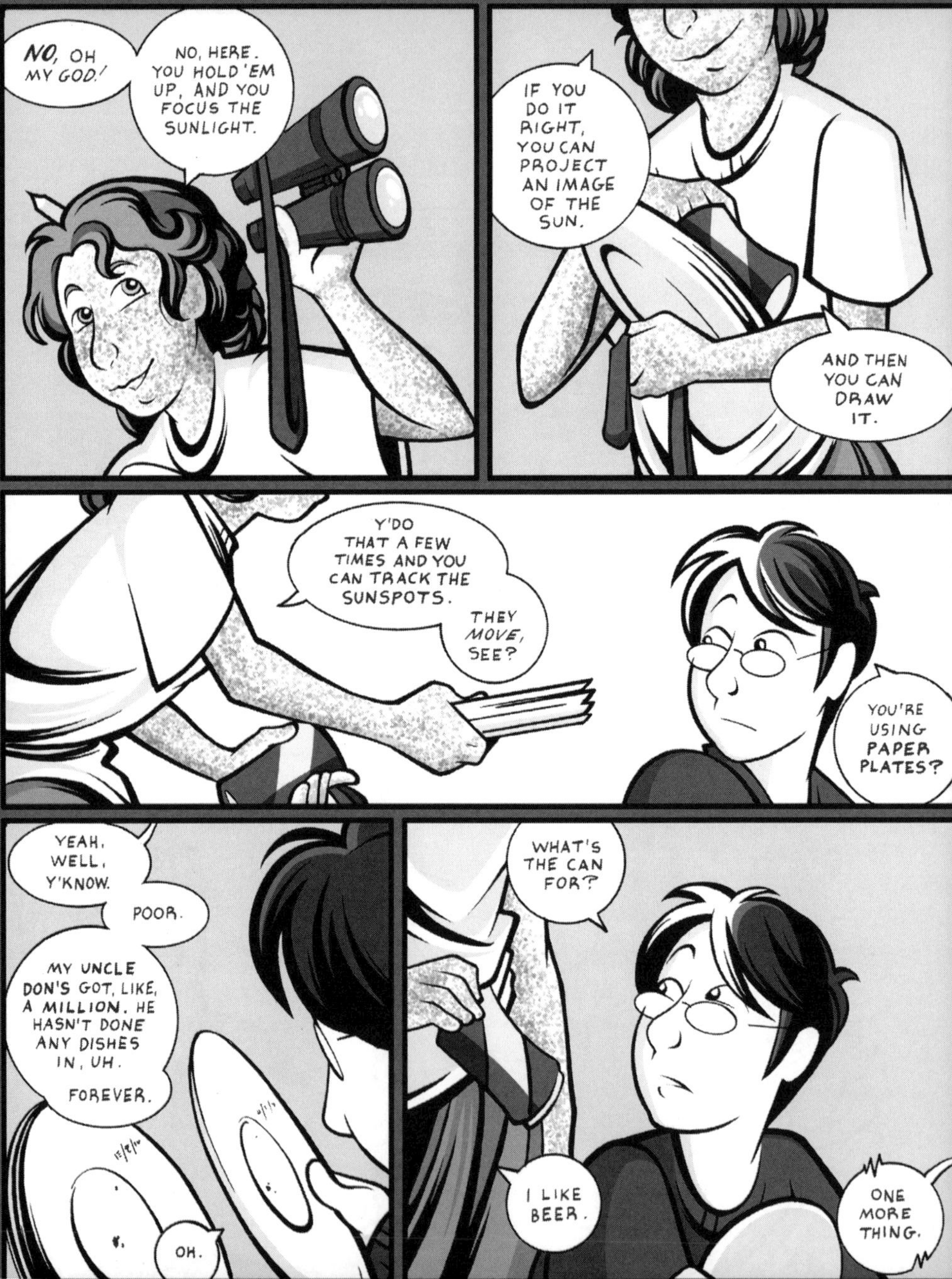
NO, OH MY GOD!
NO, HERE. YOU HOLD 'EM UP, AND YOU FOCUS THE SUNLIGHT.
IF YOU DO IT RIGHT, YOU CAN PROJECT AN IMAGE OF THE SUN.
AND THEN YOU CAN DRAW IT.
Y'DO THAT A FEW TIMES AND YOU CAN TRACK THE SUNSPOTS.
THEY MOVE, SEE?
YOU'RE USING PAPER PLATES?
YEAH. WELL. Y'KNOW.
POOR.
MY UNCLE DON'S GOT, LIKE, A MILLION. HE HASN'T DONE ANY DISHES IN, UH.
FOREVER.
OH.
WHAT'S THE CAN FOR?
I LIKE BEER.
ONE MORE THING.

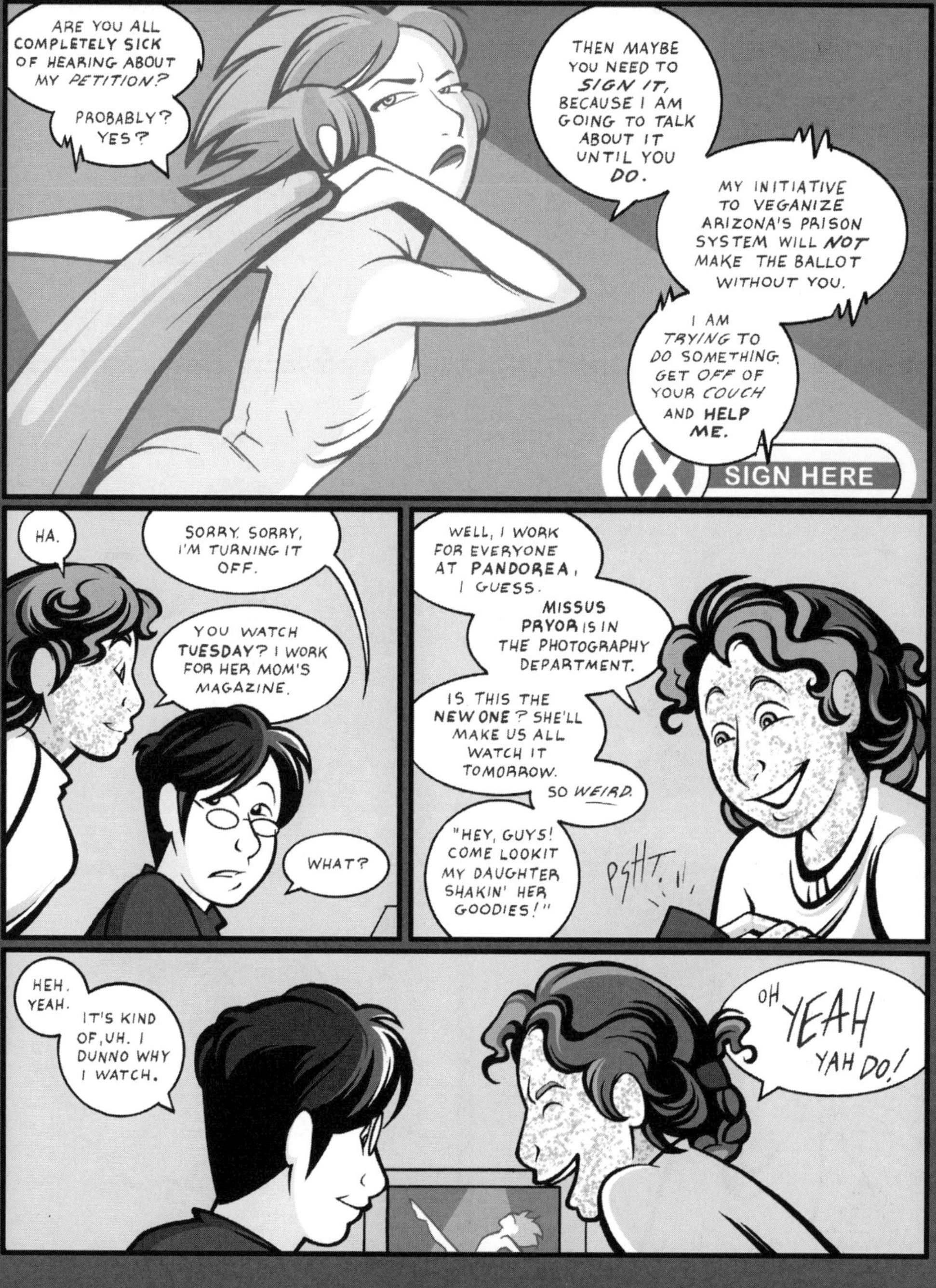

ARE YOU ALL COMPLETELY SICK OF HEARING ABOUT MY *PETITION*?
PROBABLY? YES?
THEN MAYBE YOU NEED TO *SIGN IT*, BECAUSE I AM GOING TO TALK ABOUT IT UNTIL YOU *DO*.
MY INITIATIVE TO VEGANIZE ARIZONA'S PRISON SYSTEM WILL *NOT* MAKE THE BALLOT WITHOUT YOU.
I AM *TRYING* TO DO SOMETHING. GET *OFF* OF YOUR *COUCH* AND **HELP ME.**
SIGN HERE
HA.
SORRY. SORRY, I'M TURNING IT OFF.
YOU WATCH **TUESDAY**? I WORK FOR HER MOM'S MAGAZINE.
WHAT?
WELL, I WORK FOR EVERYONE AT **PANDOREA**, I GUESS.
MISSUS PRYOR IS IN THE PHOTOGRAPHY DEPARTMENT.
IS THIS THE **NEW ONE**? SHE'LL MAKE US ALL WATCH IT TOMORROW.
SO *WEIRD*.
"HEY, GUYS! COME LOOKIT MY DAUGHTER SHAKIN' HER GOODIES!"
PSHT!
HEH. YEAH.
IT'S KIND OF, UH. I DUNNO WHY I WATCH.
OH YEAH YAH DO!

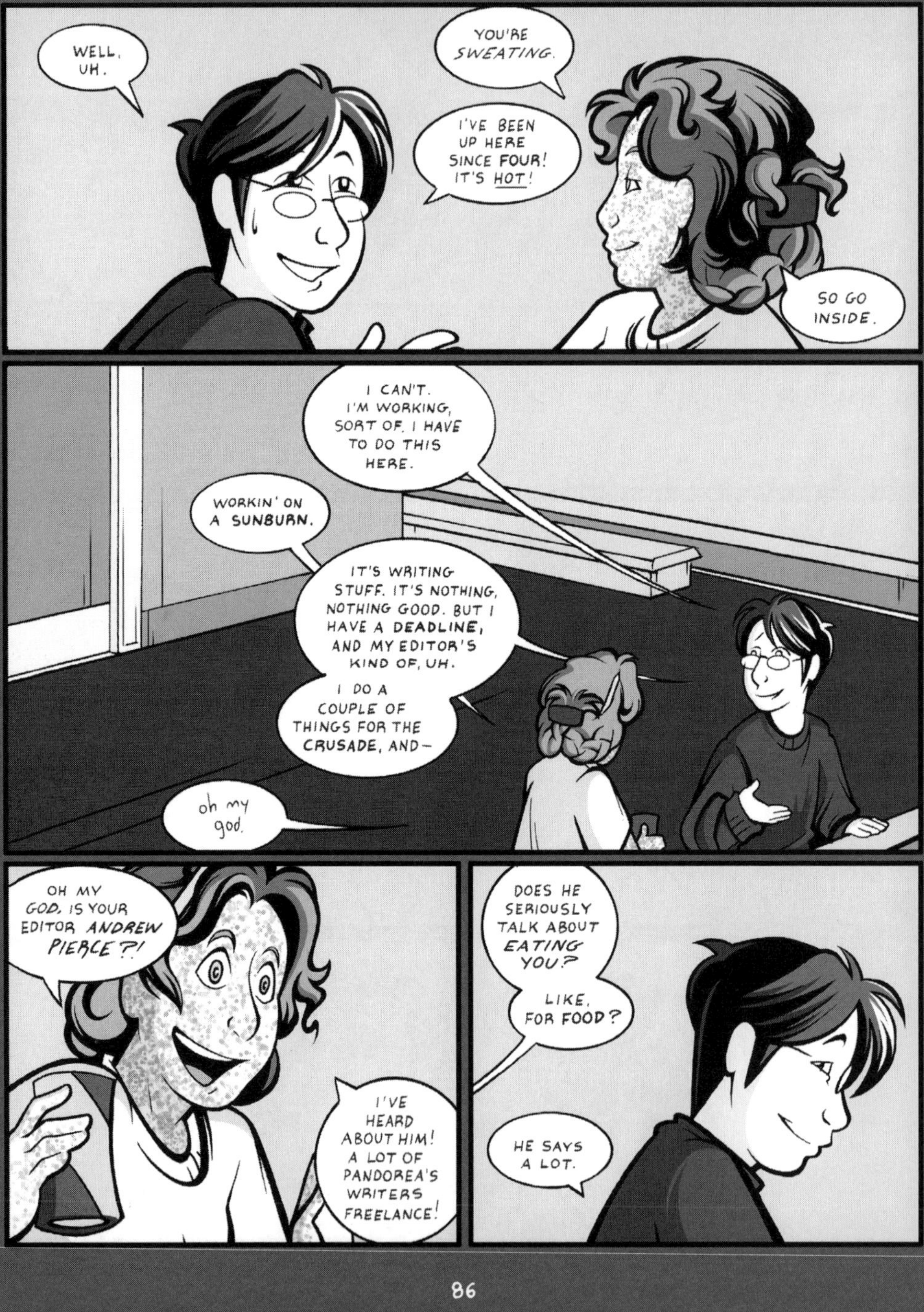
WELL, UH.
YOU'RE SWEATING.
I'VE BEEN UP HERE SINCE FOUR! IT'S HOT!
SO GO INSIDE.
I CAN'T. I'M WORKING, SORT OF. I HAVE TO DO THIS HERE.
WORKIN' ON A SUNBURN.
IT'S WRITING STUFF. IT'S NOTHING, NOTHING GOOD. BUT I HAVE A DEADLINE, AND MY EDITOR'S KIND OF, UH.
I DO A COUPLE OF THINGS FOR THE CRUSADE, AND—
oh my god.
OH MY GOD, IS YOUR EDITOR ANDREW PIERCE?!
I'VE HEARD ABOUT HIM! A LOT OF PANDOREA'S WRITERS FREELANCE!
DOES HE SERIOUSLY TALK ABOUT EATING YOU?
LIKE, FOR FOOD?
HE SAYS A LOT.

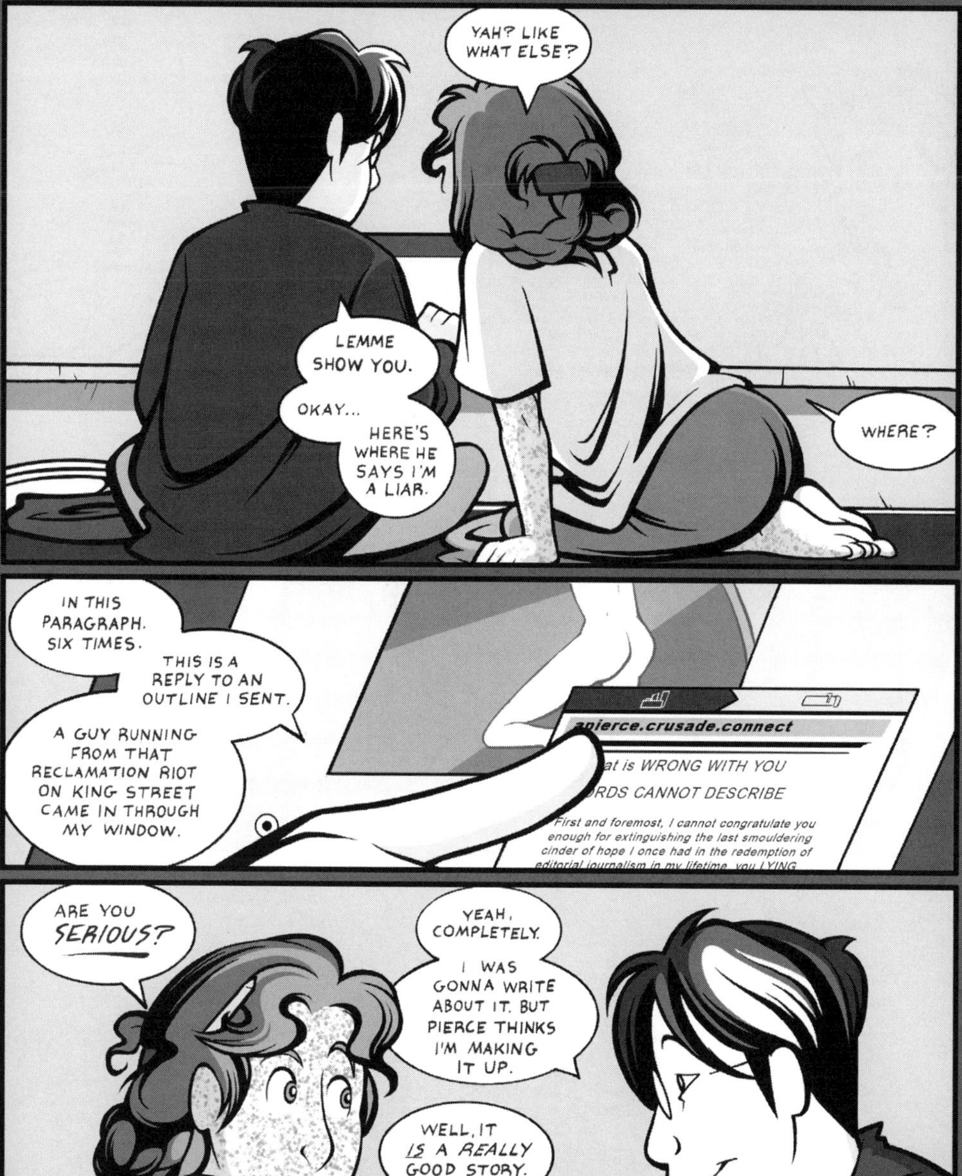
YAH? LIKE WHAT ELSE?
LEMME SHOW YOU.
OKAY...
HERE'S WHERE HE SAYS I'M A LIAR.
WHERE?
IN THIS PARAGRAPH. SIX TIMES.
THIS IS A REPLY TO AN OUTLINE I SENT.
A GUY RUNNING FROM THAT RECLAMATION RIOT ON KING STREET CAME IN THROUGH MY WINDOW.
apierce.crusade.connect
at is WRONG WITH YOU
ORDS CANNOT DESCRIBE
First and foremost, I cannot congratulate you enough for extinguishing the last smouldering cinder of hope I once had in the redemption of
ARE YOU *SERIOUS?*
YEAH, COMPLETELY.
I WAS GONNA WRITE ABOUT IT. BUT PIERCE THINKS I'M MAKING IT UP.
WELL, IT *IS* A *REALLY* GOOD STORY.
IF I WERE GONNA LIE, I'D LIE LIKE THAT.
ME, TOO.

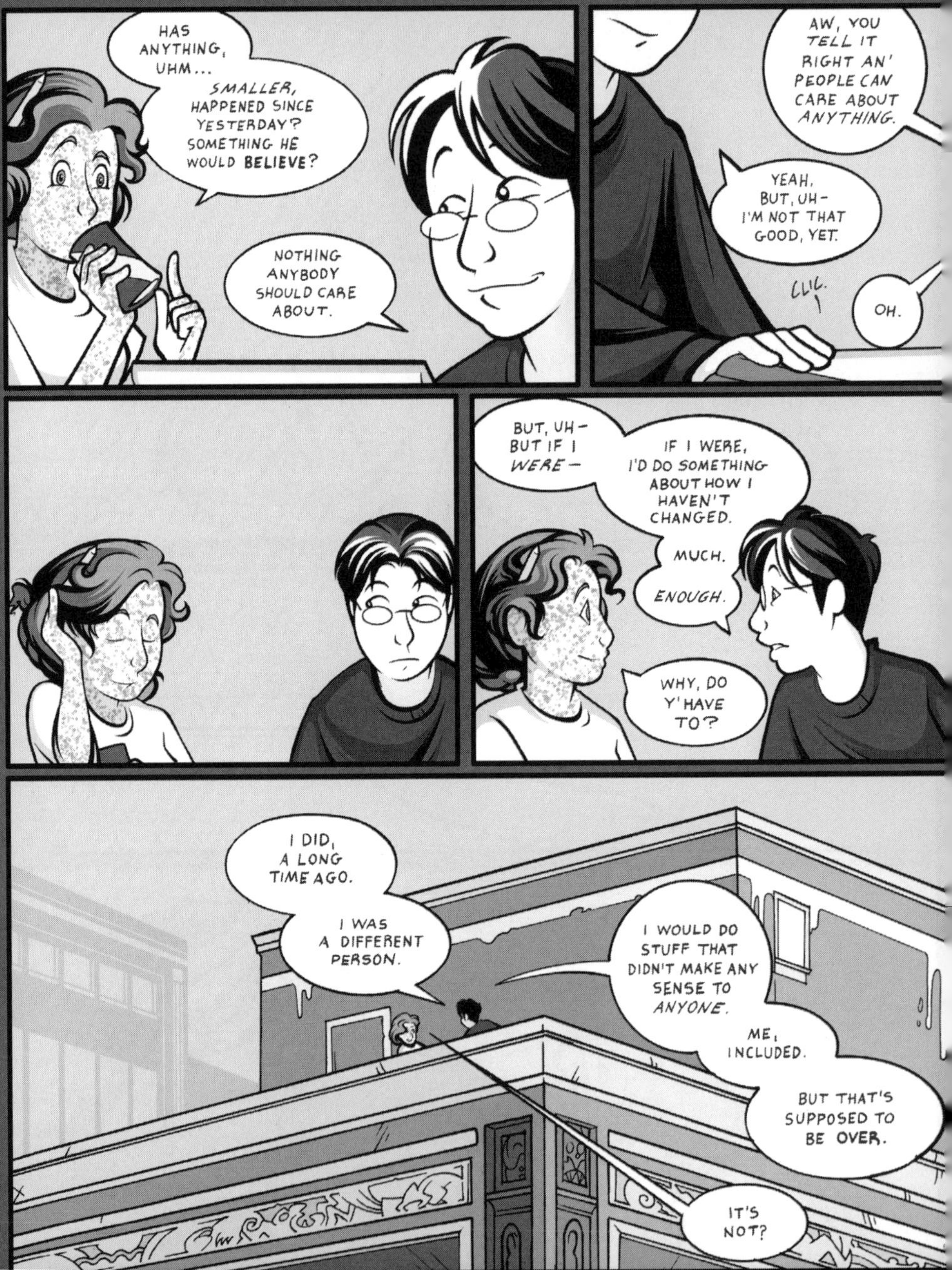
HAS ANYTHING, UHM... SMALLER, HAPPENED SINCE YESTERDAY? SOMETHING HE WOULD BELIEVE?
NOTHING ANYBODY SHOULD CARE ABOUT.
AW, YOU TELL IT RIGHT AN' PEOPLE CAN CARE ABOUT ANYTHING.
YEAH, BUT, UH- I'M NOT THAT GOOD, YET.
CLIC.
OH.
BUT, UH- BUT IF I WERE-
IF I WERE, I'D DO SOMETHING ABOUT HOW I HAVEN'T CHANGED.
MUCH.
ENOUGH.
WHY, DO Y'HAVE TO?
I DID, A LONG TIME AGO.
I WAS A DIFFERENT PERSON.
I WOULD DO STUFF THAT DIDN'T MAKE ANY SENSE TO ANYONE.
ME, INCLUDED.
BUT THAT'S SUPPOSED TO BE OVER.
IT'S NOT?

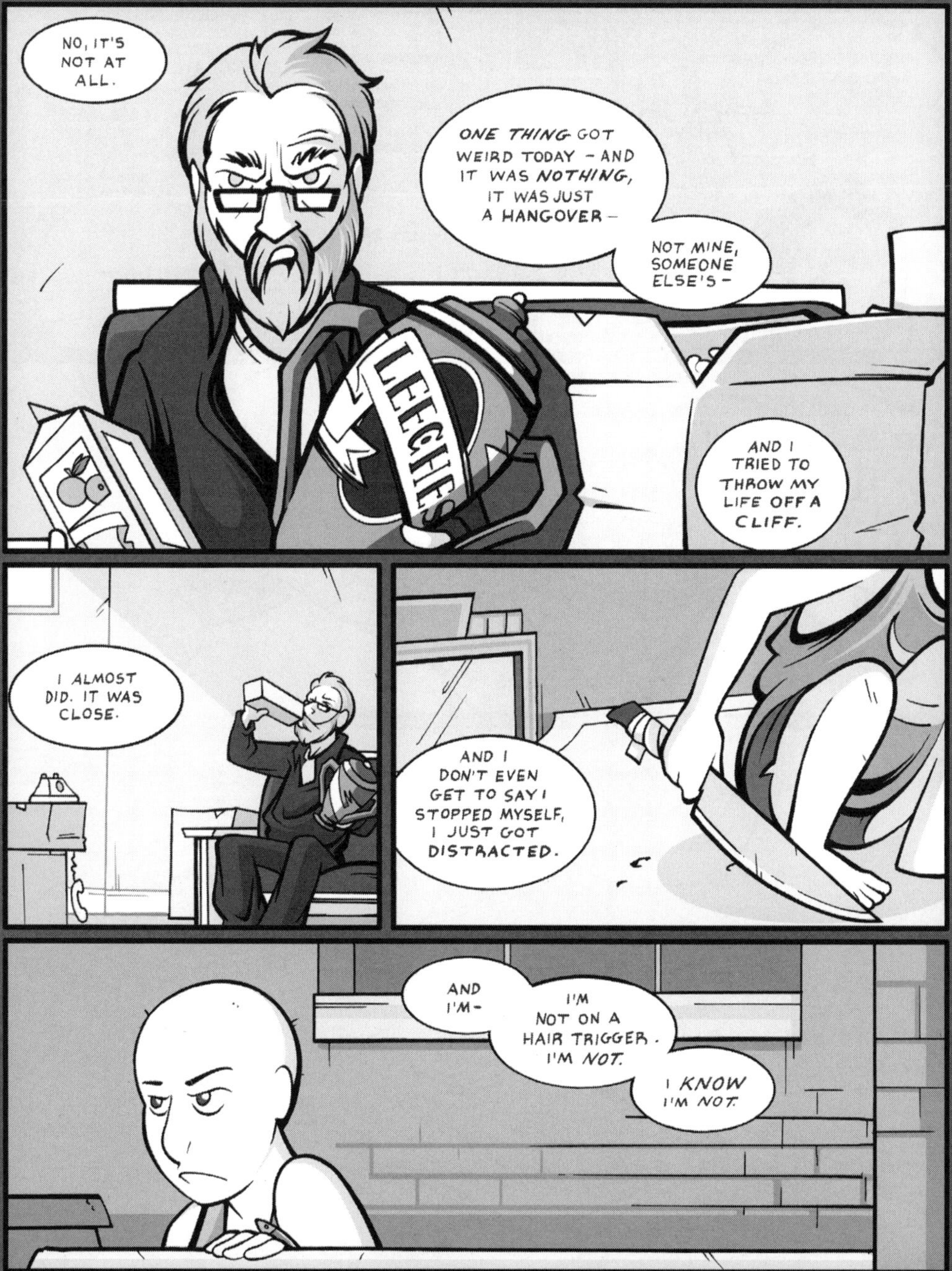
NO, IT'S NOT AT ALL.
ONE THING GOT WEIRD TODAY - AND IT WAS NOTHING, IT WAS JUST A HANGOVER -
NOT MINE, SOMEONE ELSE'S -
LEECHES
AND I TRIED TO THROW MY LIFE OFF A CLIFF.
I ALMOST DID. IT WAS CLOSE.
AND I DON'T EVEN GET TO SAY I STOPPED MYSELF, I JUST GOT DISTRACTED.
AND I'M-
I'M NOT ON A HAIR TRIGGER. I'M NOT.
I KNOW I'M NOT.

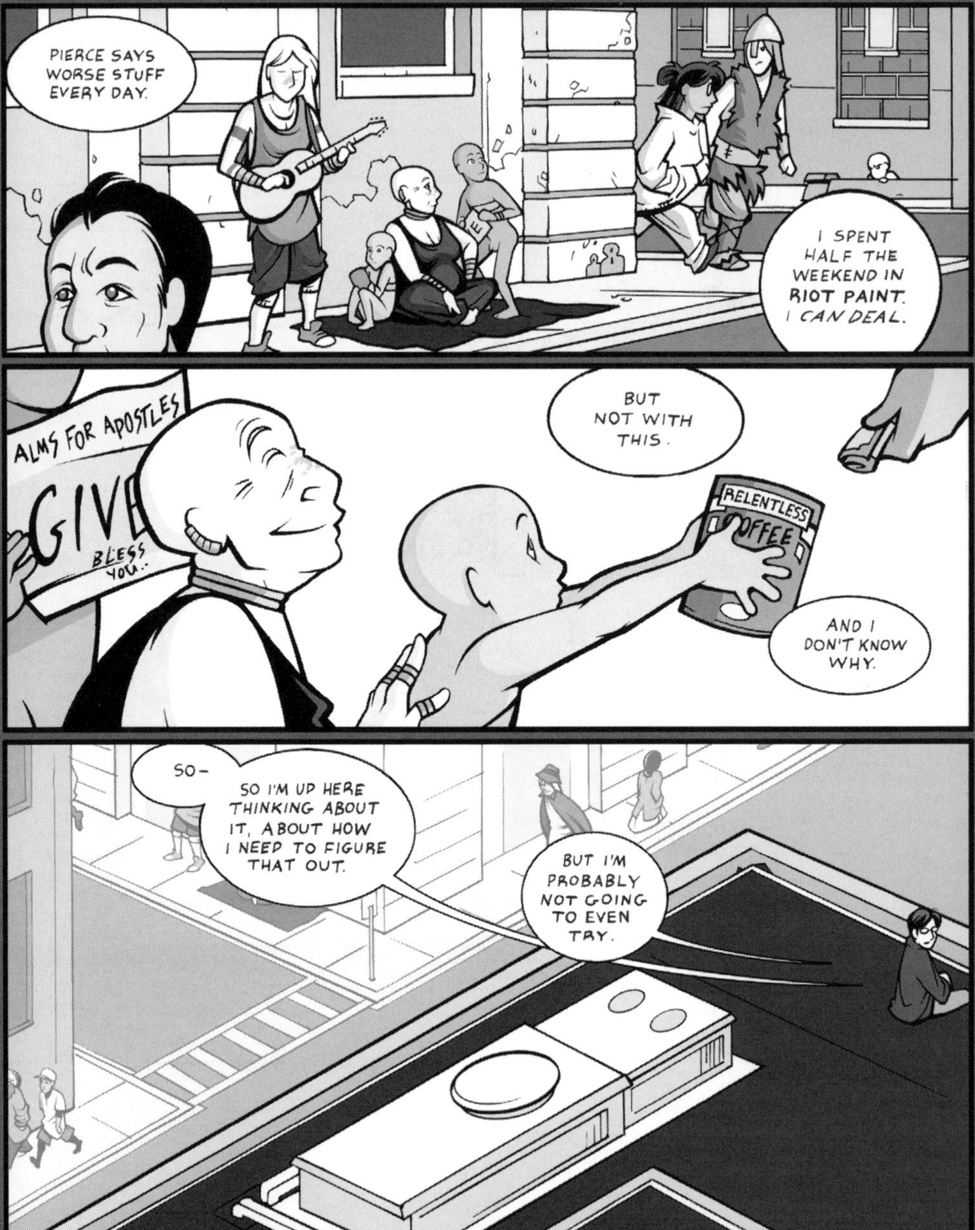

PIERCE SAYS WORSE STUFF EVERY DAY.
I SPENT HALF THE WEEKEND IN RIOT PAINT. I CAN DEAL.
ALMS FOR APOSTLES
GIVE
BLESS YOU..
BUT NOT WITH THIS.
RELENTLESS
COFFEE
AND I DON'T KNOW WHY.
SO-
SO I'M UP HERE THINKING ABOUT IT, ABOUT HOW I NEED TO FIGURE THAT OUT.
BUT I'M PROBABLY NOT GOING TO EVEN TRY.

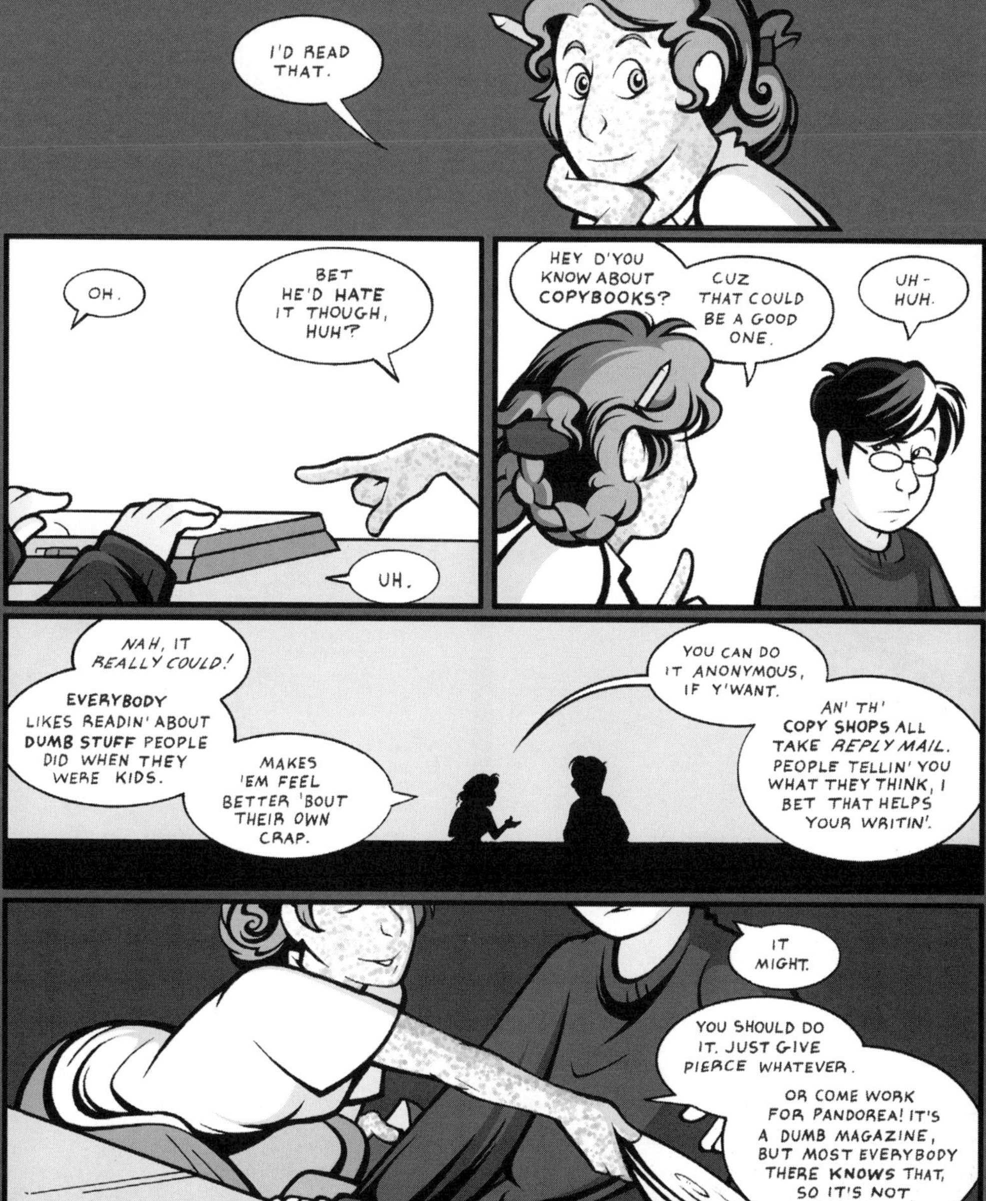

I'D READ THAT.
OH.
BET HE'D HATE IT THOUGH, HUH?
UH.
HEY D'YOU KNOW ABOUT COPYBOOKS?
CUZ THAT COULD BE A GOOD ONE.
UH-HUH.
NAH, IT REALLY COULD!
EVERYBODY LIKES READIN' ABOUT DUMB STUFF PEOPLE DID WHEN THEY WERE KIDS.
MAKES 'EM FEEL BETTER 'BOUT THEIR OWN CRAP.
YOU CAN DO IT ANONYMOUS, IF Y'WANT.
AN' TH' COPY SHOPS ALL TAKE REPLY MAIL. PEOPLE TELLIN' YOU WHAT THEY THINK, I BET THAT HELPS YOUR WRITIN'.
IT MIGHT.
YOU SHOULD DO IT. JUST GIVE PIERCE WHATEVER.
OR COME WORK FOR PANDOREA! IT'S A DUMB MAGAZINE, BUT MOST EVERYBODY THERE KNOWS THAT, SO IT'S NOT THAT BAD.
'SCUZE.

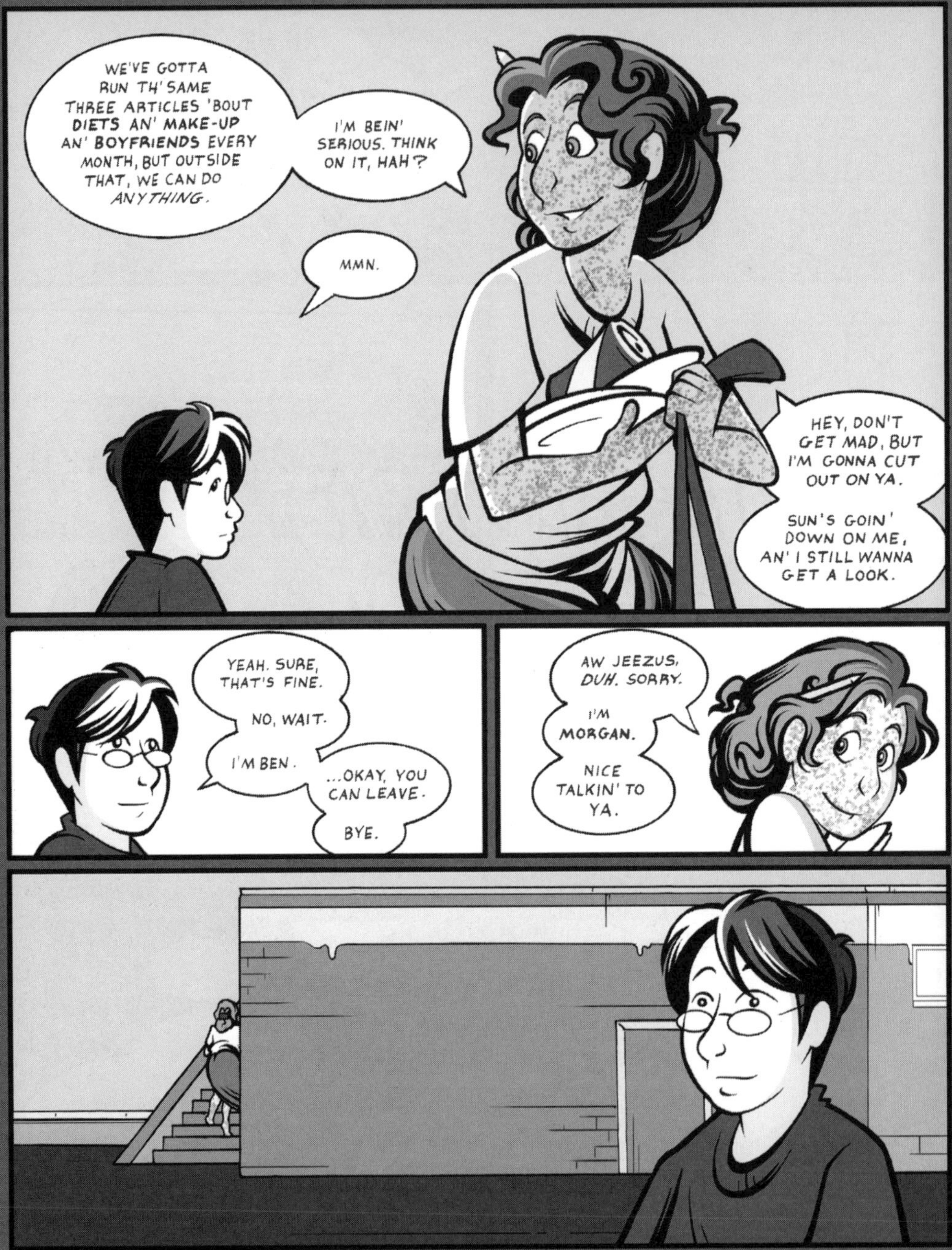
WE'VE GOTTA RUN TH' SAME THREE ARTICLES 'BOUT DIETS AN' MAKE-UP AN' BOYFRIENDS EVERY MONTH, BUT OUTSIDE THAT, WE CAN DO ANYTHING.
I'M BEIN' SERIOUS. THINK ON IT, HAH?
MMN.
HEY, DON'T GET MAD, BUT I'M GONNA CUT OUT ON YA.
SUN'S GOIN' DOWN ON ME, AN' I STILL WANNA GET A LOOK.
YEAH. SURE, THAT'S FINE.
NO, WAIT.
I'M BEN.
...OKAY, YOU CAN LEAVE.
BYE.
AW JEEZUS, DUH. SORRY.
I'M MORGAN.
NICE TALKIN' TO YA.

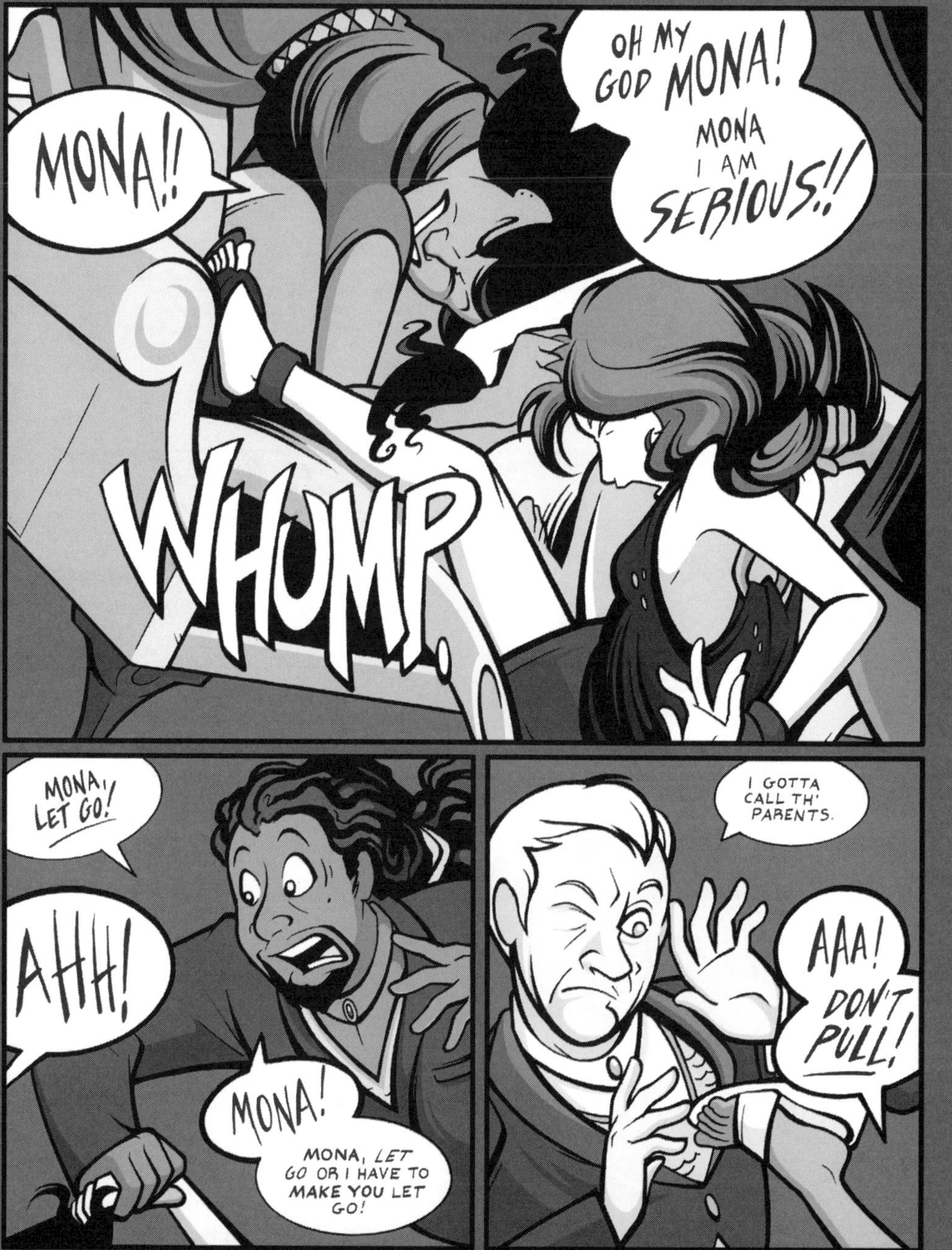
MONA!!
OH MY GOD MONA!
MONA I AM SERIOUS!!
WHUMP.
MONA, LET GO!
AHH!
MONA!
MONA, LET GO OR I HAVE TO MAKE YOU LET GO!
I GOTTA CALL TH' PARENTS.
AAA!
DON'T PULL!

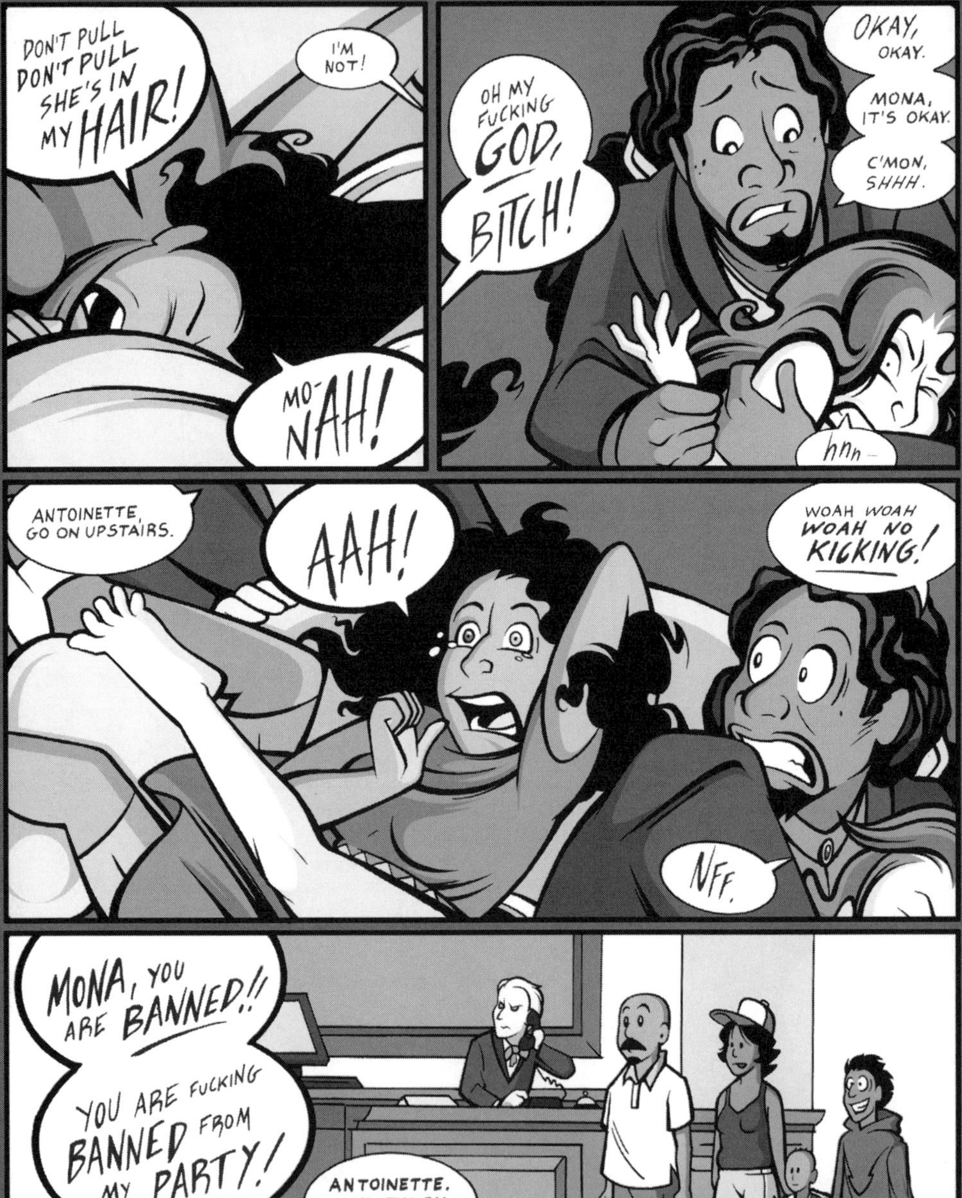
DON'T PULL DON'T PULL SHE'S IN MY HAIR!
I'M NOT!
MO-NAH!
OH MY FUCKING GOD, BITCH!
OKAY, OKAY.
MONA, IT'S OKAY.
C'MON, SHHH.
hnn...
ANTOINETTE, GO ON UPSTAIRS.
AAH!
WOAH WOAH WOAH NO KICKING!
NFF.
MONA, YOU ARE BANNED!!
YOU ARE FUCKING BANNED FROM MY PARTY!
ANTOINETTE. IT'S TAKEN CARE OF.
HEAD ON BACK TO TH' SUITE.

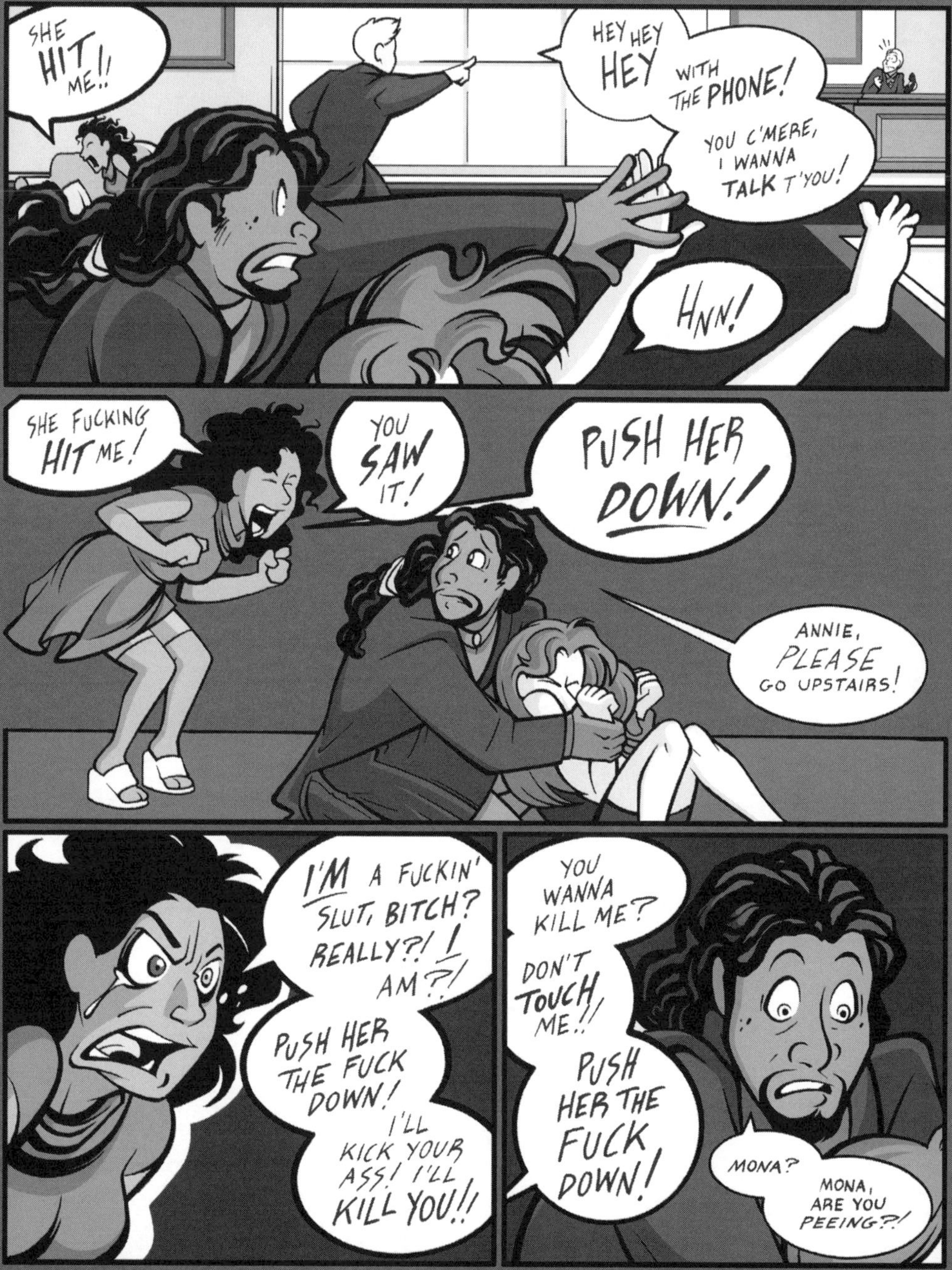
SHE HIT ME!!
HEY HEY HEY
WITH THE PHONE!
YOU C'MERE, I WANNA TALK T'YOU!
HNN!
SHE FUCKING HIT ME!
YOU SAW IT!
PUSH HER DOWN!
ANNIE, PLEASE GO UPSTAIRS!
I'M A FUCKIN' SLUT, BITCH? REALLY?! I AM?!
PUSH HER THE FUCK DOWN!
I'LL KICK YOUR ASS! I'LL KILL YOU!!
YOU WANNA KILL ME?
DON'T TOUCH ME!!
PUSH HER THE FUCK DOWN!
MONA?
MONA, ARE YOU PEEING?!

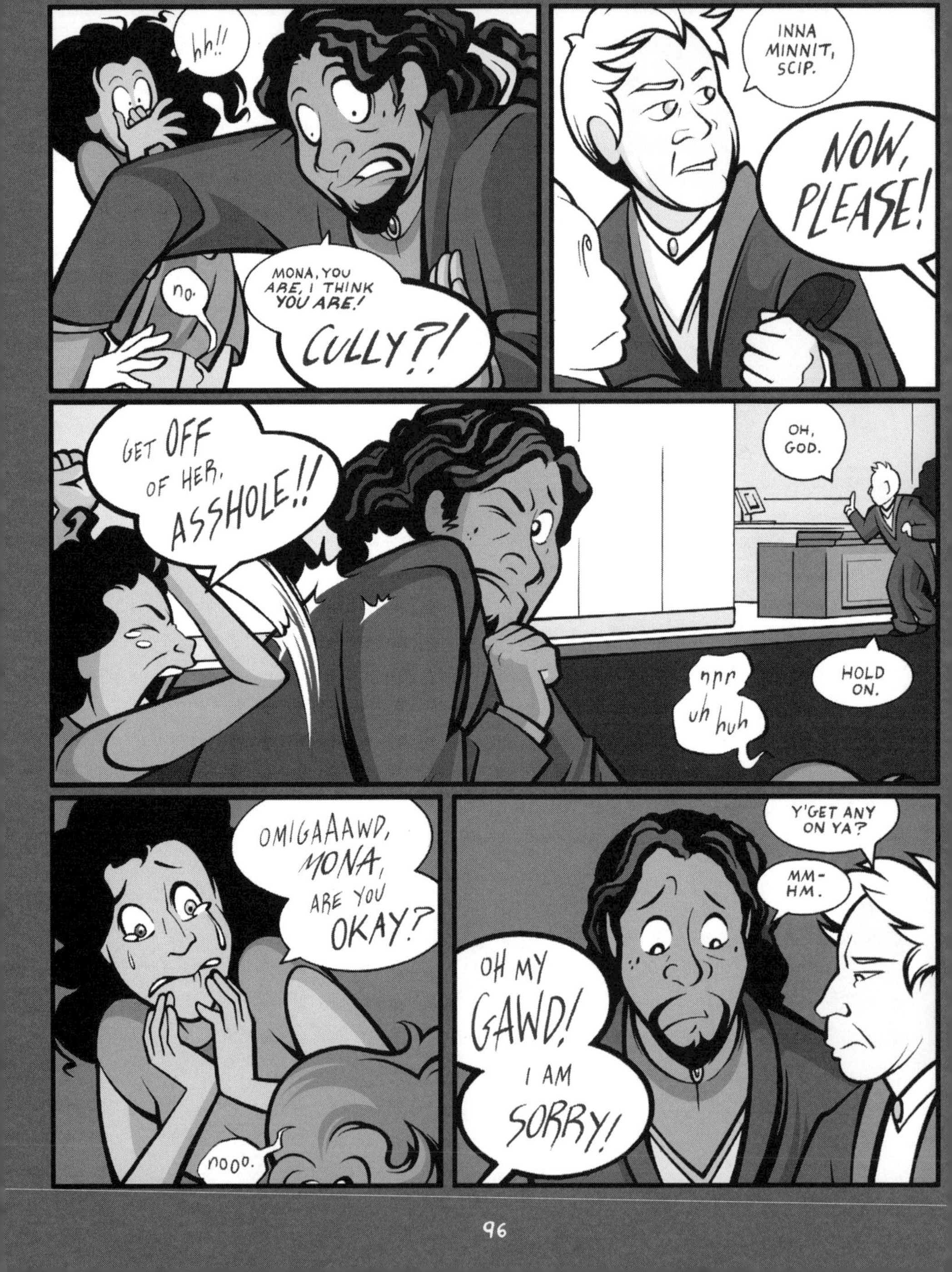
hh!!
no.
MONA, YOU ARE, I THINK YOU ARE!
CULLY?!
INNA MINNIT, SCIP.
NOW, PLEASE!
GET OFF OF HER, ASSHOLE!!
OH, GOD.
npr uh huh
HOLD ON.
OMIGAAAWD, MONA, ARE YOU OKAY?
nooo.
Y'GET ANY ON YA?
MM-HM.
OH MY GAWD! I AM SORRY!

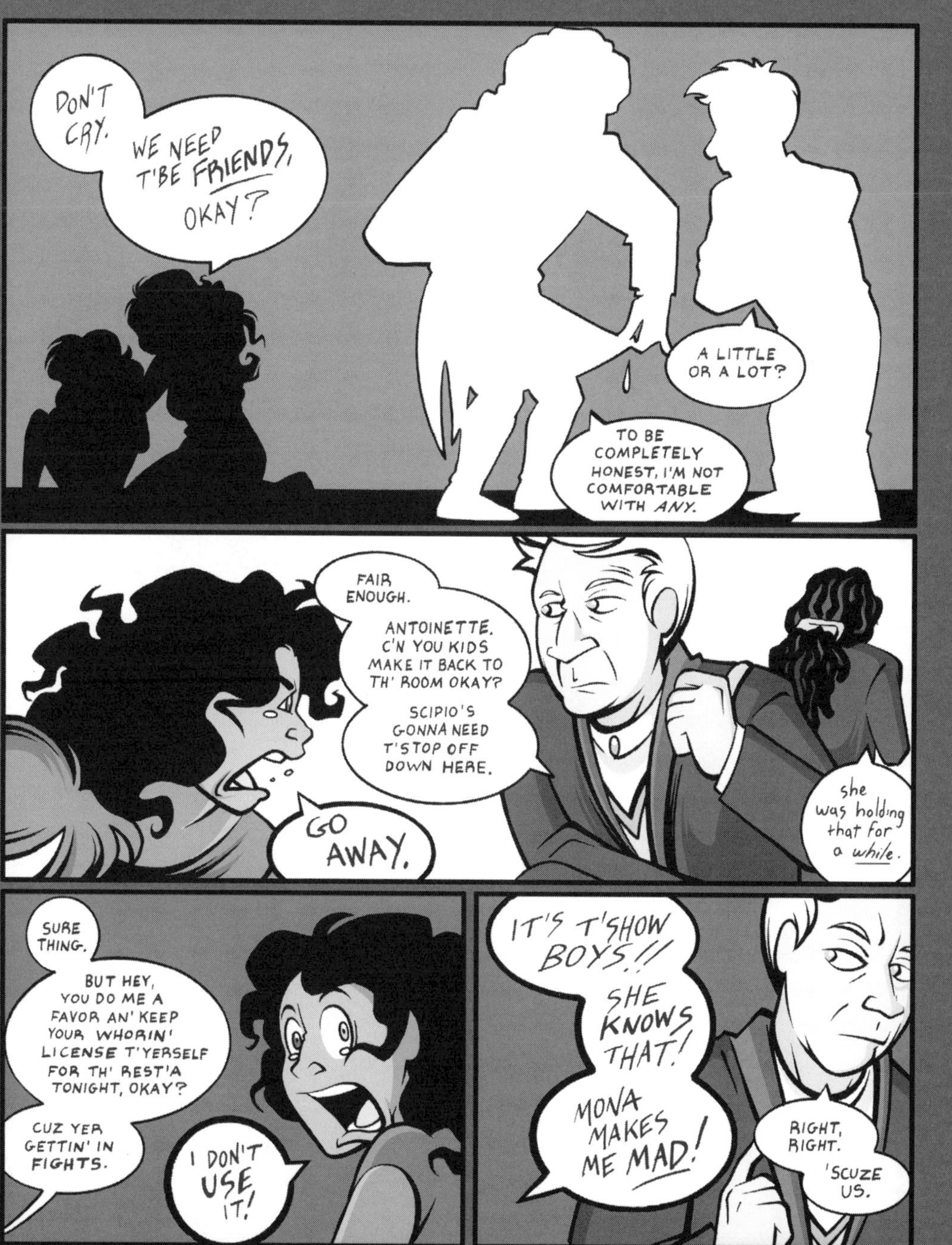
DON'T CRY.
WE NEED T'BE FRIENDS, OKAY?
A LITTLE OR A LOT?
TO BE COMPLETELY HONEST, I'M NOT COMFORTABLE WITH ANY.
FAIR ENOUGH.
ANTOINETTE. C'N YOU KIDS MAKE IT BACK TO TH' ROOM OKAY?
SCIPIO'S GONNA NEED T'STOP OFF DOWN HERE.
GO AWAY.
she was holding that for a while.
SURE THING.
BUT HEY, YOU DO ME A FAVOR AN' KEEP YOUR WHORIN' LICENSE T'YERSELF FOR TH' REST'A TONIGHT, OKAY?
CUZ YER GETTIN' IN FIGHTS.
I DON'T USE IT!
IT'S T'SHOW BOYS!!
SHE KNOWS THAT!
MONA MAKES ME MAD!
RIGHT, RIGHT.
'SCUZE US.

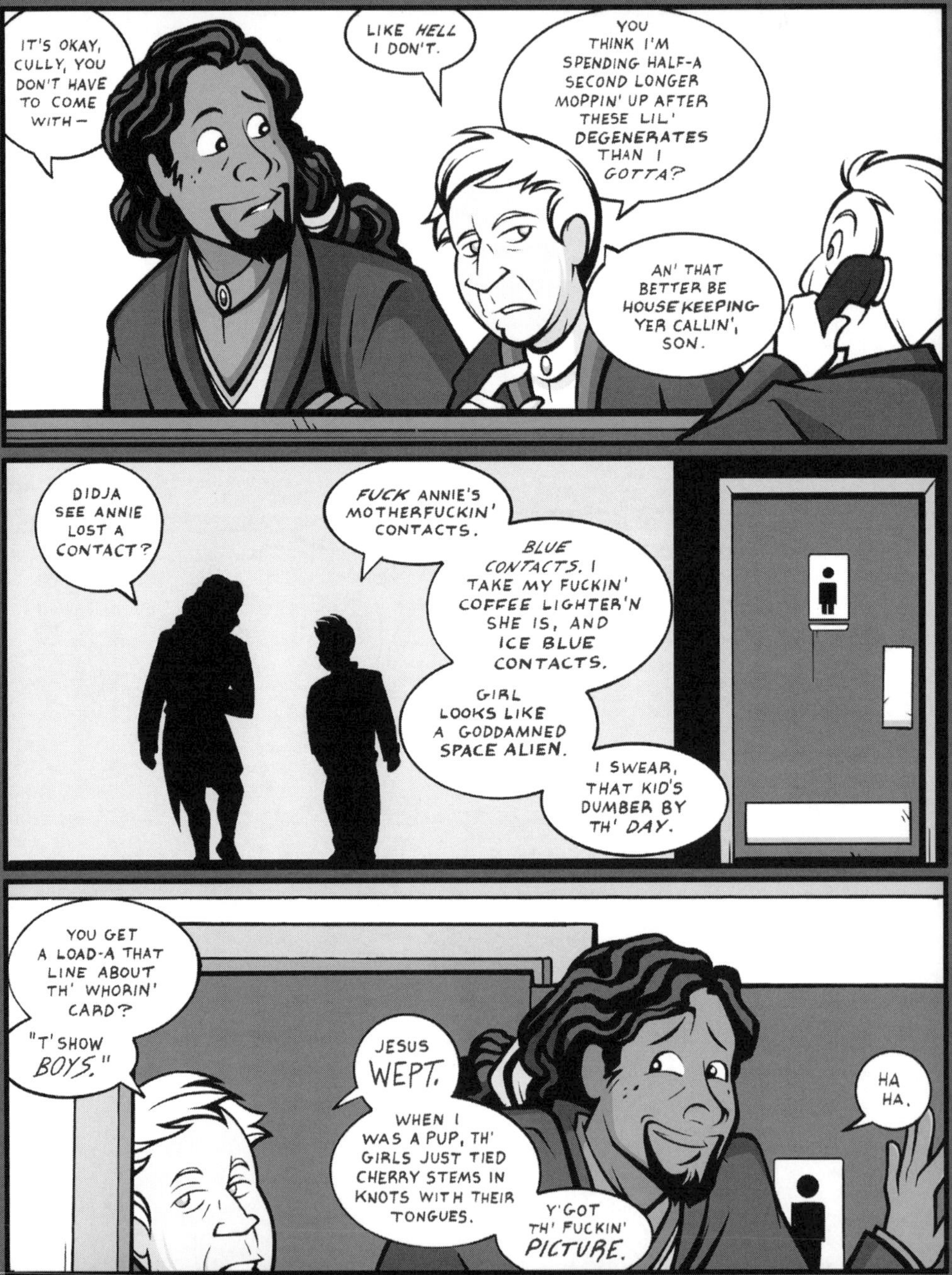
IT'S OKAY, CULLY, YOU DON'T HAVE TO COME WITH—
LIKE HELL I DON'T.
YOU THINK I'M SPENDING HALF-A SECOND LONGER MOPPIN' UP AFTER THESE LIL' DEGENERATES THAN I GOTTA?
AN' THAT BETTER BE HOUSEKEEPING YER CALLIN', SON.
DIDJA SEE ANNIE LOST A CONTACT?
FUCK ANNIE'S MOTHERFUCKIN' CONTACTS.
BLUE CONTACTS. I TAKE MY FUCKIN' COFFEE LIGHTER'N SHE IS, AND ICE BLUE CONTACTS.
GIRL LOOKS LIKE A GODDAMNED SPACE ALIEN.
I SWEAR, THAT KID'S DUMBER BY TH' DAY.
YOU GET A LOAD-A THAT LINE ABOUT TH' WHORIN' CARD?
"T'SHOW BOYS."
JESUS WEPT.
WHEN I WAS A PUP, TH' GIRLS JUST TIED CHERRY STEMS IN KNOTS WITH THEIR TONGUES.
Y'GOT TH' FUCKIN' PICTURE.
HA HA.

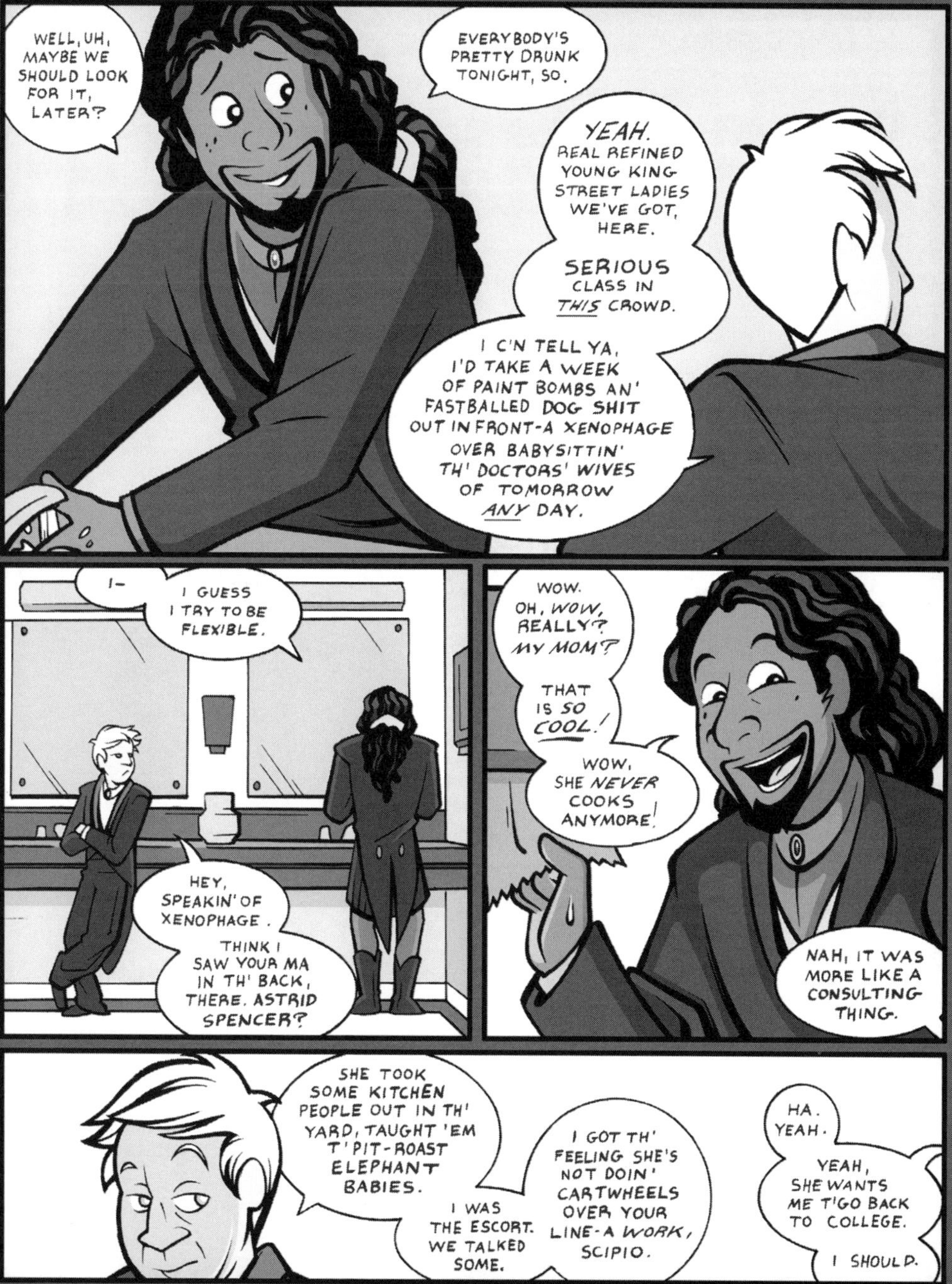
WELL, UH, MAYBE WE SHOULD LOOK FOR IT, LATER?
EVERYBODY'S PRETTY DRUNK TONIGHT, SO.
YEAH. REAL REFINED YOUNG KING STREET LADIES WE'VE GOT, HERE.
SERIOUS CLASS IN THIS CROWD.
I C'N TELL YA, I'D TAKE A WEEK OF PAINT BOMBS AN' FASTBALLED DOG SHIT OUT IN FRONT-A XENOPHAGE OVER BABYSITTIN' TH' DOCTORS' WIVES OF TOMORROW ANY DAY.
I–
I GUESS I TRY TO BE FLEXIBLE.
HEY, SPEAKIN' OF XENOPHAGE.
THINK I SAW YOUR MA IN TH' BACK, THERE. ASTRID SPENCER?
WOW. OH, WOW, REALLY? MY MOM?
THAT IS SO COOL!
WOW, SHE NEVER COOKS ANYMORE!
NAH, IT WAS MORE LIKE A CONSULTING THING.
SHE TOOK SOME KITCHEN PEOPLE OUT IN TH' YARD, TAUGHT 'EM T' PIT-ROAST ELEPHANT BABIES.
I WAS THE ESCORT. WE TALKED SOME.
I GOT TH' FEELING SHE'S NOT DOIN' CARTWHEELS OVER YOUR LINE-A WORK, SCIPIO.
HA. YEAH.
YEAH, SHE WANTS ME T'GO BACK TO COLLEGE.
I SHOULD.

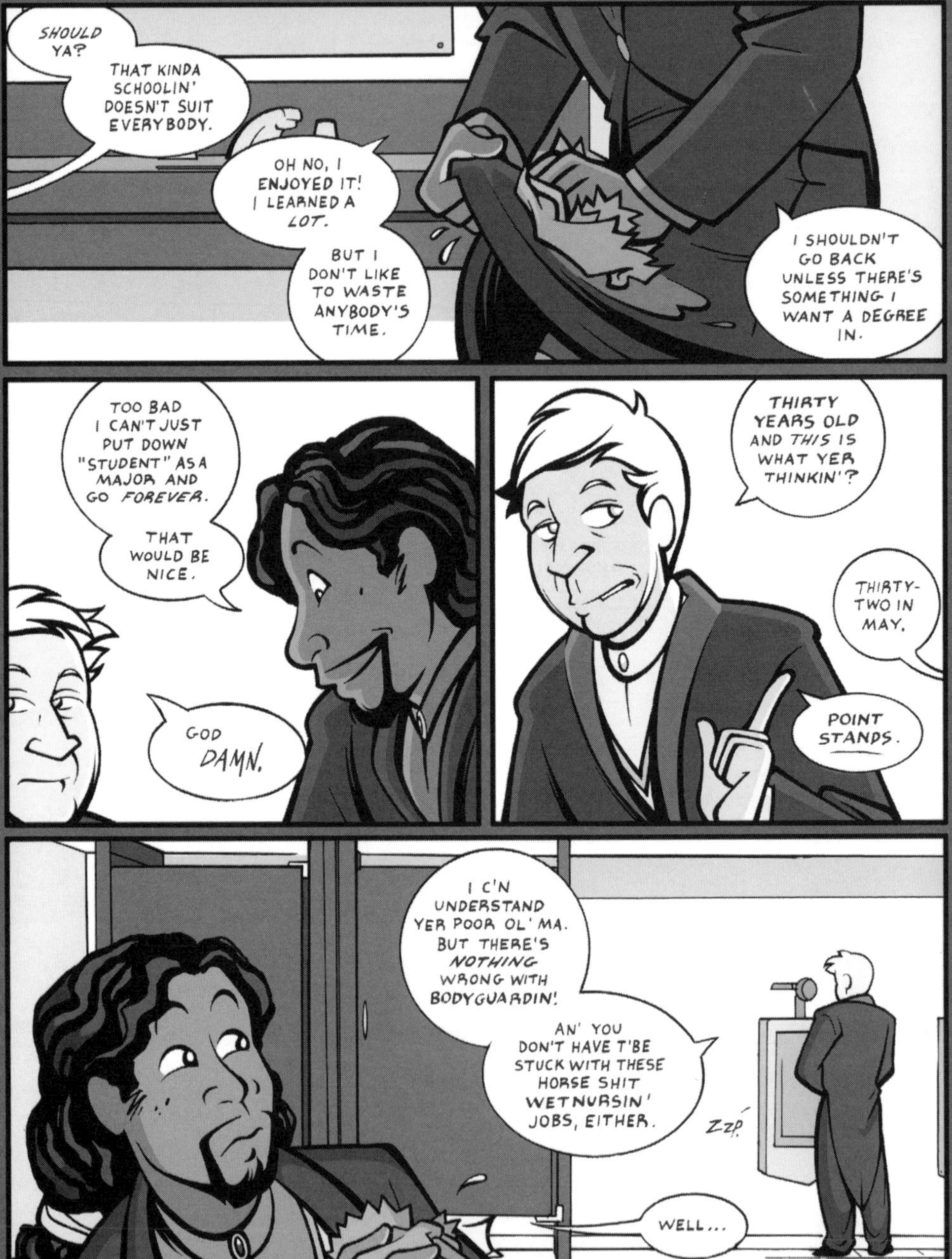
SHOULD YA?
THAT KINDA SCHOOLIN' DOESN'T SUIT EVERYBODY.
OH NO, I ENJOYED IT! I LEARNED A LOT.
BUT I DON'T LIKE TO WASTE ANYBODY'S TIME.
I SHOULDN'T GO BACK UNLESS THERE'S SOMETHING I WANT A DEGREE IN.
TOO BAD I CAN'T JUST PUT DOWN "STUDENT" AS A MAJOR AND GO FOREVER.
THAT WOULD BE NICE.
GOD DAMN.
THIRTY YEARS OLD AND THIS IS WHAT YER THINKIN'?
THIRTY-TWO IN MAY.
POINT STANDS.
I C'N UNDERSTAND YER POOR OL' MA. BUT THERE'S NOTHING WRONG WITH BODYGUARDIN'.
AN' YOU DON'T HAVE T'BE STUCK WITH THESE HORSE SHIT WETNURSIN' JOBS, EITHER.
ZZP!
WELL...

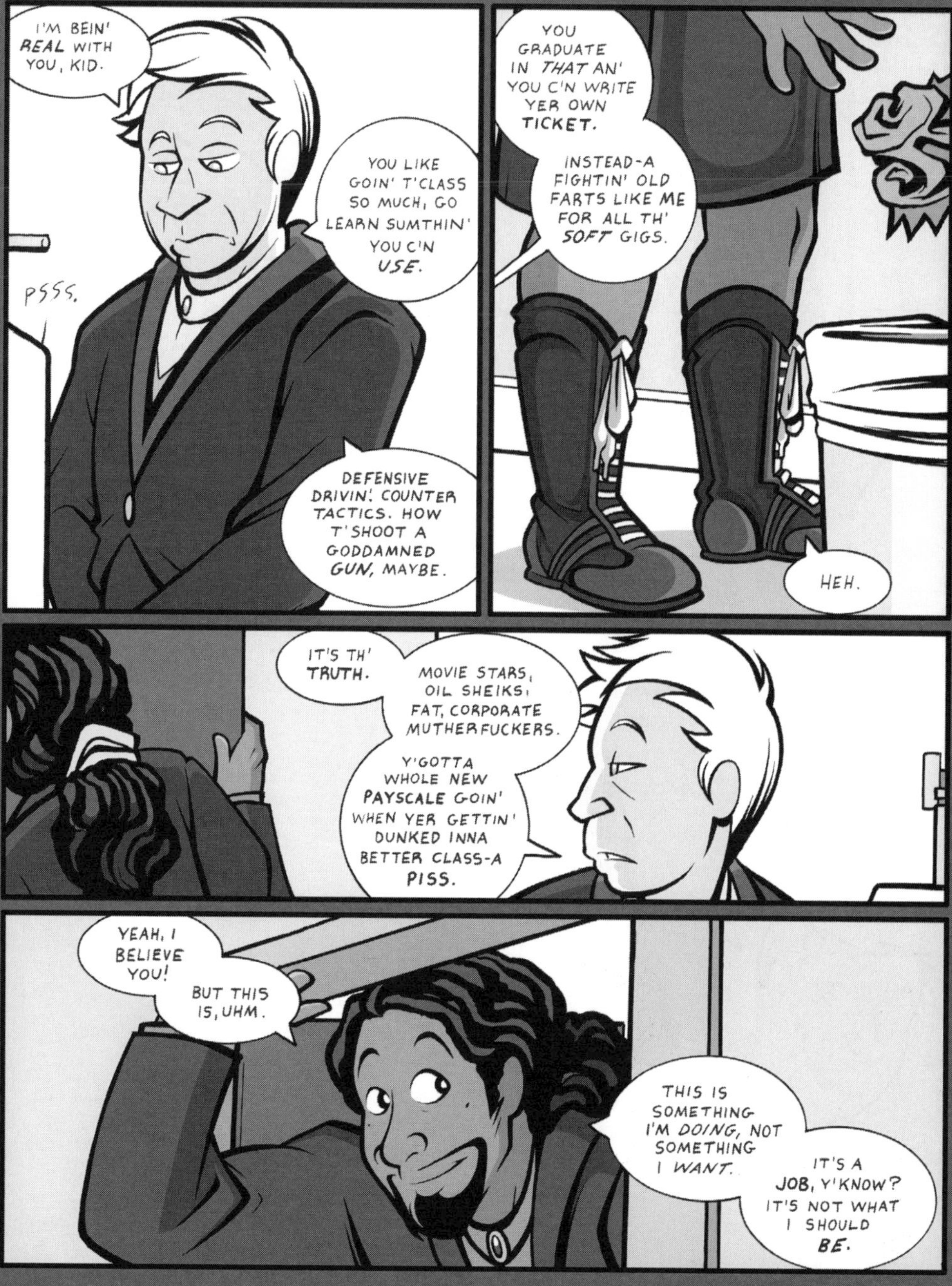
I'M BEIN' REAL WITH YOU, KID.
YOU LIKE GOIN' T'CLASS SO MUCH, GO LEARN SUMTHIN' YOU C'N USE.
PSSS.
DEFENSIVE DRIVIN'. COUNTER TACTICS. HOW T'SHOOT A GODDAMNED GUN, MAYBE.
YOU GRADUATE IN THAT AN' YOU C'N WRITE YER OWN TICKET.
INSTEAD-A FIGHTIN' OLD FARTS LIKE ME FOR ALL TH' SOFT GIGS.
HEH.
IT'S TH' TRUTH.
MOVIE STARS, OIL SHEIKS, FAT, CORPORATE MUTHERFUCKERS.
Y'GOTTA WHOLE NEW PAYSCALE GOIN' WHEN YER GETTIN' DUNKED INNA BETTER CLASS-A PISS.
YEAH, I BELIEVE YOU!
BUT THIS IS, UHM.
THIS IS SOMETHING I'M DOING, NOT SOMETHING I WANT.
IT'S A JOB, Y'KNOW? IT'S NOT WHAT I SHOULD BE.

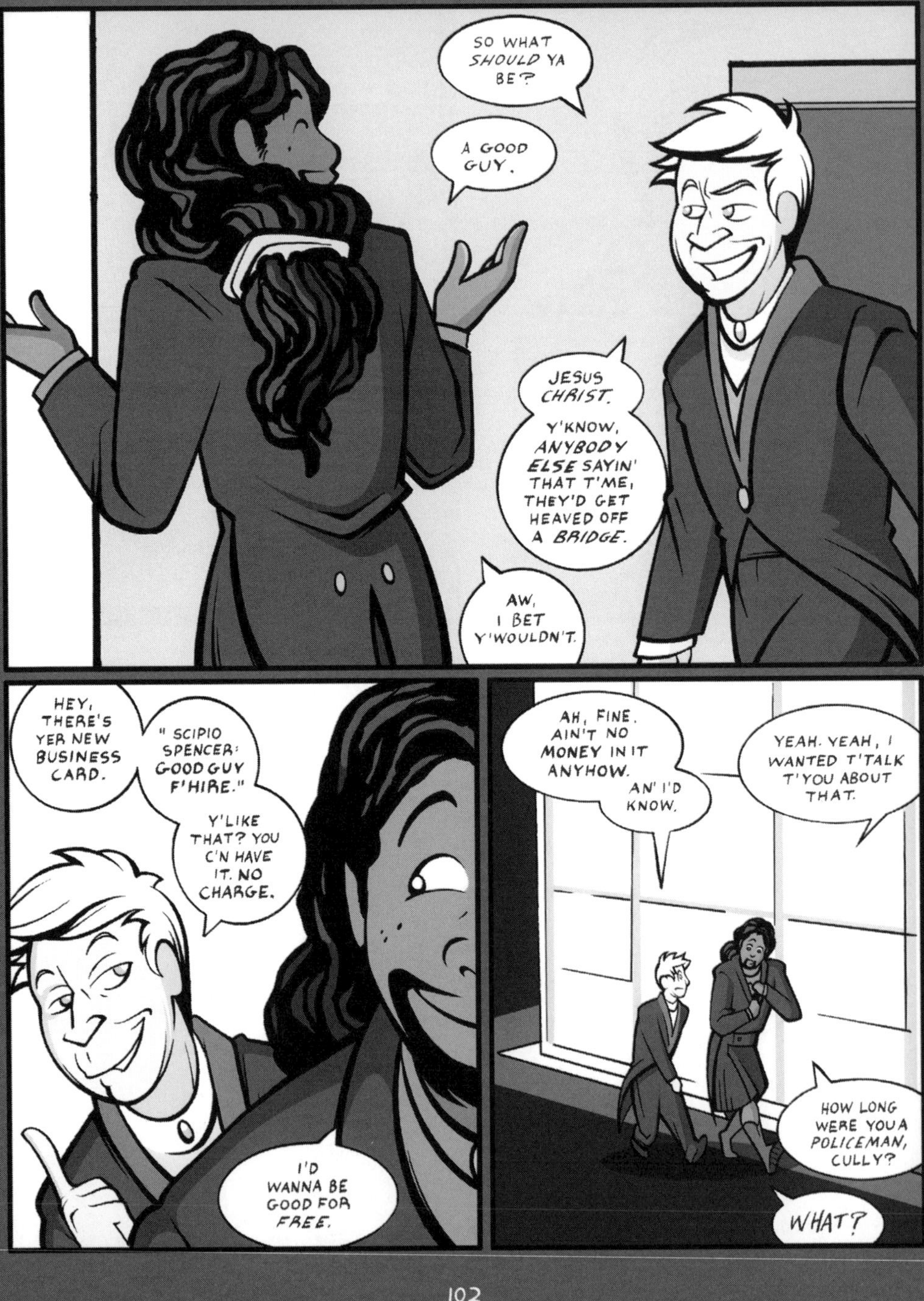

SO WHAT SHOULD YA BE?
A GOOD GUY.
JESUS CHRIST.
Y'KNOW, ANYBODY ELSE SAYIN' THAT T'ME, THEY'D GET HEAVED OFF A BRIDGE.
AW, I BET Y'WOULDN'T.
HEY, THERE'S YER NEW BUSINESS CARD.
"SCIPIO SPENCER: GOOD GUY F'HIRE."
Y'LIKE THAT? YOU C'N HAVE IT. NO CHARGE.
I'D WANNA BE GOOD FOR FREE.
AH, FINE. AIN'T NO MONEY IN IT ANYHOW.
AN' I'D KNOW.
YEAH. YEAH, I WANTED T'TALK T'YOU ABOUT THAT.
HOW LONG WERE YOU A POLICEMAN, CULLY?
WHAT?

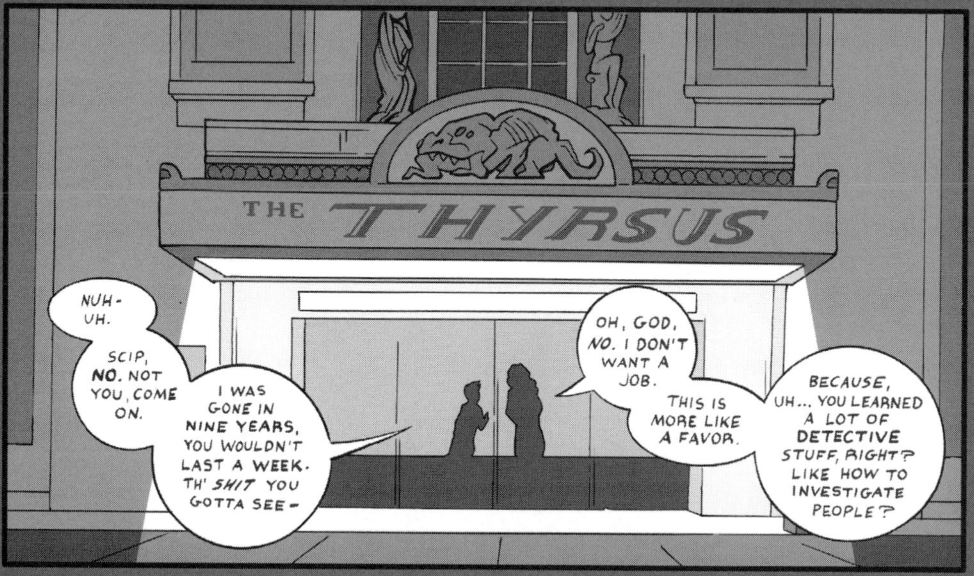
THE THYRSUS
NUH-UH.
SCIP, NO. NOT YOU, COME ON.
I WAS GONE IN NINE YEARS, YOU WOULDN'T LAST A WEEK. TH' SHIT YOU GOTTA SEE-
OH, GOD, NO. I DON'T WANT A JOB.
THIS IS MORE LIKE A FAVOR.
BECAUSE, UH... YOU LEARNED A LOT OF DETECTIVE STUFF, RIGHT? LIKE HOW TO INVESTIGATE PEOPLE?

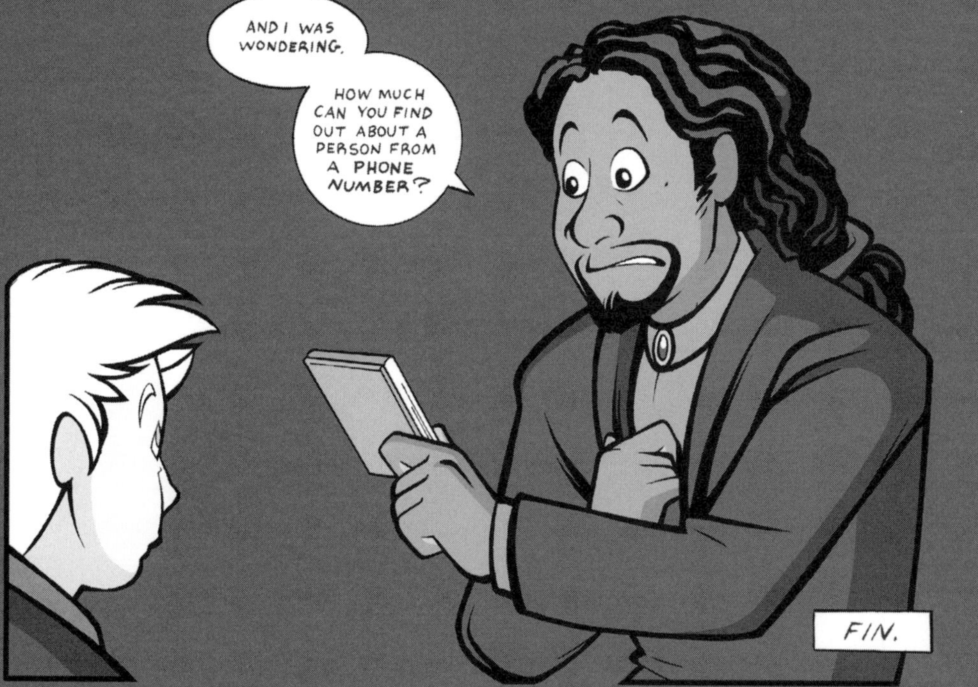
AND I WAS WONDERING.
HOW MUCH CAN YOU FIND OUT ABOUT A PERSON FROM A PHONE NUMBER?
FIN.

TEMPLAR, ARIZONA.

INTERMISSION:
LITTLE CAIRO.

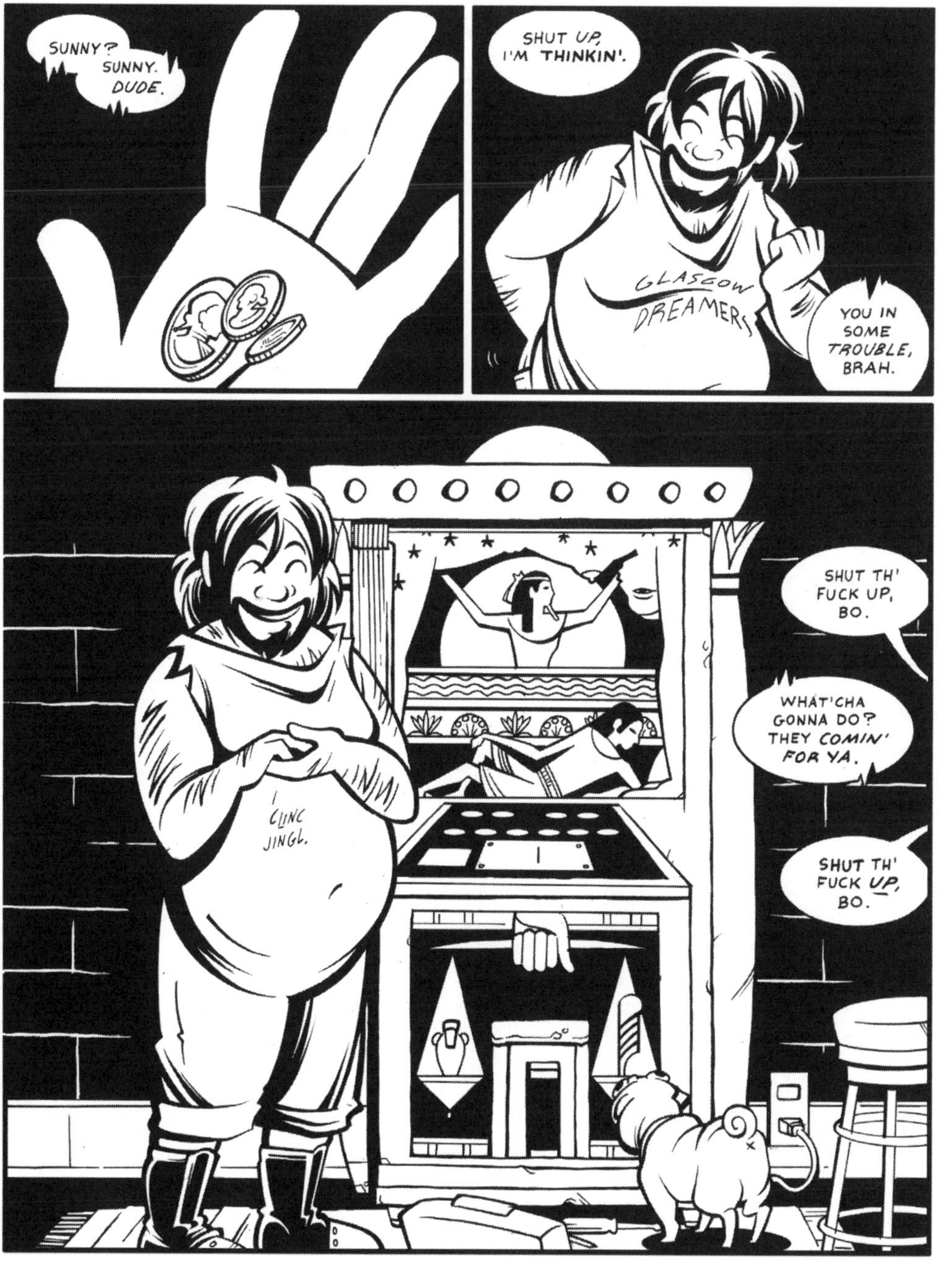
SUNNY? SUNNY. DUDE.
SHUT UP, I'M THINKIN'.
GLASGOW DREAMERS
YOU IN SOME TROUBLE, BRAH.
SHUT TH' FUCK UP, BO.
WHAT'CHA GONNA DO? THEY COMIN' FOR YA.
CLINC JINGL.
SHUT TH' FUCK UP, BO.

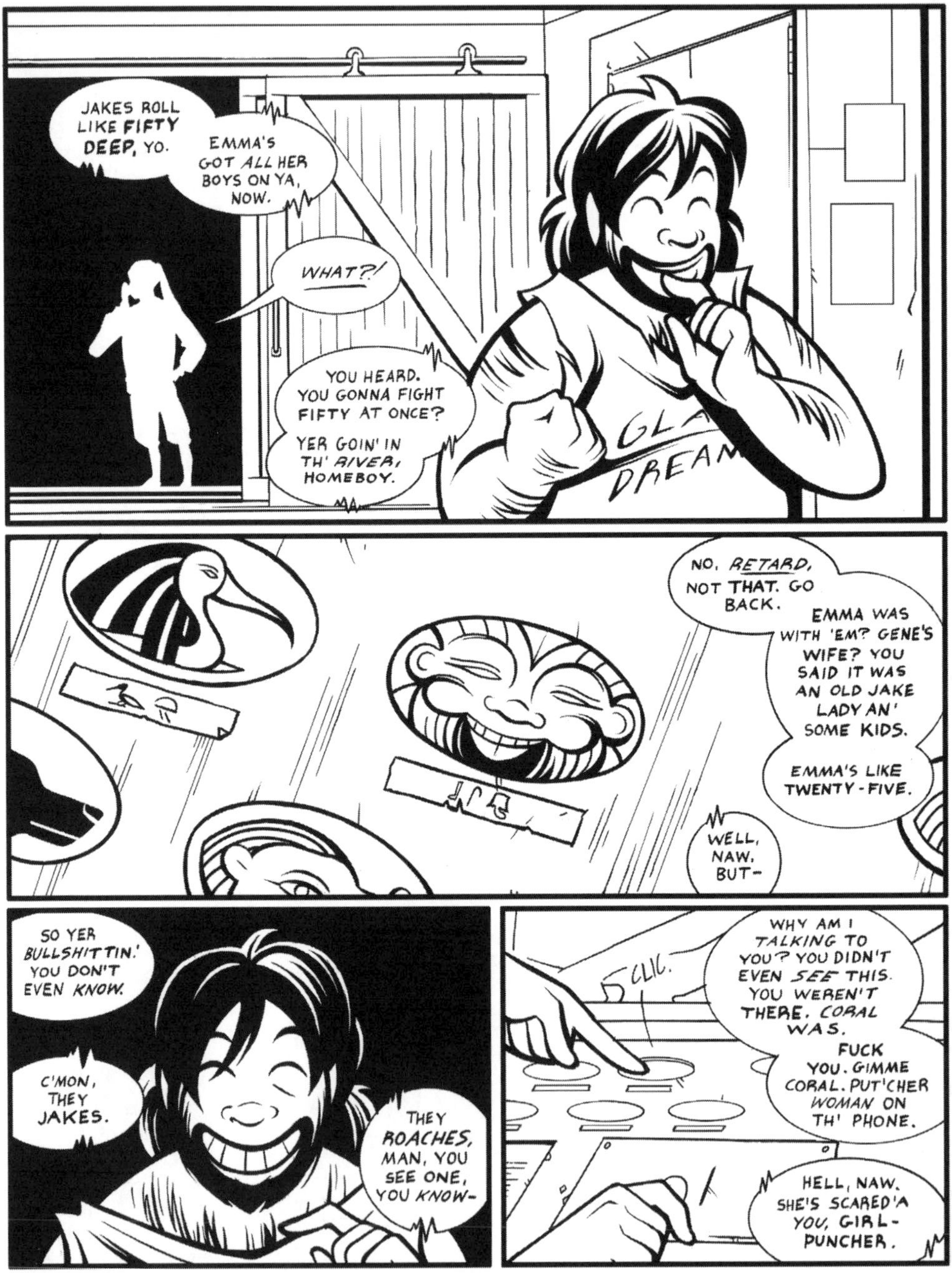
JAKES ROLL LIKE FIFTY DEEP, YO.
EMMA'S GOT ALL HER BOYS ON YA, NOW.
WHAT?!
YOU HEARD. YOU GONNA FIGHT FIFTY AT ONCE?
YER GOIN' IN TH' RIVER, HOMEBOY.
NO, RETARD, NOT THAT. GO BACK.
EMMA WAS WITH 'EM? GENE'S WIFE? YOU SAID IT WAS AN OLD JAKE LADY AN' SOME KIDS.
EMMA'S LIKE TWENTY-FIVE.
WELL, NAW, BUT-
SO YER BULLSHITTIN.' YOU DON'T EVEN KNOW.
C'MON, THEY JAKES.
THEY ROACHES, MAN, YOU SEE ONE, YOU KNOW-
CLIC.
WHY AM I TALKING TO YOU? YOU DIDN'T EVEN SEE THIS. YOU WEREN'T THERE. CORAL WAS.
FUCK YOU. GIMME CORAL. PUT'CHER WOMAN ON TH' PHONE.
HELL, NAW. SHE'S SCARED'A YOU, GIRL-PUNCHER.

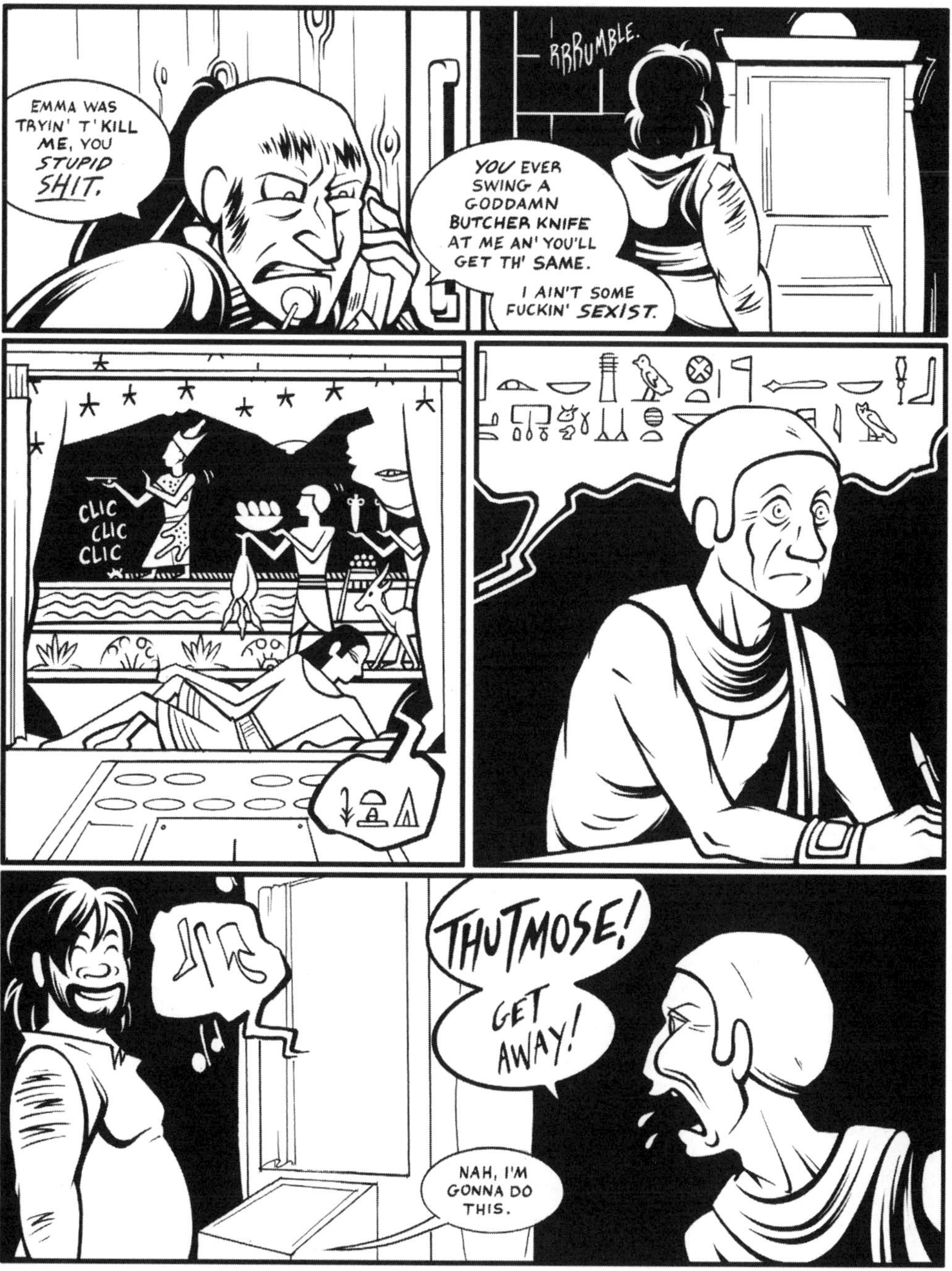
EMMA WAS TRYIN' T'KILL ME, YOU STUPID SHIT.
RRRUMBLE.
YOU EVER SWING A GODDAMN BUTCHER KNIFE AT ME AN' YOU'LL GET TH' SAME.
I AIN'T SOME FUCKIN' SEXIST.
CLIC CLIC CLIC
THUTMOSE! GET AWAY!
NAH, I'M GONNA DO THIS.

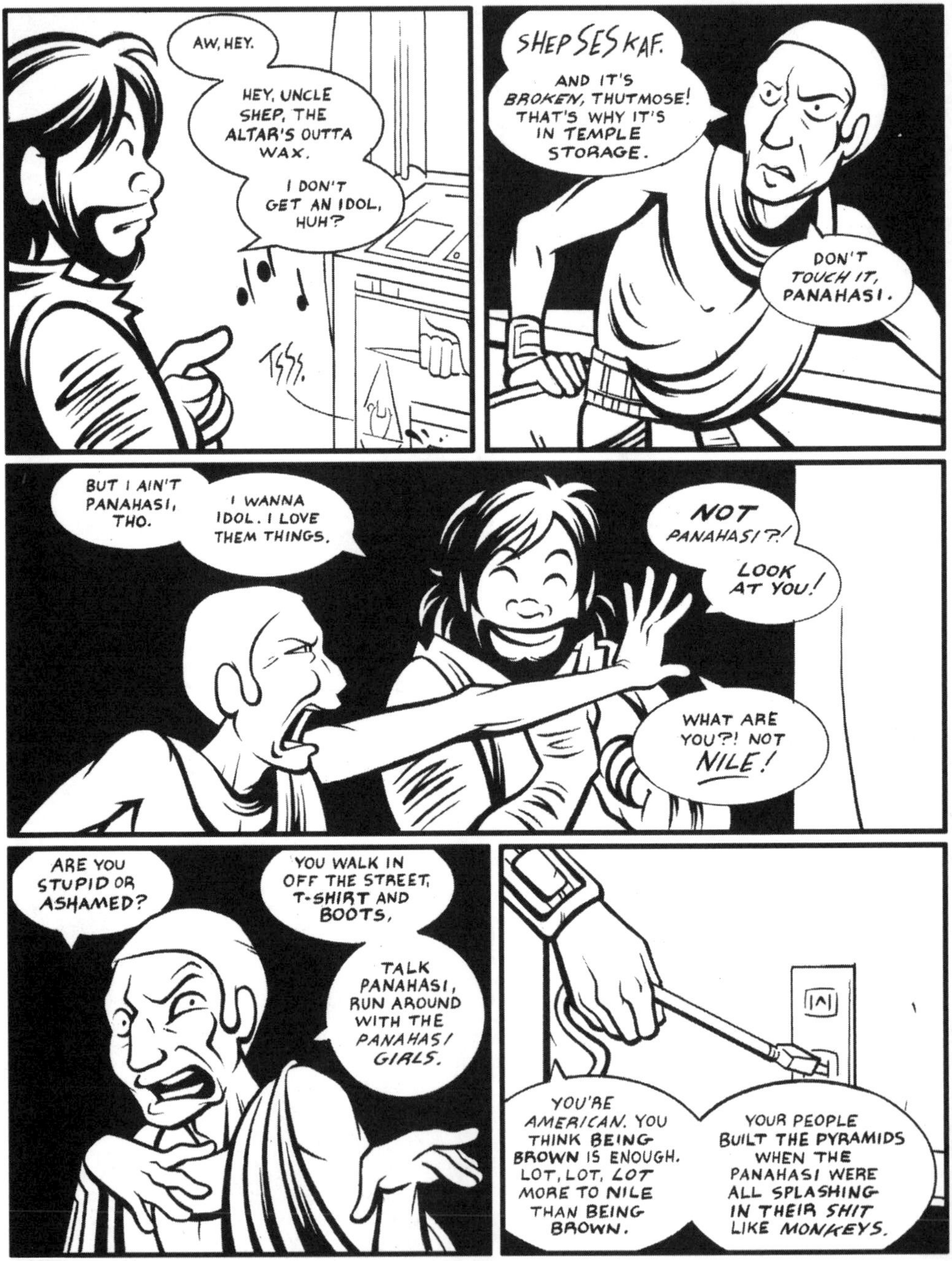
AW, HEY.
HEY, UNCLE SHEP, THE ALTAR'S OUTTA WAX.
I DON'T GET AN IDOL, HUH?
TSSS.
SHEPSESKAF.
AND IT'S *BROKEN*, THUTMOSE! THAT'S WHY IT'S IN TEMPLE STORAGE.
DON'T *TOUCH IT*, PANAHASI.
BUT I AIN'T PANAHASI, THO.
I WANNA IDOL. I LOVE THEM THINGS.
NOT PANAHASI?!
LOOK AT YOU!
WHAT ARE YOU?! NOT NILE!
ARE YOU STUPID OR ASHAMED?
YOU WALK IN OFF THE STREET, T-SHIRT AND BOOTS,
TALK PANAHASI, RUN AROUND WITH THE *PANAHASI GIRLS.*
YOU'RE *AMERICAN*. YOU THINK BEING BROWN IS ENOUGH. LOT, LOT, *LOT* MORE TO NILE THAN BEING BROWN.
YOUR PEOPLE BUILT THE PYRAMIDS WHEN THE PANAHASI WERE ALL SPLASHING IN THEIR *SHIT* LIKE *MONKEYS*.

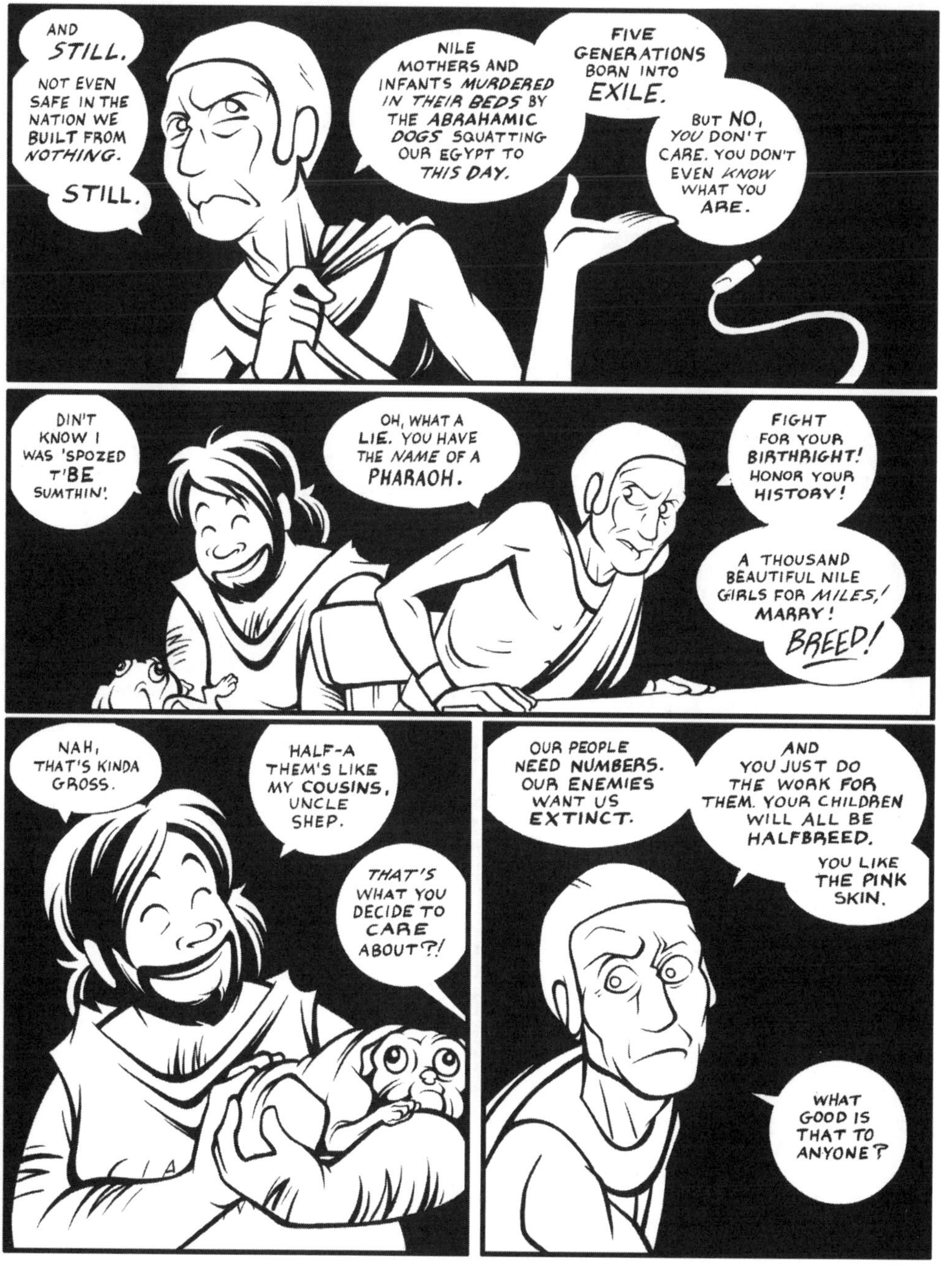
AND STILL. NOT EVEN SAFE IN THE NATION WE BUILT FROM NOTHING. STILL.
NILE MOTHERS AND INFANTS MURDERED IN THEIR BEDS BY THE ABRAHAMIC DOGS SQUATTING OUR EGYPT TO THIS DAY.
FIVE GENERATIONS BORN INTO EXILE.
BUT NO, YOU DON'T CARE. YOU DON'T EVEN KNOW WHAT YOU ARE.
DIN'T KNOW I WAS 'SPOZED T'BE SUMTHIN'.
OH, WHAT A LIE. YOU HAVE THE NAME OF A PHARAOH.
FIGHT FOR YOUR BIRTHRIGHT! HONOR YOUR HISTORY!
A THOUSAND BEAUTIFUL NILE GIRLS FOR MILES! MARRY! BREED!
NAH, THAT'S KINDA GROSS.
HALF-A THEM'S LIKE MY COUSINS, UNCLE SHEP.
THAT'S WHAT YOU DECIDE TO CARE ABOUT?!
OUR PEOPLE NEED NUMBERS. OUR ENEMIES WANT US EXTINCT.
AND YOU JUST DO THE WORK FOR THEM. YOUR CHILDREN WILL ALL BE HALFBREED.
YOU LIKE THE PINK SKIN.
WHAT GOOD IS THAT TO ANYONE?

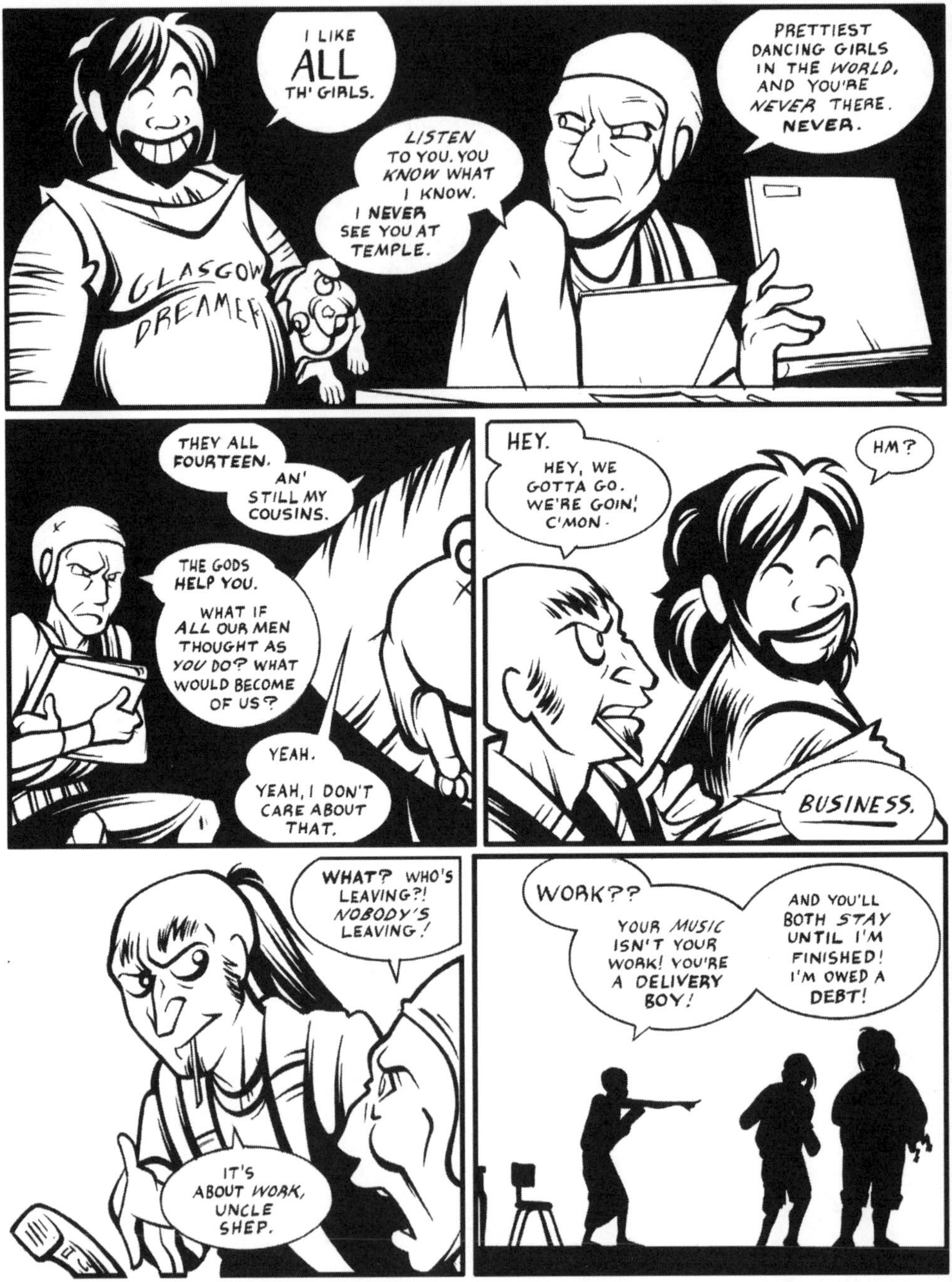
I LIKE ALL TH' GIRLS.
PRETTIEST DANCING GIRLS IN THE WORLD, AND YOU'RE NEVER THERE. NEVER.
LISTEN TO YOU. YOU KNOW WHAT I KNOW.
I NEVER SEE YOU AT TEMPLE.
GLASGOW DREAMER
THEY ALL FOURTEEN.
AN' STILL MY COUSINS.
THE GODS HELP YOU.
WHAT IF ALL OUR MEN THOUGHT AS YOU DO? WHAT WOULD BECOME OF US?
YEAH.
YEAH, I DON'T CARE ABOUT THAT.
HEY.
HEY, WE GOTTA GO. WE'RE GOIN', C'MON.
HM?
BUSINESS.
WHAT? WHO'S LEAVING?! NOBODY'S LEAVING!
IT'S ABOUT WORK, UNCLE SHEP.
WORK??
YOUR MUSIC ISN'T YOUR WORK! YOU'RE A DELIVERY BOY!
AND YOU'LL BOTH STAY UNTIL I'M FINISHED! I'M OWED A DEBT!

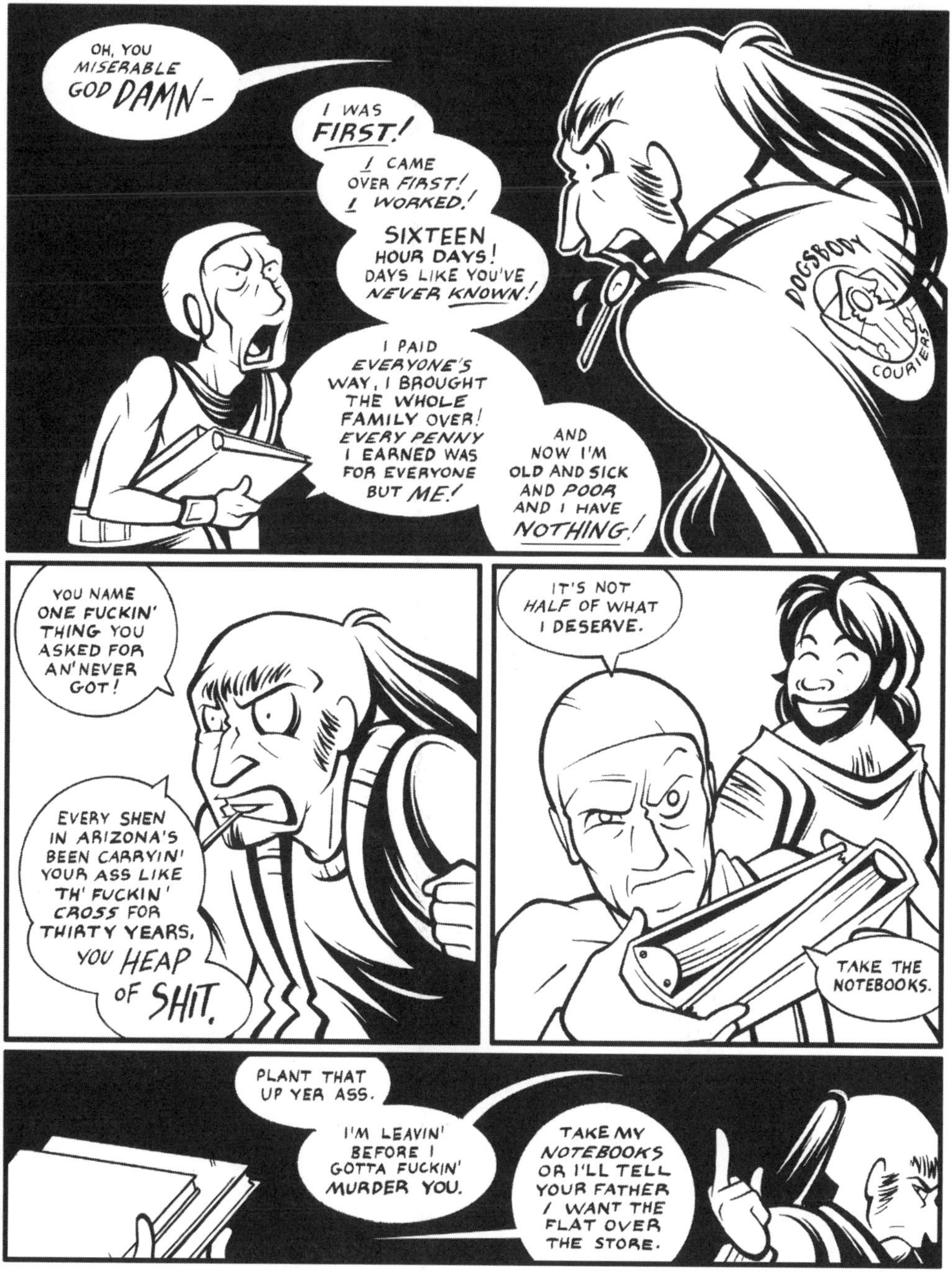
OH, YOU MISERABLE GOD DAMN-
I WAS FIRST!
I CAME OVER FIRST! I WORKED!
SIXTEEN HOUR DAYS! DAYS LIKE YOU'VE NEVER KNOWN!
I PAID EVERYONE'S WAY, I BROUGHT THE WHOLE FAMILY OVER! EVERY PENNY I EARNED WAS FOR EVERYONE BUT ME!
AND NOW I'M OLD AND SICK AND POOR AND I HAVE NOTHING!
DOGSBODY COURIERS
YOU NAME ONE FUCKIN' THING YOU ASKED FOR AN' NEVER GOT!
EVERY SHEN IN ARIZONA'S BEEN CARRYIN' YOUR ASS LIKE TH' FUCKIN' CROSS FOR THIRTY YEARS, YOU HEAP OF SHIT.
IT'S NOT HALF OF WHAT I DESERVE.
TAKE THE NOTEBOOKS.
PLANT THAT UP YER ASS.
I'M LEAVIN' BEFORE I GOTTA FUCKIN' MURDER YOU.
TAKE MY NOTEBOOKS OR I'LL TELL YOUR FATHER I WANT THE FLAT OVER THE STORE.

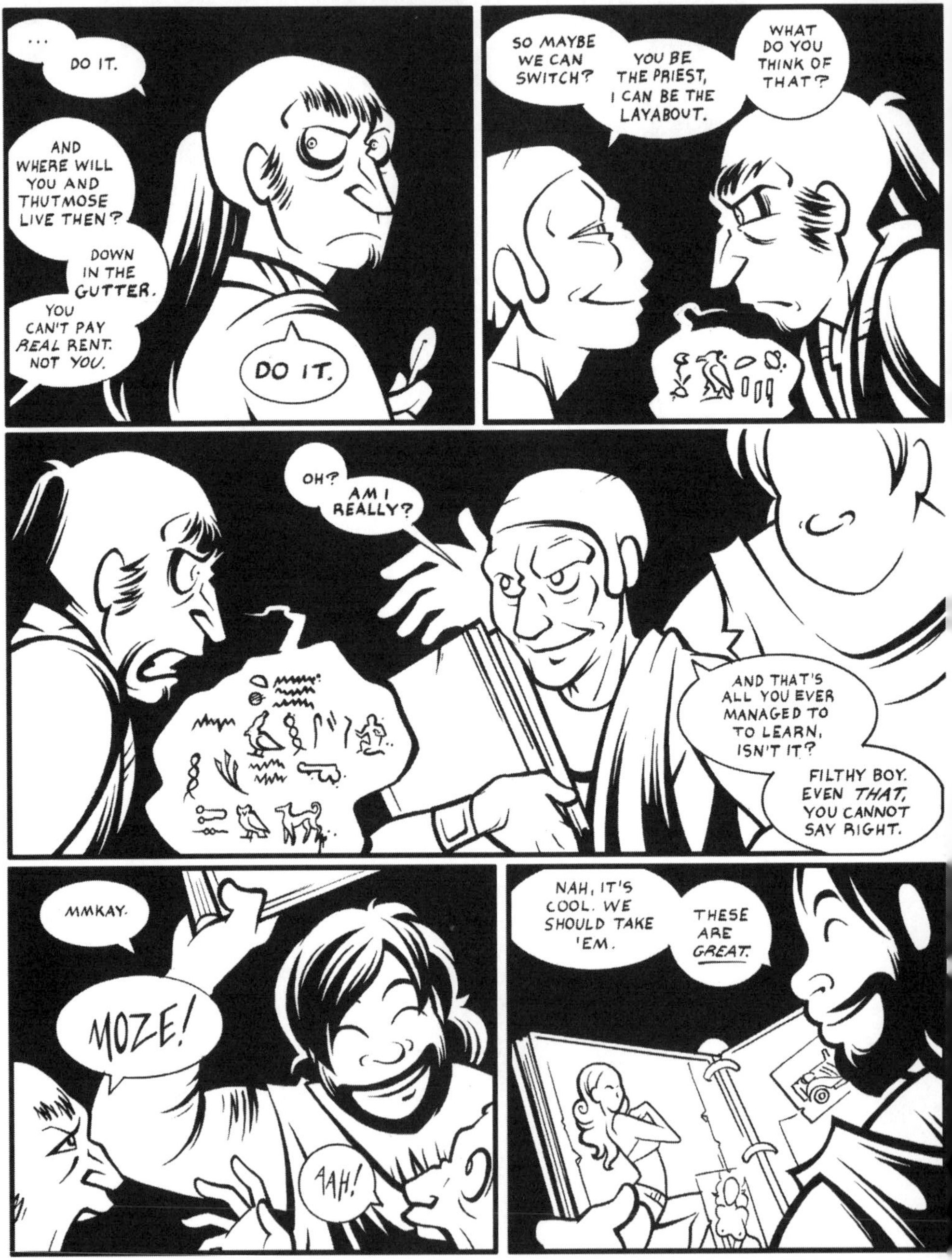
...
DO IT.
AND WHERE WILL YOU AND THUTMOSE LIVE THEN?
DOWN IN THE GUTTER.
YOU CAN'T PAY REAL RENT. NOT YOU.
DO IT.
SO MAYBE WE CAN SWITCH?
YOU BE THE PRIEST, I CAN BE THE LAYABOUT.
WHAT DO YOU THINK OF THAT?
OH? AM I REALLY?
AND THAT'S ALL YOU EVER MANAGED TO TO LEARN, ISN'T IT?
FILTHY BOY. EVEN THAT, YOU CANNOT SAY RIGHT.
MMKAY.
MOZE!
AAH!
NAH, IT'S COOL. WE SHOULD TAKE 'EM.
THESE ARE GREAT.

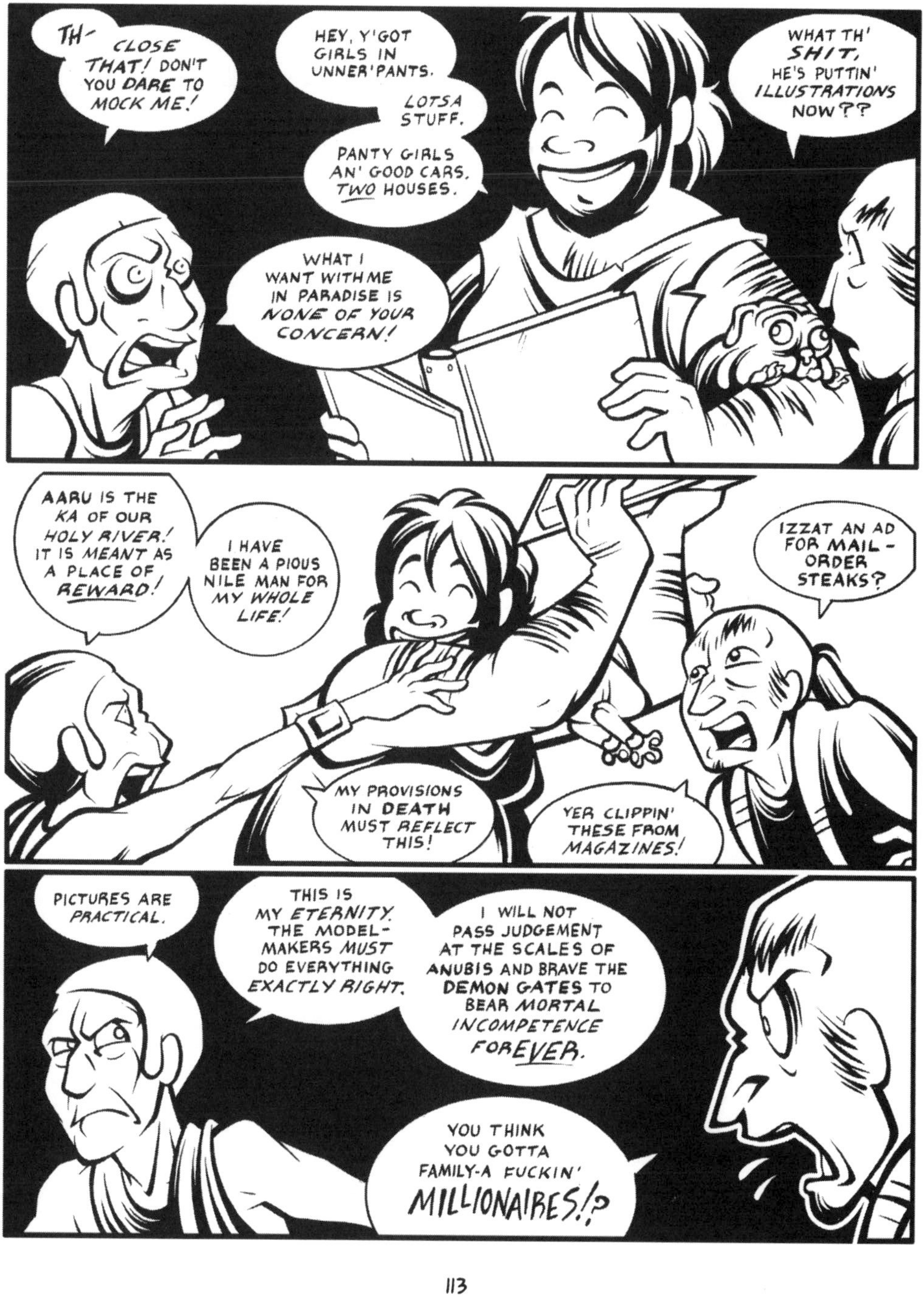
TH- CLOSE THAT! DON'T YOU DARE TO MOCK ME!
HEY, Y'GOT GIRLS IN UNNER'PANTS.
LOTSA STUFF.
PANTY GIRLS AN' GOOD CARS. TWO HOUSES.
WHAT TH' SHIT, HE'S PUTTIN' ILLUSTRATIONS NOW??
WHAT I WANT WITH ME IN PARADISE IS NONE OF YOUR CONCERN!
AARU IS THE KA OF OUR HOLY RIVER! IT IS MEANT AS A PLACE OF REWARD!
I HAVE BEEN A PIOUS NILE MAN FOR MY WHOLE LIFE!
IZZAT AN AD FOR MAIL-ORDER STEAKS?
MY PROVISIONS IN DEATH MUST REFLECT THIS!
YER CLIPPIN' THESE FROM MAGAZINES!
PICTURES ARE PRACTICAL.
THIS IS MY ETERNITY. THE MODEL-MAKERS MUST DO EVERYTHING EXACTLY RIGHT.
I WILL NOT PASS JUDGEMENT AT THE SCALES OF ANUBIS AND BRAVE THE DEMON GATES TO BEAR MORTAL INCOMPETENCE FOREVER.
YOU THINK YOU GOTTA FAMILY-A FUCKIN' MILLIONAIRES!?

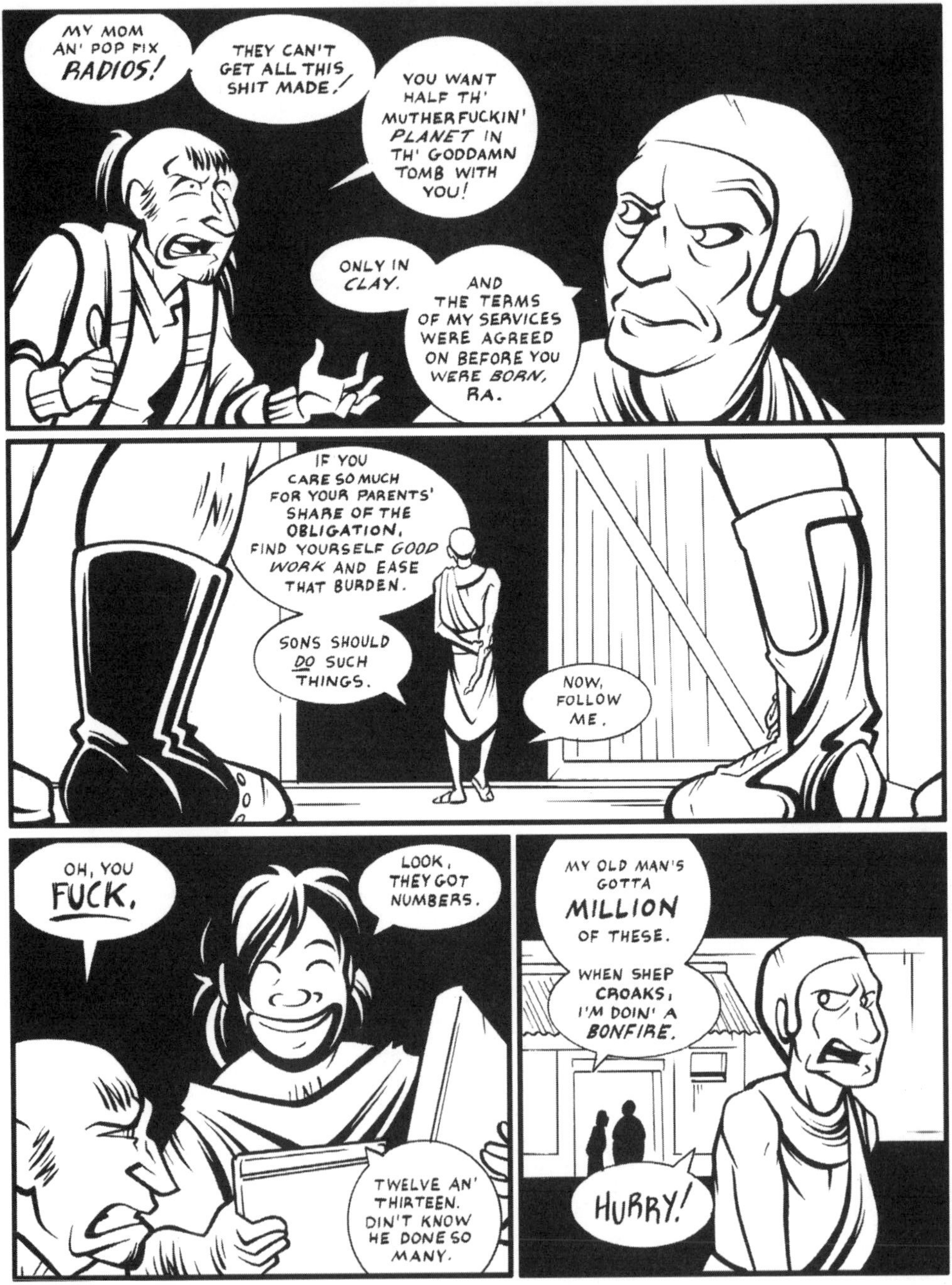
MY MOM AN' POP FIX RADIOS!
THEY CAN'T GET ALL THIS SHIT MADE!
YOU WANT HALF TH' MUTHERFUCKIN' PLANET IN TH' GODDAMN TOMB WITH YOU!
ONLY IN CLAY.
AND THE TERMS OF MY SERVICES WERE AGREED ON BEFORE YOU WERE BORN, RA.
IF YOU CARE SO MUCH FOR YOUR PARENTS' SHARE OF THE OBLIGATION, FIND YOURSELF GOOD WORK AND EASE THAT BURDEN.
SONS SHOULD DO SUCH THINGS.
NOW, FOLLOW ME.
OH, YOU FUCK.
LOOK, THEY GOT NUMBERS.
TWELVE AN' THIRTEEN. DIN'T KNOW HE DONE SO MANY.
MY OLD MAN'S GOTTA MILLION OF THESE.
WHEN SHEP CROAKS, I'M DOIN' A BONFIRE.
HURRY!

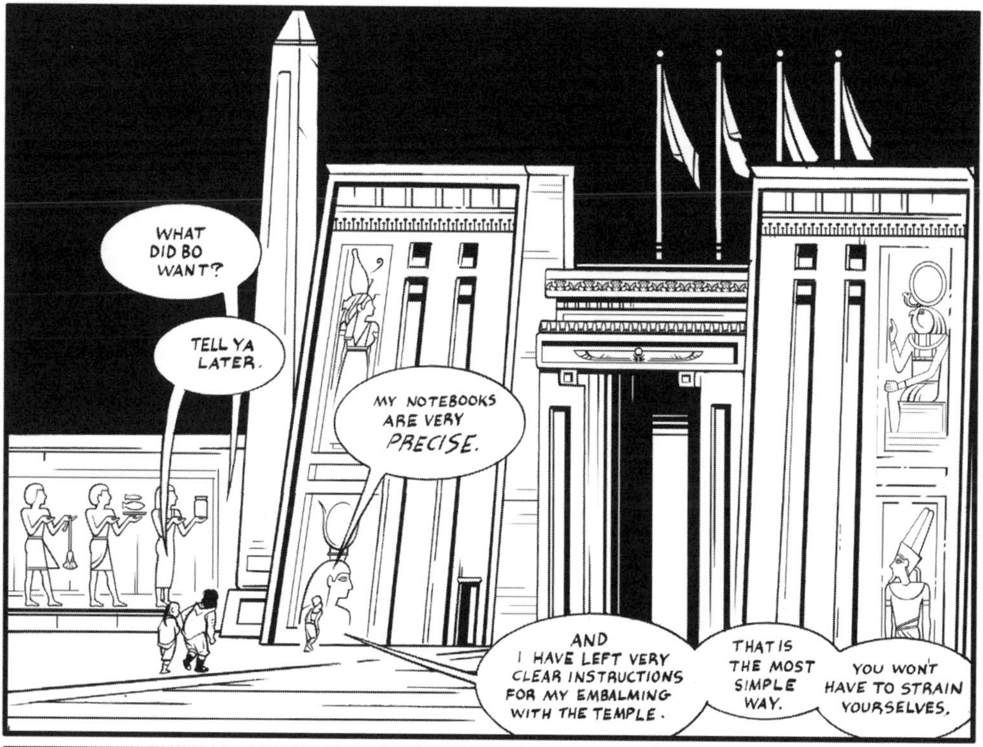
WHAT DID BO WANT?
TELL YA LATER.
MY NOTEBOOKS ARE VERY *PRECISE*.
AND I HAVE LEFT VERY CLEAR INSTRUCTIONS FOR MY EMBALMING WITH THE TEMPLE.
THAT IS THE MOST SIMPLE WAY.
YOU WON'T HAVE TO STRAIN YOURSELVES.

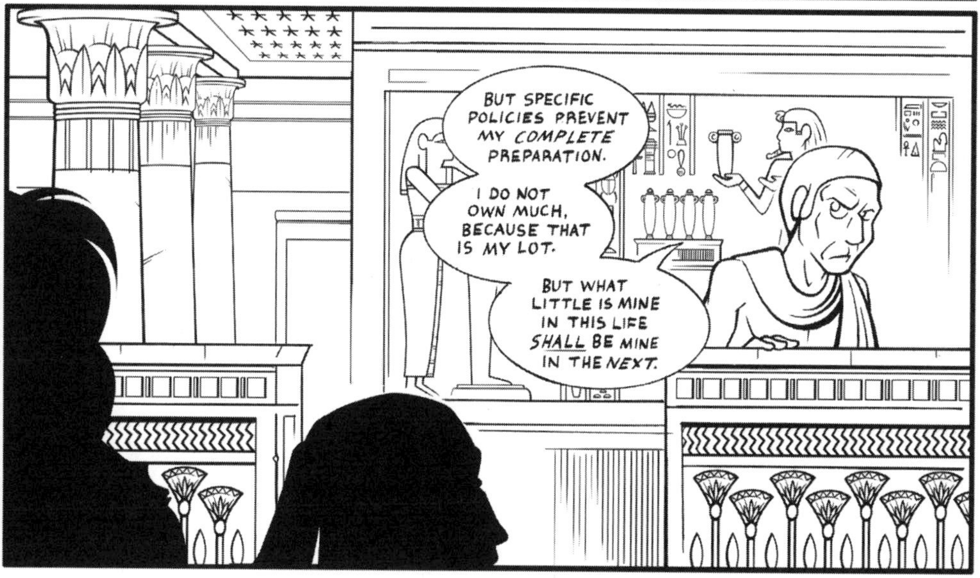
BUT SPECIFIC POLICIES PREVENT MY *COMPLETE* PREPARATION.
I DO NOT OWN MUCH, BECAUSE THAT IS MY LOT.
BUT WHAT LITTLE IS MINE IN THIS LIFE *SHALL* BE MINE IN THE *NEXT*.

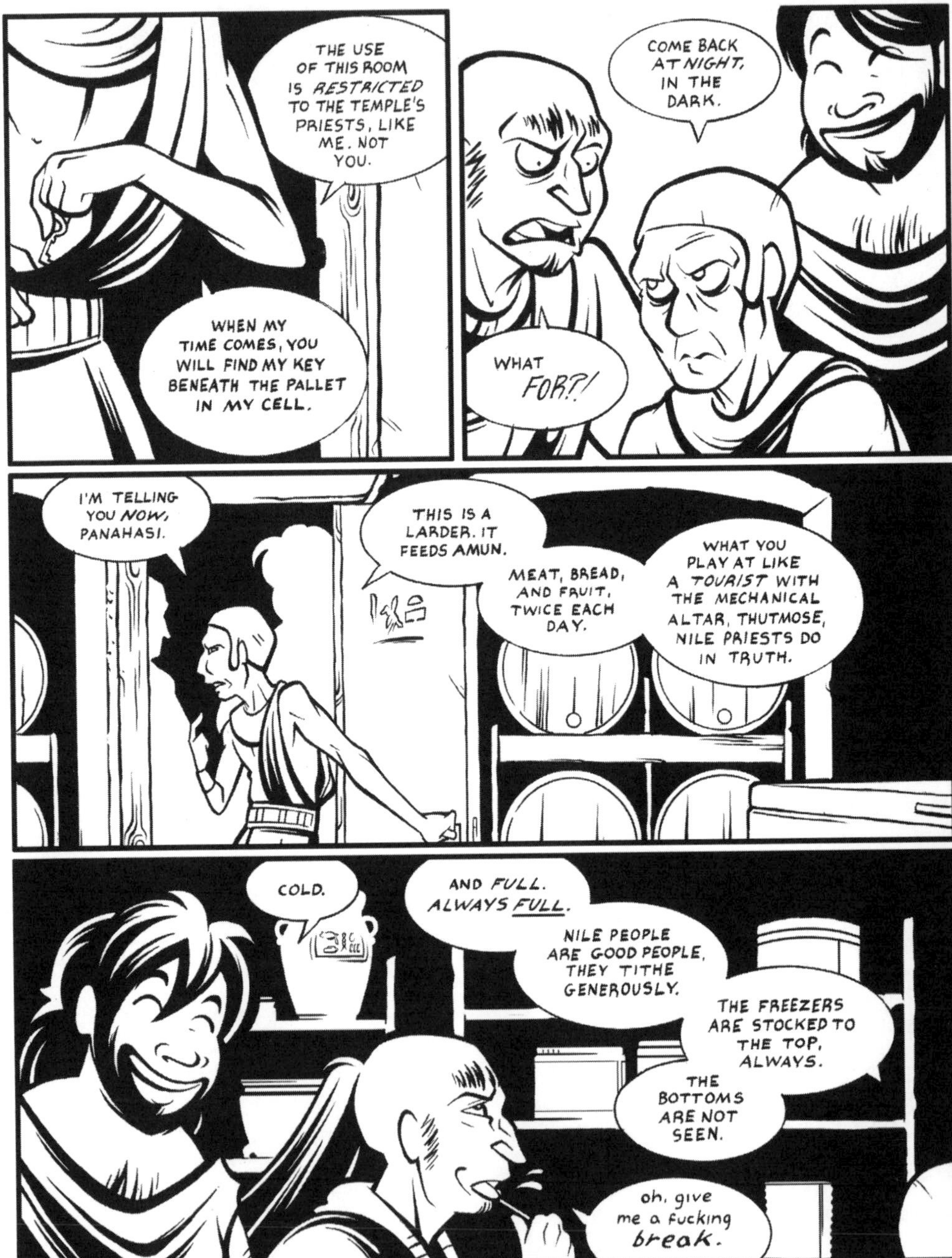
THE USE OF THIS ROOM IS RESTRICTED TO THE TEMPLE'S PRIESTS, LIKE ME. NOT YOU.
WHEN MY TIME COMES, YOU WILL FIND MY KEY BENEATH THE PALLET IN MY CELL.
COME BACK AT NIGHT, IN THE DARK.
WHAT FOR?!
I'M TELLING YOU NOW, PANAHASI.
THIS IS A LARDER. IT FEEDS AMUN.
MEAT, BREAD, AND FRUIT, TWICE EACH DAY.
WHAT YOU PLAY AT LIKE A TOURIST WITH THE MECHANICAL ALTAR, THUTMOSE, NILE PRIESTS DO IN TRUTH.
COLD.
AND FULL. ALWAYS FULL.
NILE PEOPLE ARE GOOD PEOPLE. THEY TITHE GENEROUSLY.
THE FREEZERS ARE STOCKED TO THE TOP, ALWAYS.
THE BOTTOMS ARE NOT SEEN.
oh, give me a fucking break.

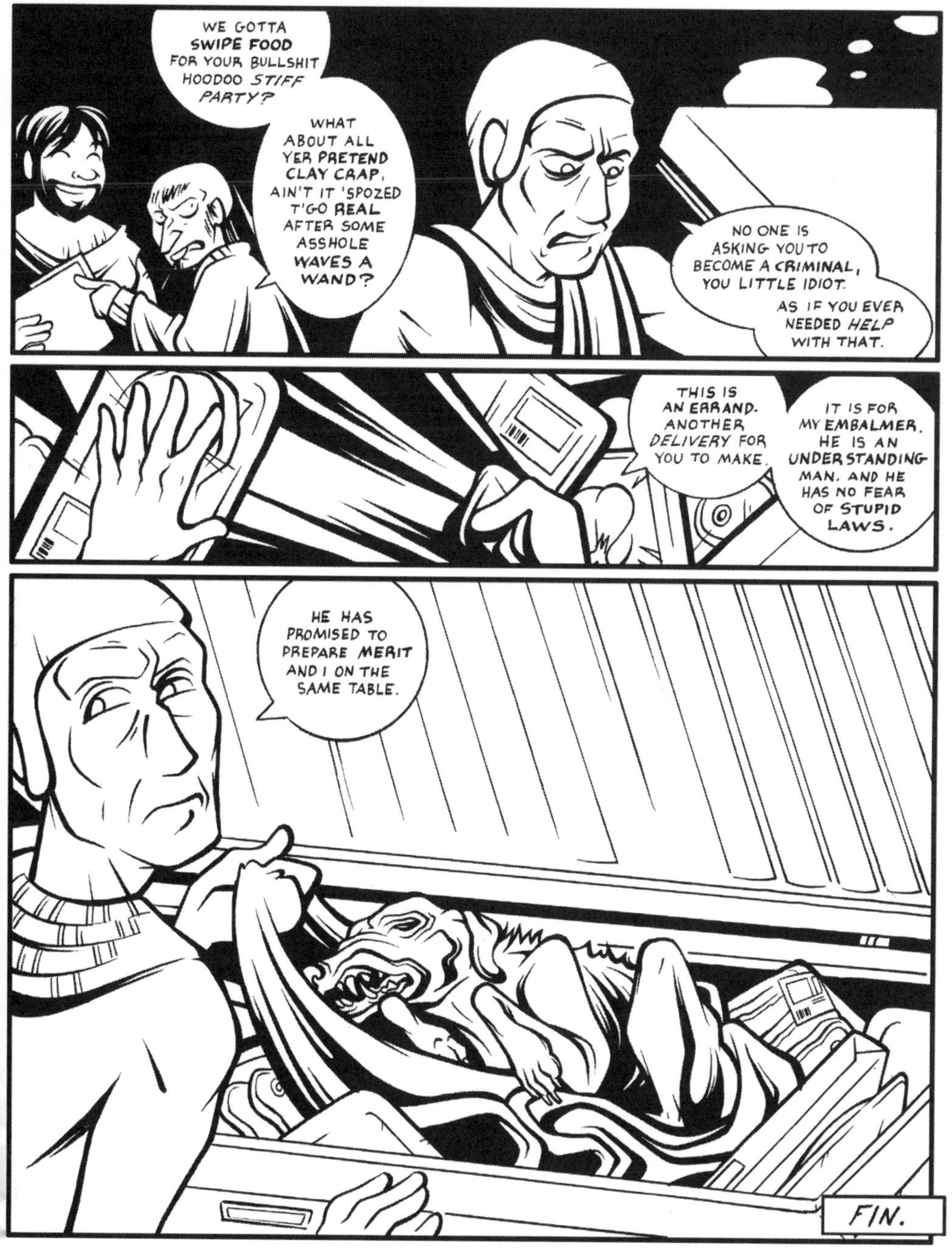
WE GOTTA SWIPE FOOD FOR YOUR BULLSHIT HOODOO STIFF PARTY?
WHAT ABOUT ALL YER PRETEND CLAY CRAP, AIN'T IT 'SPOZED T'GO REAL AFTER SOME ASSHOLE WAVES A WAND?
NO ONE IS ASKING YOU TO BECOME A CRIMINAL, YOU LITTLE IDIOT.
AS IF YOU EVER NEEDED HELP WITH THAT.
THIS IS AN ERRAND. ANOTHER DELIVERY FOR YOU TO MAKE.
IT IS FOR MY EMBALMER. HE IS AN UNDERSTANDING MAN, AND HE HAS NO FEAR OF STUPID LAWS.
HE HAS PROMISED TO PREPARE MERIT AND I ON THE SAME TABLE.
FIN.

Footnotes.

Page 1

As a child, I lived about half an hour from a neighborhood of beautifully maintained Victorian houses. The owners kept them up in the original style, with brightly-colored paint jobs and traditionally shingled roofs. You can find pictures of them in coffee table books about Victorian architecture.

This house isn't Victorian, though. The style's called Queen Anne, and it was popular around 1900. When you moved to Yakima at the turn of the century and made a fortune farming, this is what you built.

Page 3

A little calculated misdirection.

Shaking down the city of Seattle in search of one runaway son would take months, and not being able to find Ben would never convince his parents he's not actually there. Especially since they're gonna find around fifteen guides to living in Seattle when they toss his room in a total panic in about five hours.

Page 7

Ben's papers are based on a real certificate of naturalization I found online. It was for a South Korean foreign adoptee, too. And coincidentally, the person was adopted roughly around the same time that I always imagined Ben was.

A few laws were recently changed so that children adopted by American citizens are now instantly granted American citizenship, but back when *he* was a little kid, Ben's adoptive parents had to apply for it.

A fragment of his original Korean name persists as a middle name.

Also present: Patton the cat. Why Patton? Because it needed a name Ben would never have given it.

Page 9

Can't let the microwave time out. It'll go *ding*. And someone upstairs might wonder who's using the microwave at four in the morning.

Page 13

A better shrink would have figured out "nothing" didn't really mean "nothing."

Page 14

Most people writing porno are a lot happier about it than this.

Page 17

Scipio has probably started his mornings this same exact way for about twenty-five years: oatmeal with Master Wu, time-traveling Buddhist crime fighter. I imagine the show's like a cross between **Doctor Who**, **Kung Fu**, and **Quantum Leap**. It's not explicitly for children, considering the beat-downs Wu just finished handing out in the first panel. But if Scip had first become aware of it as an adult, he would have never begun watching it.

Master Wu's look is based on an ancient Chinese statue of the Buddha, from around the time the Buddhist faith was just beginning to take hold after being imported from India.

On Scip's laptop: a Triceratops. His computer's a lot nicer than Ben's Trilobite model.

Page 19

Our first glimpse of the loathed Nicky Collision. The fact that a guy like this has his own show inspired a lot of questions from readers about the nature of Templar television.

Nicky isn't doing a public access show, here. He has a sponsor building his sets, coordinating his shows, and paying him a salary. "Damage Report" would have been proposed to that sponsor in a sales pitch, just like network television shows are proposed to network executives. And a show on Templar television can be sponsored by just about anyone. An indulgent parent, a brothel, a shoe manufacturer, a foreign country. *Anyone.*

As a result, there are a huge number of shows and dozens of genres, and no such thing as "development hell." This means having a television show to your name is notable, but not exceptional.

The real path to first-class fame on Templar-style TV is running your show on a major channel. Templar Connect will air anything locally produced and legal that meets the minimum standards for watchability, but multiple sponsorships and the backing of a big, international network would afford a show's cast the kind of acclaim, production values, payscale, and recognition we would equate with film stars. Some Templars with TV shows want this desperately, some couldn't care less. I'll let you figure out who's who.

Page 21

The Doves of the Oarlock—the neighborhood's governing pimps and madams—work under pseudonyms to avoid potentially shaming or irritating the less open-minded members of their families. There's no MBA-powered fast track into management when it comes to Oarlock whoring; all the Doves worked their way up the ranks. Male or female, they all started out as prostitutes.

Dove aliases are names that were popular in the Edwardian and Victorian eras, but have since fallen out of fashion. This is in reference to the era in which the Oarlock was founded.

Only one of the current Doves, Zebulon, is male.

Page 23

She's... kind of got a point. A point she doesn't realize she's making and a point being filtered through colossal teenage hubris, inexperience, and too much TV, but a point all the same.

Buying into Nicky's act probably isn't a fantastic idea. But if you don't *know* it's an act and you're seventeen years old, it's probably hard to resist being impressed by his blatant disrespect.

Page 24

Nicky's schedule: Calculated to offend as many people as possible.

Page 28

It's very easily possible to harbor truly demented levels of racial prejudice without being overtly insulting about it. The Jakes do it every day, by reducing the enormous complexity of the human condition to five categories determined by genetic inheritance. They're five non-hierarchical categories that do their best to flatter, though, which makes them pretty unusual. Race theory isn't normally this friendly.

When I was first writing Jakeskin scripture, my goal was to give it a tangy dash of pop-eyed lunacy, without making said lunacy completely impossible to swallow. I had to believe that somebody, somewhere, even one in a thousand people, could read what I was about to write and think, "Well, that sounds pretty reasonable."

For the record, a few people have.

Page 29

Gene is playing a musical game called "Gvidon Piece Ultra." "Gvidon" is a reference to Prince Gvidon, a character from the Russian opera **The Tale of Tsar Saltan**. In the third act of the opera, Prince Gvidon is transformed into an insect so he can visit his father incognito; he exits the scene to the tune of "Flight of the Bumblebee."

That's why the mascot for the game is a little conducting bee.

And Gene is, indeed, about to finish the game with an even billion points. That's because he's scored a perfect ten million points on every level.

The music notation on the screen isn't for "Flight of the Bumblebee," though. It's an arrangement by Kaikhosru Shapurji Sorabji, a British composer of Parsi origin notorious for writing exceptionally difficult arrangements, most notably the **Opus Clavicembalisticum**.

Gene has both an Unagi and a more advanced Super Unagi system. He's playing the older console because Gvidon Piece Ultra isn't available on the newer one. Not yet, anyway.

Page 31

Did you catch the naked and shameless confession to felony child neglect and endangerment? Blink and you'll miss it.

A breech birth with an infantile epilepsy chaser would send most new mothers to the closest hospital screaming. Not Feather.

Her powers of denial must be extraordinary if she's referring to an adult son who can't spell his own name as "fixed."

Page 32

The Jakes use a lot of chemistry terms in their scripture.

Page 34

You're not misreading anything. Jakes think mixed-race children will save humanity through the physical and psychological advantages afforded to 'em by their selectively bred multiracial ancestry.

Really.

By the way, I don't think those are Jackie's kids. Not both of 'em, anyway.

Page 35

I really have no idea what to make of Jackie. Seriously. Like Kasper and the Shen cousins, she's one of those characters who was meant as scenery, to be granted two or three lines of dialog before being nudged offstage. But she takes up a lot of my mental real estate for supporting cast.

She hasn't inherited her mother's ability to command, or whatever terrible capabilities her father is quietly harboring. She doesn't strike me as very bright, very religious, or... very *anything*, really. She grew up Jake, and she's content to stay Jake. She does as she's told, believes everything she was taught, and doesn't complain. Something about that makes me suspicious. I guess every big organization needs members like her, though.

Page 38

Scipio and Reagan's arguments are a lot of fun to write. They're close friends and reasonable, intelligent people who are completely incapable of harboring the same opinions. So, they can get their bitch on for pages and pages, but stay civil, be totally honest, and end things in a stalemate every time. That pretty much guarantees we'll always know exactly how they both feel about anything.

Page 48

This is my favorite page in the whole chapter. It's just so stark and miserable. It's Eli Bash's entire life in four panels.

Page 53

Ransom Bash is a pretty cool name, actually. Even if I'm sure the kid himself is probably incredibly obnoxious.

Don't ask me why. I'm just convinced of it.

Cascade Abalone, I just feel sorry for.

Page 54

Not an amicable break-up, I'm assuming.

Dr. Bash has no idea how insane his spasms of sub-rational, foam-flecked loathing make him look and sound. People like him never do. Being married to Eli was probably pretty hard work.

Page 55

Anatomical waxes (wax moulages) can usually only be found in the archives of medical museums, these days, but private collections do exist; Christie's auctioned one off piece by piece in 2001. Bash's pride and joy probably cost him about $2,500, if the estimates calculated for similar waxes from that lot are accurate. But hey, maybe Bash got a deal. Hideously diseased faces aren't the easiest things to sell, particularly outside of esoteric collectors' circles.

And "syphilology" was a real field, before the advent of simple antibiotics. Syphilis was capable of some truly heinous disfigurement when left unchecked; syphilology and dermatology were practically interchangeable specialties prior to penicillin.

Page 59

Ben isn't usually this socially abnormal. Most of his quirks can be passed off as introversion or shyness, but neither of those explain why his reaction to the conversational equivalent of the Titanic slamming into an iceberg is an attempt to go down with the ship.

Who here thought this scene was gonna end in a wacky, **Three's Company**-style misunderstanding instead of mutual retreat and enraged confusion? Pft. C'mon, I wouldn't do that to you guys.

Page 65

I never draw Ben's little prescription bottle as if it's actually big enough to hold a six-month supply of medication.

Page 67

You can almost hear Zora recounting this scene to her court-appointed therapist fifteen years from now.

Page 70

Like a lot of seers, Gene specializes in telling you a bunch of stuff you kinda already knew, and retreating into scripture when pressed for specifics.

Is he the real deal? His family thinks so. And Gene does, too. Everyone involved here believes he can be possessed by clairvoyant supernatural spirits, and they listen to what those spirits have to say. So, for all intents and purposes, yes. This is real. Gene is an oracle, in the Delphic sense.

Feather's shameless displays of favoritism for her firstborn still aren't okay, but probably a little easier to understand, given that fact she's convinced Gene occasionally harbors angels.

Page 74

This gun is modeled after a homemade Chechen number. A friend who actually knows something about guns has given me some very helpful insight into how it's probably used, adding that the only purpose of a gun like this in our world is to shoot someone else with a better gun and take theirs.

I think the Jakes would pride themselves on their ability to build something like this out of rusty scrap, though. When your entire belief system is focused around developing the survival skills you'll need when civilization collapses, being able to cobble together a single-shot zip gun is one hell of an advantage to have.

Page 80

I bet a lot of people watch "Mondays with Tuesday" muted.

Page 84

Try this sometime. It's fun.

Page 85

I apologize for Tuesday's surname. I couldn't resist.

Some readers have asked if "Tuesday Pryor" is a reference to "Thursday Next," a character from a series of novels by Jasper Fforde. After reading a little about Fforde's books, I'm tempted to say yes. But sadly, that would be a lie. I don't have good taste in alternate history and comedic fantasy. I just like horrible puns.

Page 92

A cute girl paying cheerful, friendly attention to you for three minutes. It's like a Red Bull for male self-esteem.

Page 94

We've heard Antoinette's name before. Tuesday called her an invertebrate at the beginning of chapter two.

When I was a little kid, I had a babysitter named Antoinette.

She was black, like me, but a bit darker; maybe the color of upmarket "70% cacao" chocolate. Her parents were friends with my parents, so watching me was a steady and reliable source of income for her. I saw a lot of her , and I would like to stress that I don't remember her negatively in any way.

But one day, when I was still pretty young, *way* too young to have any idea why everyone was so upset, our families went to brunch together, and Antoinette showed up with colored contacts. They were electric blue. Swimming pool blue. Unmistakably, undeniably blue.

I didn't know it then, since I was still a child. But I now understand Antoinette spent the entire meal irritated and defensive, my own parents were disturbed and asking probing questions, and Annie's parents were uncomfortably silent.

I don't think she ever babysat for me again, in retrospect.

Page 99

Xenophage is where we first saw Cully. Check chapter one.

Page 100

A little insight into why Scip took Epiphany's "fuck school" speech so badly.

Page 101

There's not much good work for bodyguards like Scipio.

He hasn't got a license to carry, or even a gun license. A city-dweller for his entire adult life, he's never learned to drive, and so obviously doesn't know any defensive or evasive driving techniques. He's never been in a military or law enforcement position, either. The only extra "bodyguard training" he's got is a working knowledge of CPR and general first aid, and he just learned that on his own, because that's the kind of guy he is.

Scipio gets all of his gigs assigned to him by a central office, and really, all the firm has in Scip is an extra warm body. Good for show, good for impressing and intimidating people (as long as he doesn't talk to them), good for plugging holes in those 12-18 hour shifts when someone calls in sick. Not good for guarding anyone important, or under any actual threat.

Which is why he's getting urinated on by drunk teenage girls.

Page 104

A cute little ceramic Osiris figurine, the kind available in every tourist trap in Little Cairo. Ancient Egyptians considered incense the food of the gods, so I guess this would be Osiris having lunch, in the form of lump frankincense and myrrh. A scene like this would be a daily occurrence in observant Nile Revivalist homes, on a family altar.

Page 105

Oh hey, speaking of altars: Here's a coin-operated one.

Coin-operated religious devices, although a classic of sci-fi illustration and certain kinds of satire, really do exist. Some Catholic churches have rows of electric candles worshipers turn on with a donation, instead of the classic wax devotionals a person actually has to light.

This Nile altar features Nut the sky goddess, dotted with stars and held aloft by Shu, god of the air. Reclining beneath them both is Geb, god of the Earth. A stylized river and vegetation are present as well, along with an enormous sun.

The panel below the machine's buttons and coin slot features a heart and a feather, both in their iconic hieroglyphic forms, balanced on a scale. Revivalists, like their ancient forebears, believe the hearts of dead Egyptians are weighed against Ma'at, the feather of truth. A heart lighter than the feather earns the recently deceased a place in the afterlife; a heart heavy with wickedness, deceit and impiety means a second death in the jaws of Ammit, a crocodile-hippo-lion goddess. This depiction of a perfectly-balanced scale is probably meant to inspire the faithful to drop a few coins in the machine and tip things in their favor.

Between the heart and feather sits a representation of a false door. The wax models ordered by customers would drop out here in a working altar. False doors were considered passageways to the supernatural realm, and used by the ka, an element of the Egyptian soul, to pass between this world and the next.

Page 106

Thoth, Bes, the snout of Anubis and a fragment of Taweret. They all want Moze's pocket change. Bes wins.

Bes is a god of the good life. Music, dancing, sex, healing, protection, and the defeat of evil spirits. There's also a passing resemblance between Moze and Bes, although I don't think Moze is self-aware enough to realize that.

Page 107

The hieroglyphs here are what Egyptologists call the Ancient Egyptian Offering Formula. It was basically a fill-in-the-blank prayer, so you could honor multiple gods and goddesses just by changing a few words. Most Revivalists would use this machine to make offerings on behalf of a deceased relative; Moze just wants a little wax Bes.

Page 109

It's hard to care about kissin' cousins when multiple generations of sibling incest are part of your faith's creation myth.

Page 112

Care for a translation?

Panel Two: "Corpse."

Panel Three: "Drink deeply from the uncircumcised penis of a Nubian, dog."

Or at least, that's what Sunny's going for.

Page 114

Funeral arrangements are something many ancient Egyptians spent a good deal of their lives organizing. A lavish and well-appointed tomb guaranteed a comfortable afterlife, and models of luxuries were considered just as good as being buried with the real thing. Model breweries, bakeries, and brickworks, all fully staffed with little model workmen, were buried with wealthy ancient Egyptians, along with model servants, farms, homes, and livestock. Aaru was considered a paradise, an eternal hunting ground in the reeds. But that didn't mean you wouldn't need someone to build your house for you when you got there.

I'm sure Shepseskaf believes the sacrifices he's made in this life have earned him everything he's asking for in the next.

Page 115

This temple is elaborately painted. It would look a little tacky and out of line with modern tastes, but a lot of Egyptian temples and statues were painted. The paint just wore off a thousand years ago, leaving us with nothing but stoic, monochromatic stone.

Note the stars on the ceiling of the temple, echoing the stars on Nut's belly.

Page 117

The payoff.

Ancient Egyptian dogs were named (names like "The Brave One" or "Black" weren't unusual) and cherished, and often mummified and buried along with their owners. Merit has pre-deceased Shep, and really, could have been mummified instead of being stuck in with Amun's steaks. But Shep is a cheap bastard who fully expects the costs of his funeral, in their entirety, to be covered by his family. He's not paying for anything he doesn't have to, including the mummification of his own dog.

And in this context, "Merit" means "Beloved One." His dog is basically named Sweetie Pie.

And that's chapter three. Thanks again, guys. As usual, there's lots more to read online at http://www.templaraz.com.

Bye!

Sketches.

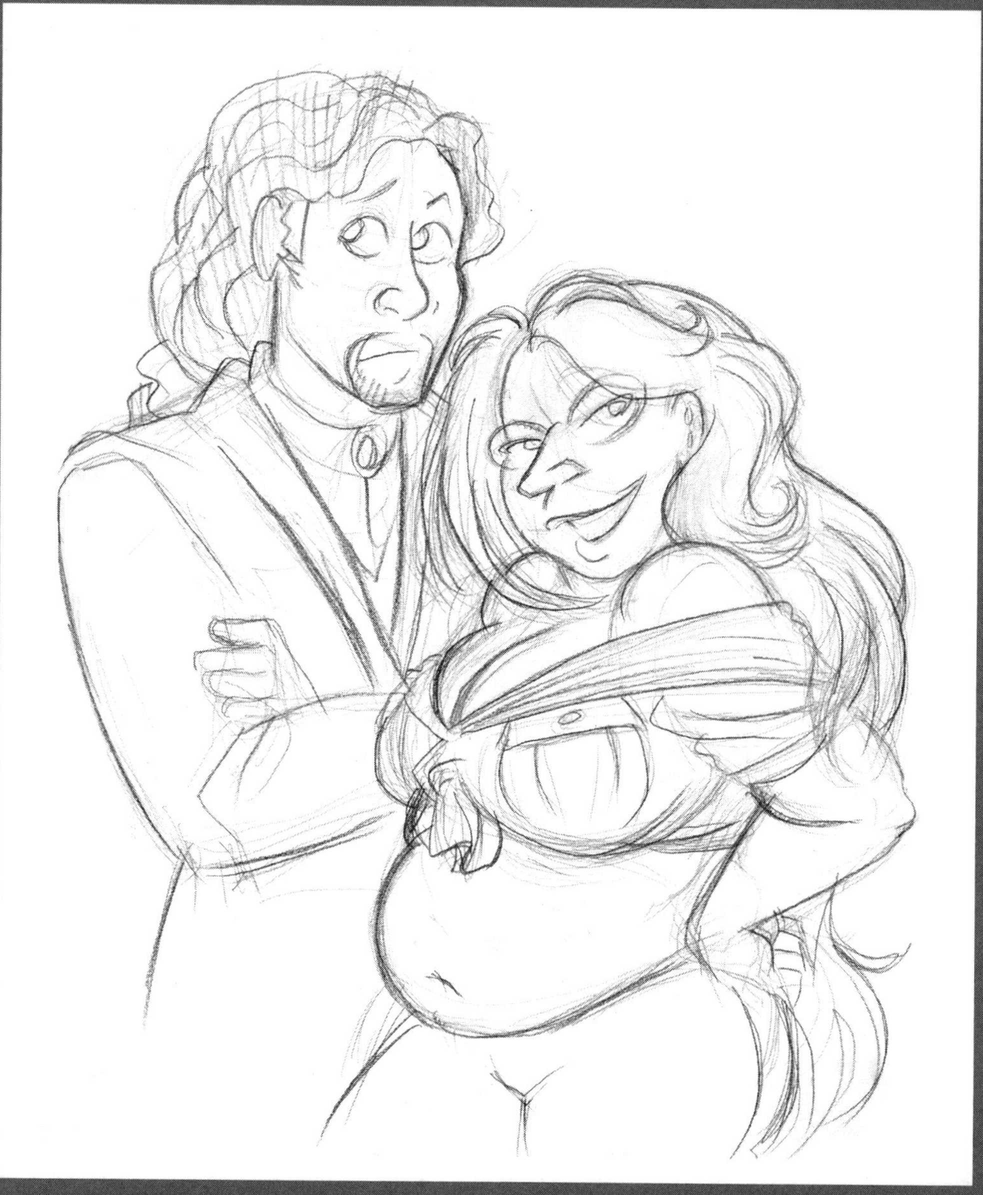

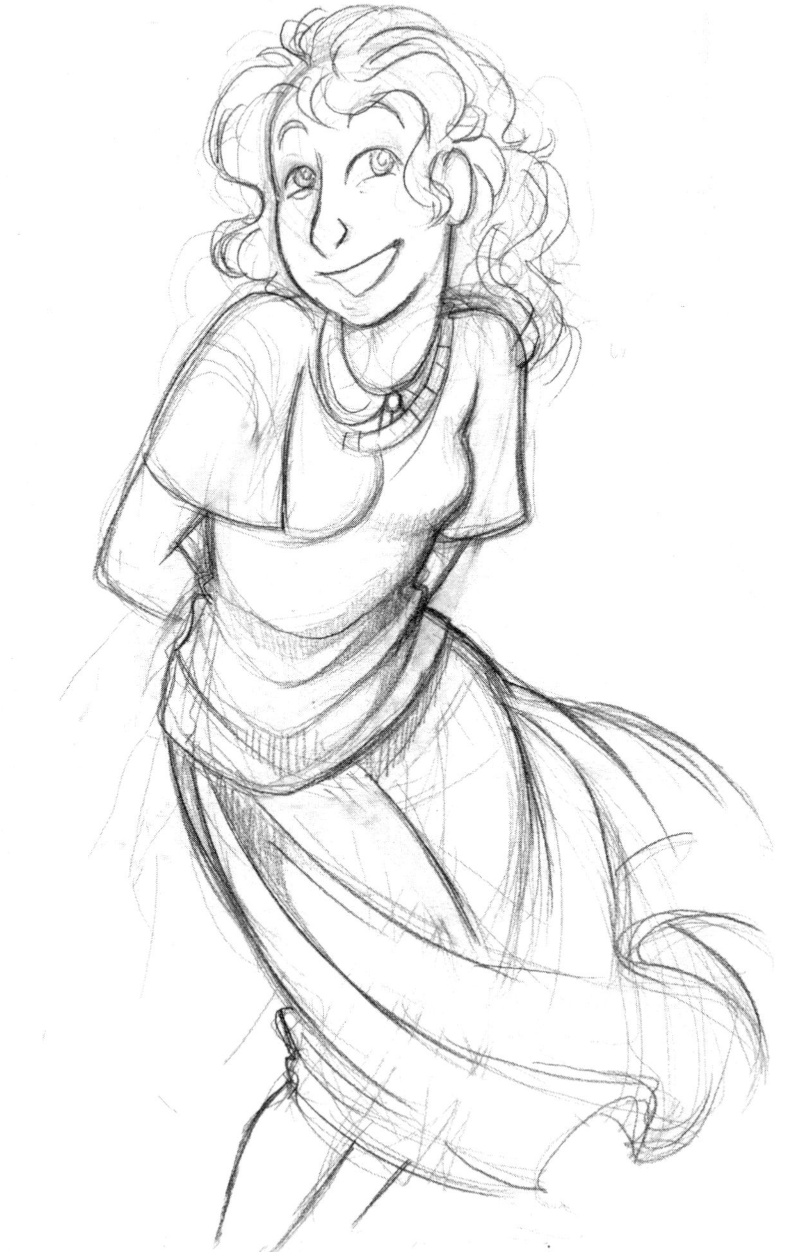

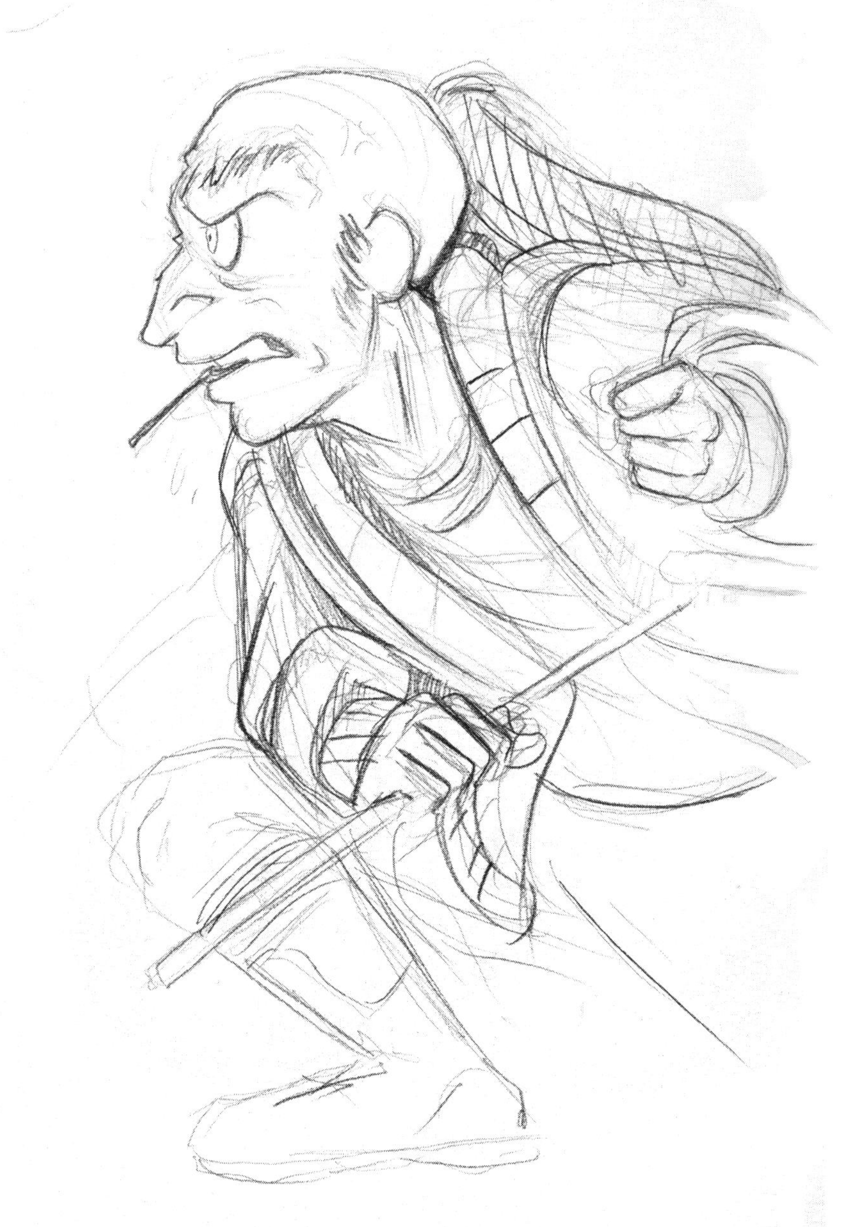

About the artist.

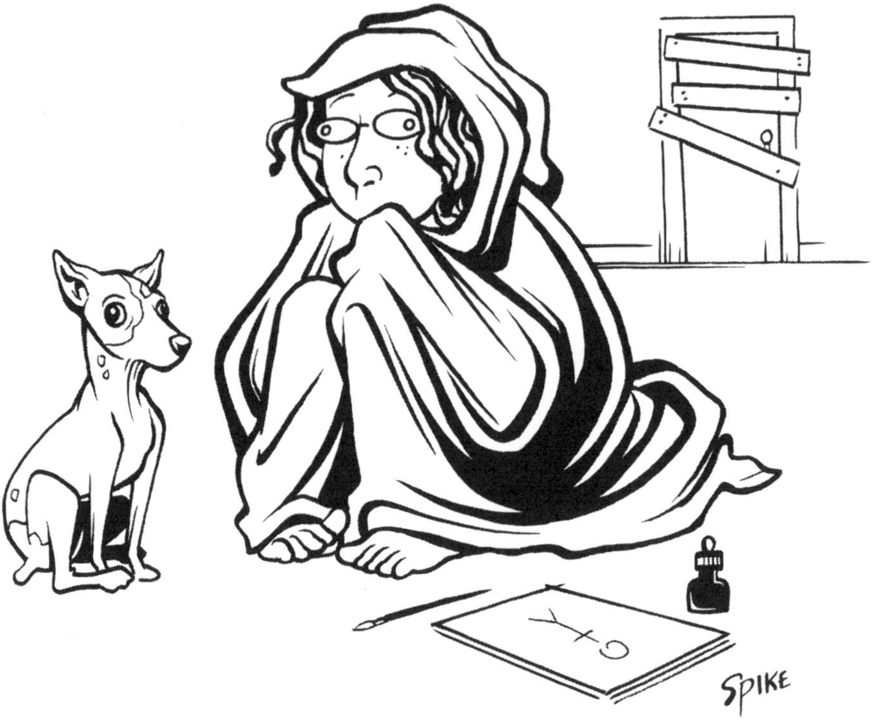
SPIKE

Spike likes to lie on the floor in her pajamas and refuse to move. She regards anything that distracts her from this—including writing, drawing, and publishing Templar—with suspicion and disdain.

She misses her cave, which was warm, muggy, and filled with crawdads. But until the curse is broken, she must stay in Chicago.

She has married a man named Matt, who suspects nothing, and owns a dog named Harvey, who devours meddlers.